Praise for *Restoring Eden*

"*Restoring Eden* is **a passionate, science-based ecological detective story that teaches us to observe nature, to notice when things are amiss, and to right wrongs.** As she discovers the sources of agricultural chemicals extinguishing life in her wetland, Hilborn reveals the personal tolls the loss exacts and the costs she endures to coax neighboring farmers to rethink their practices for the health of their interconnected realms."

—**John M. Marzluff**, coauthor of *Gifts of the Crow* and author of *In Search of Meadowlarks*

"*Restoring Eden* is a must read. In its pages you will **discover the secret agribusiness toxic chemicals that are contaminating the lives of everyone they touch.** This means you. If you think this is someone else's problem, or that you're safe because you eat organic, read this. If you think one person can't make a difference, read this. If you think one community can't come together, read this. We owe big thanks to Elizabeth Hilborn for her courage, tenacity, and love of life in all its forms."

—**Hob Osterlund, APRN**, Senior Fellow, Safina Center, and author of *Holy Mōlī: Albatross and Other Ancestors*

"**A thoroughly engrossing environmental murder mystery** that challenges accepted wisdom and exposes the toxic price of conventional farming."

—**David R. Montgomery**, MacArthur Fellow, coauthor of *What Your Food Ate: How to Heal Our Land and Reclaim Our Health*, and author of *Growing a Revolution*

"When Elizabeth Hilborn sets out to protect a struggling wetland on her North Carolina farm, she discovers that its fate—and her care for it—is shaped by family histories, neighborly relations, the limits of science, and the long reach of global agribusiness. *Restoring Eden* is **a mystery, a memoir, a warning, and a powerful testament to one person's stubborn love for a place and all its inhabitants.**"

—**Michelle Nijhuis**, author of *Beloved Beasts: Fighting for Life in an Age of Extinction*

RESTORING
EDEN

UNEARTHING THE
AGRIBUSINESS SECRET
THAT POISONED MY FARMING COMMUNITY

ELIZABETH D. HILBORN

CHICAGO
REVIEW
PRESS

Disclaimer
This story describes my lived experience. I present all events truthfully and
as accurately as memory and research allow. Conversations and dialogue are
re-created from memory, but many phrases are "as spoken" because they are
so memorable to me. All characters represent actual individuals; there are
no composite characters. Place names, most individuals' names, and some
identifying characteristics of living persons have been changed to protect their
privacy. The views and opinions expressed here are solely my own.

Library of Congress Control Number: 2023938304

Cover design: Preston Pisellini
Cover photographs: Roxana Bashyrova/Shutterstock (farm); varuna/Shutterstock (roots)
Typesetting: Nord Compo
All photos were taken by the author or are in the author's collection unless
otherwise noted.

Printed in the United States of America

CONTENTS

For the farmers who feed us.

Preface

AT HOME IN
THE NATURAL WORLD

THE CAT LIFTS ITS HEAD. Or did it?

I look away from the bumper in front of me to catch a second glimpse of its pale form stretched across the white line to my right. There it was again. It clearly moved.

I interrupt sweet toddler song to say over my shoulder, "Melissa honey, Mommy has to turn around. I have to check on an animal."

"OK." She continues singing. Melissa is strapped into a car seat in the back of my ancient Volvo sedan. She embellishes her improvised song with graceful, then emphatic hand gestures. She smacks her lips to keep loose baby-time.

Wind whips the trees arched above the road, and sunset-colored leaves drift down upon the steady stream of cars below. Behind the wheel, exhausted from a full day of classes at the veterinary college in Raleigh, I'd navigated rush hour traffic while I considered what I would feed our two-year-old for dinner. But I top the hill and take a left onto a side street, turn around, and join the downhill traffic. The cat's still there. I park the car well off the road to the right on the wide grassy shoulder. I set the brake.

I turn and grab a light-gray lap robe from the back seat. "Stay here and wait for Mommy." Melissa's busy with her song and simply nods.

I look in the side mirror for a short break in traffic, open the car door, and slip out. I stand, back to my car, eyes fixed upon the cat across two lines of tightly spaced vehicles. My stomach clenches with every car wheel that passes within inches of the cat's head. Some cars have turned on their headlights. In the twilight, it could easily be crushed.

I lean into the lane, extend a leg, but again and again, I must pull it back behind my white line. The cat and I keep our positions. The flow of cars separates us—a rolling wall. Drivers stare straight ahead as they pass me.

Time slows. I want to give up, but no one else has stopped for the cat. The cat struggles to rise again but fails. I can't leave it. Finally, a dark-haired woman, driving alone, comes to a full stop and lets me cross the lane in front of her. She waits. I turn toward the line of cars to my right, toes behind the double yellow line. Another car stops and lets me cross.

I pull the cat off the pavement and kneel beside her on the weed-choked shoulder—she's lovely, with long, silky gray hair. She looks up at me with deep green eyes full of fear. She pants through an open mouth. I gently scoop her up, tuck the robe around her in a swaddle, and turn back toward my car. I feel her tremble and feel the flutter of her rapid, shallow breaths against my chest as I wait again for each line of traffic to stop and let me pass.

Melissa watches me from the back seat and I can feel our connection, the pull, but can't move toward her. I struggle to control my need to get to my car but feel the danger of our position. I turn the light-colored robe toward headlights and stay focused on the stream of cars. I leave room in my embrace so the cat can draw her vital, shallow breaths, but I want to scream, "I have an injured animal, let me pass!"

When I finally reach the car, I set the rolled-up cat on the front passenger floorboard. I take my place behind the wheel and use the next gap to pull into traffic. I continue downhill to the closest vet in town.

Within ten minutes, Melissa and I burst into the lobby of the veterinary hospital, the wrapped cat cradled in my arms. "I found a cat hit by a car," I tell the woman behind the reception desk. "It's still breathing but is badly injured."

The woman stands up, opens the door behind her, and calls into the back hallway, "Walk-in, cat hit by car. Who's free?" She ushers us into an exam room. I set the cat on the table, taking care to leave the robe between her and cold stainless steel. A technician and doctor enter together. The veterinarian asks, "What happened?" I briefly explain that I don't know much. I was just passing by. The vet places his stethoscope on the cat's chest and listens. He feels her abdomen and examines the color of her mouth. I stand next to the technician at the end of the table, a wide-eyed Melissa's hand in mine.

"The collision may have ruptured the diaphragm," he says. "Her intestines have been drawn by low pressure into her chest. The shallow breaths and rapid pulse are because her lungs and heart are working extra hard to keep her alive. To confirm, we'll need an X-ray." The technician applies an oxygen mask.

What now? I wonder. This is a cat with no identification in urgent need of surgery to survive. I can't take ownership. Not with full-time school during the week, twelve-hour nursing shifts each weekend day, and a toddler to care for. My partner, Howard, doesn't like cats. He would not want me to adopt it. I wavered—*Did I do the right thing? Yes*, I concluded. *I did.* Even if the cat can't be saved, I believe that a death in this quiet, warm office with kind people is more humane than last breaths taken in frigid fear beside rolling tires.

We thank the staff and walk to the parking lot. I buckle my stunned child back into her car seat.

Later, at home, as I prepare dinner, Melissa rattles off a stream of questions about what she'd seen that evening. I tell her that although cars are useful to carry us around, they're also big and heavy, and can move fast. "Moving cars can hurt us," I say, "so when we're near the road we have to stay far away from them. The cat got too close."

Howard arrives home after Melissa is tucked in for the night. He stops by the bedroom to kiss our daughter, then joins me in the kitchen. He pours himself a beer and sits down. As I prepare plates of food for us, I tell him about the cat.

He puts the beer down and stares at me. "What were you thinking? You parked the car by the road? What if someone had hit it? Our
daughter was in there."

I'm silent in the face of his intensity—his eyes, fixed on mine, show
anger, maybe fear. I look down. He isn't finished. "You were out there
in that traffic—what if someone had struck you? *You* could have been
hit in front of our daughter."

I struggle to explain. I knew there was some risk, but I'm careful. "I
couldn't leave the animal, Howie. It was clearly alive, and no one else was
stopping. I had to get it off the road. How could I sleep if I'd left it there?"

"Betsy, I know you care and I love you for it. But tonight was a big
mistake. You can't save them all."

That's not how I saw things. I was studying to become a veterinarian because I wanted to save them. After all, animals and the amazing
world they live in—the trees, streams, and meadows—had saved me.

———————

When I was six, my family lived in a house above a lively brook. When
the walls of our small wooden house closed tighter, when everything
vibrated with my parents' screams, when objects flew through the air, I
slipped outside. I followed the music of tumbling water as it wound its
way through the neighborhood. I followed the animals, was charmed far
away from houses into the forest and marsh. I followed butterflies and
dragonflies as they foraged. I splashed after small fish and tadpoles in the
water. I scouted for turtles and caught frogs. I climbed high into trees to
watch birds building nests—I sat still, hidden. Evenings in the house on
cold winter nights after dinner, I burrowed under thick bedcovers and
sought comfort with pet cats.

The animals pushed me, pulled me toward veterinary medicine. I
became a registered nurse along the way and learned some of the secrets
of sustaining life. I gathered my skills together and put them to use as
a veterinary scientist. I now work to improve the health of populations
of people and animals—more beings than I ever could have helped one
at a time in any medical center. But I do not look into the eyes of my

patients anymore; I have not had to gaze upon the face of death and suffering. Until one day death came to me.

One fine afternoon in early spring 2017, a curious discovery, a wetland with quiet, stained waters, disrupted our lives and the lives of the animals we lived among. Our farm, which we had built from a raw clearing in the forest to a place where we grew most of the fruits and vegetables we ate, a wildlife-sustaining oasis of native shrubs and trees, was transformed into an unfamiliar, ruined landscape.

I watched as spring unfolded as it always had: pear leaves emerged when hazelnut trees bloomed, migratory warblers filled the tops of trees as buds broke open into new leaves, and birds revisited their familiar houses, holes, and thickets to start new families. But as summer approached, we found our bountiful farm crippled. I understood that if I wanted to save our way of life, I had to fight for it. Not just for our family, but for those animals, plants, and people at our farm and in my rural community.

My quest strained my marriage and my relationships with neighbors. But I never had a choice to turn away and to ignore the death that stalked our farm. I witnessed life fade around us—it was like watching a household from afar as midnight approaches—where bright windows go dark, one by one.

I knew that solving the mystery was urgent; once bird or insect populations have disappeared, there's no guarantee that they'll recover. Some of our farming helpers disappeared—the specialist bees that pollinated my blueberries and the bumblebees that gave us a thousand tomatoes each summer. They didn't travel from afar to find us, we lived among them. Much wildlife is local, and when depleted it must be replenished from nearby populations. But our farm was an oasis built to support wildlife. If the lives of wild pollinators and other animals with small territories were destroyed at the farm, would others find us? Were there others left?

I came to understand that the bright lights of migratory birds and wild pollinators, our partners in food production, were winking out one by one, not only at our place but across the country. I had to fight because I was forced to look, to see. I was given a front-row seat, a close-up view of the ongoing insect apocalypse.

1

THE MYSTERY

WE LIVE FAR OUT IN THE COUNTRYSIDE, so we're never alone. At the end of a dirt road is our farm, set in a clearing in the green, green forest of central North Carolina. Two people, hundreds of animals. Thousands if I squint a bit or pull out the magnifying glass. There are billions more to see if I use a microscope. We live among multitudes.

Travel down the road in mid-May. Early morning. The sun is shining and high enough to clear the trees. A checkered pattern of deep shadow and glaring light lays upon the packed gravel ahead. Watch. Box turtles cross while the day is cool. Warm sun on crushed rock helps snakes lose their night chill. Gnats gather and swirl in select beams of sunlight, confusing the still air.

In meadows beside the way, twitchy rabbits forage for sweet herbs in self-made tracks. Resting grasshoppers extend their legs with explosive force and seem to disappear. Beetles explore the surface of the earth among new green shoots. Stout plants partner and support webs of sheet-weaver spiders, fairy hammocks among the woody stems. They're only visible because of the dew.

Plant leaves push watery droplets out from within, offering sweet, mineral-rich refreshment to tiny mouths. Drops of dew glitter from plants along the way. Dew on leaves projects the illusion of a thousand stars, but really the drops contain a thousand tiny worlds. Sun energizes the dewdrops until leaves dry and the drops fade into faint shadows. Then, all life hunkers down and waits for evening's return of water.

Farther along, fields have transformed into forest. Treetops shelter shy members of the multitude. Song of wood thrush and red-eyed vireo emerge from deep within. The air is saturated with the rich scent of moist earth, leaf mold, and pine needle. Tentative breezes thrill bare skin.

If, as I learned to do, one lowers the threshold of perception to notice the shy things, the tiny things, the obvious things that seem to merit no special attention, one can perceive some of the individual threads that create the fabric of our living world.

Cicadas, katydids, and crickets buzz and pulse from the canopy; the forest vibrates in response. Colorful butterflies and moths float by, apparently aimlessly, but what do we know? Bees, serious and focused, create a new generation of plants with the pollen they gather on their bodies. Insects act as an engine of transformation and renewal in this place.

We would struggle to survive without them.

I pulled the front door open. Soft light filled the foyer, and living air moved across our skin, awakening our senses as it carried moisture and dawn's spring chorus of blustering songbirds.

Taz arrowed out the growing gap between door and frame. She fit her snout, then shoulders, precisely through the available space. Brindled hips followed. She timed her movement so that not another millisecond of her life was wasted within stale walls. She sailed off the porch toward green grass and a banquet of new morning scents. Young Charlie followed the older dog, but misapplied his power—an awkward pogo leap turned him sideways and his hip fell into the doorframe. He corrected course on the porch, then galumphed after Taz into the high meadow. I followed.

The air was already warm; it whispered of the scorching North Carolina summer to come. Sun vaporized dew and turned the sky a soft blue-gray as humidity filled the air. I called the dogs back in as soon as they had relieved themselves; I was not in a leisurely mood. I had planned a full Saturday that day in early May. I wanted to check on the young trees I'd recently planted.

After breakfast and farm chores, I prepared for landscaping work by donning heavy khaki pants and a white T-shirt. I trapped my hair in a ponytail, donned an old straw sunhat and tall white waterproof shrimp boots, and slathered on sunscreen. I grabbed two buckets from the shed and filled them with pruners, tree stakes, gloves, a spade, and a large water bottle. Just before noon, I hiked downhill.

The flood had receded the previous week, but signs persisted in the floodplain meadow: gray silt coated the grass, and while no one had been looking, the three-foot-high sand dunes along the Eden River had been rearranged. Twigs, splintered shards of red Solo cups, brightly colored Mylar balloon husks, and lengths of straw were intertwined among tree branches four and a half feet above my head.

The height of the trash caught in branches wove a reliable mark of the maximum depth of the water: the recent event had been a major flood. Distorted plastic bottles and Lance cracker wrappers obscured sections of water-flattened grass at my feet. Large tree limbs, logs, and building materials newly littered the meadow. The river collected and the flood redistributed the buoyant detritus of the watershed into the floodplain below, like children's jacks thrown across a waxed wooden floor.

The sweet scent of the river enveloped me as I inspected the young trees. Birdsong reached me from the distant forest across the water. As I worked to straighten the trees, some of which had been forced sideways by the power of the water, I spotted paper wasp nests hanging empty within white plastic tree-protection tubes. I was unconcerned; I assumed the queens had abandoned their brood when they became submerged during the flood. As I worked to uncover the base of each tree, I was periodically aware of belted kingfishers flying upriver by their staccato rattle—a warning of my presence.

After a couple hours, I took a break in the shade and leaned against a big green ash tree on the bank ten feet above the river. I drank deeply

Eden River in flood, April 25, 2017.

from my water bottle. As I prepared to return to work, movement caught my eye: I spotted a heron below, beside the main channel. The large blue-gray bird was slowly strutting through the shallows, eyes down, ready to snatch an unwary frog or fish with its yellow dagger-beak.

By late afternoon, I'd finished my work and emptied the water bottle. I counted my tools and stooped to pick up as much of the plastic trash as fit into my buckets. I walked across the meadow toward the hill leading home. The musk of the river followed me as I left the dunes behind.

As I walked, I reviewed the day's accomplishments. None of the protective tree tubes had been lost in the flood. The saplings were all there and had been relatively easy to unearth from new mounds of silty sand. Overall, the damage was minimal. The next good rain would wash the silt off the older leaves, and new leaves had already started to emerge in the nine days since the flood had receded.

Buckets rose and fell with my stride as I crossed the meadow. Scattered spring flowers among grasses at my feet occasionally drew my gaze and slowed my pace: blackberries, blue-eyed grass, and violets. The intensity of the sun diminished as I stepped into dappled shadow at the eastern edge of forest. A light breeze dried the sweat on my face, cooled my body, and renewed my energy. As a treat to myself for a day of work well done, I turned and headed east to visit with the animals of the central swale.

The swale is a two-foot-deep, eight-foot-wide ditch. It fills periodically with rain or floodwater. When full, it forms a linear wetland almost half a mile long. That afternoon, I sought a section of brimming swale that glistened in golden light cast over the eastern portion of the meadow. From my years of experience, I knew that sunlit water would provide the best view.

Over the last century, that swale has nourished generations of amphibians: frogs, toads, and salamanders. The shallow water, warm and fish free, was premier real estate within which to deposit eggs, a safe shelter for tadpoles and larval young. The swale in springtime was well known to me; it was one of my favorite places near the farm to watch wildlife.

But amphibians are born wary. If startled, frogs and tadpoles scatter and disappear. They hide deep in swale pools, adjacent to and indistinguishable from last autumn's fallen leaves and living spikes of bulrush. But when all is still, tadpoles emerge up into the water column. Some float to the surface and gulp air; some linger, graze algae, and eat plant debris. Some turn and chase each other in a frenzied game of tag.

I anticipated my visit to that natural aquarium with pleasure. As I approached the sunlit pools, I looked for dragonflies in the air, water striders skimming the surface, diving beetles rising and falling in the water column, and I listened for frogs as they splashed to safety. I approached cautiously, tried to remain hidden by trees and shrubs. Not a single frog jumped into the water. As I neared the swale, I leaned over to view tadpoles in the sunny spot. But the sight before me froze me in place.

I did not see dragonflies in the air. I did not see water striders on the surface. I didn't see diving beetles moving up and down as they hunted. I didn't see any tadpoles. I was greeted with something I'd never seen before: still, murky, golden-brown water. Portions of the surface were clouded by a thin gray scum. I found a few small animals, still and lifeless. Two were splayed out on the sticky film, one lay beside the water. I recognized them: a yellow and black millipede, a green and black dragonfly, and a black (with yellow) hoverfly.

My eyes scanned a wider and wider area of the pool, but there was no movement, no life.

The ribbon of still, golden-brown water lay before me. My body stilled, fingers slackened, useless. Buckets tumbled to the ground. I searched for survivors. My eyes registered reassuring remnants of the place: clumps of spiky green rushes, sweetgum branches overarching the swale, shafts of sunlight illuminating the surface of golden-brown water. Plant leaves stirred slightly in the warm air, but the surface of the water was smooth. Gray scum divided the living from the dead. Nothing in the water needed to break the surface for an urgent breath of air. I pivoted in place to look up and down the swale pool. More stillness, more death.

———————

I gathered the bits of plastic that had spilled out of my buckets, picked up tools and water bottle. I turned my back to the river. Home was on the other side of the swale.

Buckets in hand, I crossed the wetland. I tentatively extended each foot as I felt for the stability of large tussocks of sedge and rush and maintained balance for a breath before shifting my weight to take the next step. I leaned my hip against tree trunks for added security. My steps were contracted and uncertain. A mistake would submerge my legs in the swale and my tall boots would fill with the sick-looking water.

Once firmly on the other side, on dry ground, I hurried across the meadow and sprinted for the hill toward home as the sun dipped below the treeline. My breath came in little gasps as I jogged up the steep slope of the trail. A tightness filled my chest and stomach as I climbed—it didn't ease with exercise.

Our small wooden house loomed near the top of the hill. I knew the house would give me shelter, a place to think. I left the path and cut the corner through the forest. My husband, Howard, was in the house, and I needed him. As I approached the porch, I dropped the buckets on the concrete walkway, climbed the porch two steps at a time, and burst into the house: "Howie! Something's wrong with the water in the swale."

My husband sat in his cluttered office next to the side door that opened into the utility room. He looked up from his work. Howard's curly gray hair was swept back from his forehead and framed his kind face. His deep blue eyes gazed at me from behind reading glasses but were calm.

"It's a weird brown color. I don't see anything alive in it." I tried to catch my breath and clutched the office doorknob as if it were an anchor. "But it doesn't make sense. I don't understand what I'm seeing."

I went on to describe the gray scum, the still brown water, and the dead insects.

Howard listened patiently but finally interjected, "Is it all like that? Did you look at other parts of the swale?"

"No, just around a tadpole pool."

He paused. "It seems strange. . . . I wonder if this is a problem with that one area. Or is it the whole wetland?" For a moment, he seemed to not believe me.

I started to gain control over my breathing. "I really—I don't know. I'm shocked . . . I ran straight home." Then I asked, "Is it possible that there was an industrial spill or something in the river during the flood? Did you hear anything about it in the news?"

"No, I haven't," he said.

"Well, I've never seen anything like this before. In the morning, can you please walk down there and look at it with me? I need a second set of eyes on this."

"Sure I can, honey," he said.

I moved into the office. Closer to him. He stood up and I leaned into him as I sought the comfort and reassurance of his arms. He held me upright in a soft, firm embrace. He let me stay there for a long while.

I wasn't able to sleep that night. I tried, but I lay listening to the ceiling fan tick off the seconds of what seemed like eternal hours. I had no frame of reference for the images appearing behind my closed eyes: the still brown water, the dead insects, the gray scum. My scientific training had given me the confidence to believe that if I reviewed all the facts, in the correct sequence, that I would understand. But I didn't understand. What could have killed the creatures in the water?

Each idea was carefully and repeatedly examined and rearranged. *Why were tadpoles gone and insects dead? Were frogs dead or had they left the area? Was the river contaminated? Was there an unreported chemical spill or toxic accident upstream? What made the water golden brown? What was that gray scum?*

The damage I'd discovered in the wetland overwhelmed me. I felt as though I'd lost a beloved pet. And that made sense. We'd built the farm and had worked to support the wildlife that lived here, including the residents of the wetland.

Howard and I arrived at this home about twenty years ago. Both of us were raised as suburban kids in New England, both drawn to country places and country people because of our experiences living in rural areas during our late teens. Decades into our partnership, after the time we raised our daughter, Melissa, in a suburban North Carolina neighborhood, our years-long search revealed this land. We found our homeplace nearby, nestled within a rural community in the heart of the state, the Piedmont.

The Piedmont rolls with green hills, abundant creeks, and rural settlements dotted with small ponds, tractor sheds, and the best of intentions. This community cradles white wooden homes with room-to-visit front porches, kitchen gardens, and azaleas planted in the yard. Small farms reside proudly upon manicured fields of fescue and orchard grass beside the road, mixed woodlots to the back. Trees are harvested at inflection points of life—for tuition, retirement, or during recession. Ancient tobacco barns, milk parlors, and cattle chutes speak of the history of the place. This community is close enough to towns for farmers to reach their salary jobs, and far enough away from towns to *have* a farm. Nationally, 90 percent of family farms need an outside income to keep farming. It's no different here.

Howard and I have claimed our roles at the farm based on our lifelong passions. I'm responsible for the living things. There is a local dog training center, and I've taken our dogs to classes, to socialize, and to play games. Taz, our rescued Cimarrón Uruguayo, trained on the agility course. She learned quickly and would have been a serious competitor if I'd been a better handler. When I fell short, she consoled me with licks of affection, leaps of joy, and tender cuddles.

But growing food has been my focus for decades. Mine is not a picture-perfect garden, but it's a place that produces a lot of food. Here on the farm, we've grown most of the fruits and vegetables we eat. In the past, from March to November, fruits and vegetables flowed steadily from our garden through the farmhouse kitchen and were distributed into our pantry and freezer, out into our neighbors' and friends' hands. Each year, I decided which plants earned their space and should be planted again. I keep records.

Fruit trees and vegetable gardens are planted in the spring and fall. During winter, we use food stored from the harvest.

The cycle of planting, harvesting, preparing, and consuming our produce feels real and deeply relevant in so many ways. Although sometimes challenging, the process of raising food is a simple partnership. We take care of the land and the inhabitants, and they take care of us. The orchard and garden have been bountiful. The work is honest. It brings me joy. Working on the farm puts me in direct contact with the natural world, the place where I thrive.

My husband, Howard, is active on the farm in a different way: he's the physical science expert. He manages the plumbing, the tractor, the electrical system. He knows the chemistry of lubricating oils, solvents, and glues. He understands the workings of batteries, transformers, and the electronic devices that analyze and run our world. He's a radio engineer with a need for quiet places and a talent for fixing mechanical things. Howard spends his time working on technically demanding jobs big and small. He winnows information from multiple disciplines and distributes it among many others. Howard has always felt the pull and power of human connections more strongly than most. He's a friend you would be grateful to have, and I am.

Howard and I have worked to build a more fertile soil and to create a productive homeplace. When we first moved here, the austere shape of the boxy house sat within a red clay sea of recently cleared forest. We spent weeks picking up small rocks and branches from the fields, returning each evening to the house with clay-encased boots like bizarre, freeform clown shoes.

Over time, we developed this farm, in this community, and made it our "forever" home. That probably makes us sound like rescued pets. But in a way, this place *did* rescue us. We settled into this community and grew into wider ways of seeing the world.

Although we arrived as sheltered suburbanites, at the farm we've built broader, deeper skills. We learned how some regard the land from the perspective of a working landscape rather than just a pretty view. How precious every drop of water can be in summertime. How electricity can't be taken for granted. How to do more for ourselves and our neighbors. The demands of our homeplace have pushed and pulled us; we've increased our physical strength, our emotional resilience, our knowledge of the land and the life it supports. We've developed an enhanced awareness of the multitude around us.

———————

The recurrent floods far below our home on the hill had always been an inconvenience for us because we used the floodplain as horse pasture. After each flood, we waited days so that we could fix the fences. When the meadows dried, the work began. I walked and Howard drove the tractor down the old farm road to the river. We wrestled branches out of intricate knots of downed fence wires, untangled trash and small limbs. Masses of dried leaves and trash tightly festooned those wires that remained taut within the fence line. When the debris was disturbed, silty river dust rose into the air. We positioned ourselves upwind of the filthy brown clouds.

We pulled logs and tree parts away from the fence with the tractor's might, and then used the tractor's bucket to carry them out of the floodplain. We straightened and replaced posts. Finally, we walked along the fence perimeter and replaced broken insulators. If we missed some, the electrified fence wire would short-circuit and allow the horses true freedom to explore the neighborhood.

Floods were hard work for us. But they were an opportunity for the amphibians and aquatic insects like dragonflies to breed. To them, the floods meant new life.

We always knew when the swales were full as even from far away, high on the hill, we could hear frog song from within our house. Normally, after heavy rains or spring floods, the swale water was deep and the songs would last all night. It was wonderful: the trills of American toads would weave together an otherworldly chorus, spring peepers earned their name, and barking tree frogs sounded like of a pack of dogs quarreling in the meadow. But after the recent flood, even with the swale brimming full that moonlit May night, the farm was strangely quiet.

The next morning, Howard and I walked downhill together to look for life in the wetland. As Howard stood over the water, I could see that he too was shocked. He took my hand and squeezed it gently. Lonely green spears of sedge leaves and tips of spikerush broke the surface of the brown water. A breeze moved sweetgum tree leaves over our heads. We turned upstream and walked slowly and quietly, looking for animals. We looked for normal signs of life in the swale.

We found none.

Howard and I climbed back up the hill to the house just before noon. There was no point in calling for help. The environmental and wildlife experts that I hoped could advise me were not in their offices. Even though I felt great urgency, I believed that this was no emergency. I thought then that the quiet, sick water had already done its damage.

Brief emails were sent off to my veterinary and environmental science colleagues. I described the water and ended with: "Have you ever seen/heard of this before? I didn't see any useful reports in the literature. I've never seen this situation in the sixteen years we've lived here." I sent the first email to a professor from the veterinary college who worked with aquatic wildlife, and then another to a state scientist knowledgeable

We looked for normal signs of life, but found none.

about water quality and types of contamination. I ended each message, "Please advise if you can help."

I hoped they would see my summaries the next day as they started their workweek. I sent another message to the Eden's Riverkeeper, a wise woman, experienced in the ways of the river and knowledgeable about most threats to it. My message had described the wetland water and ended with a question: "Was there a spill or contamination event during the flood?"

To my surprise, she answered almost immediately. "No, not to my knowledge," she wrote. "I'll let you know if I learn of anything."

Well, so much for my worst fears of the previous night.

———————

With no evidence of a major disaster in the river, I thought about the floodplain. The swale that bisects it is an overgrown remnant of an old drainage system. It was dug early in the last century to help dry the crop fields in the meadow.

The fields did not flood every year in those days, and the fertile floodplain was locally renowned for producing bountiful corn crops. As a newcomer to the community twenty years ago, even I heard the tales of the unbelievable harvests of corn pulled from those meadows. Huge ears of corn were handpicked and loaded into groaning wooden wagons hauled with difficulty up the old farm road. But now, upstream development and heavy rainfall have made river flooding an annual (or more frequent) occurrence, and the meadows near our place bore only wildflowers.

But it had been that enduring reputation of exceptional corn yields that had attracted a local farmer, Robert Feld, to rent our neighbors' land. I'd known the Felds for over twenty-five years. They're all spare—Nordic fair. Robert, wiry thin with crazy dandelion hair, has lived in the community his whole life. I can spot him from afar due to that hair and his penchant for wearing brightly colored golf shirts.

When I first met the family, Robert's dad had a thriving used-car business. He went to auctions and came home with cars and light trucks that seemed to need just a little attention to be attractive to buyers. I can imagine he learned early that at auction, it's not always obvious why the vehicle's on the block. Sometimes one discovers unpleasant details after the bid is won. So Robert's dad learned to fix engines, brakes, transmissions, whatever was needed to move the vehicle off his lot. I imagine Robert, a strong teenager at the time, helped him with those heavy jobs.

But when Robert was a young man, his dad gave it up. I imagine that Robert's father had had enough of mandatory employee withholdings, business taxes, and complicated paperwork. Enough of officials telling him where and how much of what engine fluid he could store in barrels outside, behind the showroom. I imagine that the demands and insults from people, many of whom were from outside the community, started to add up—to chafe. I wonder if the casual disrespect, the long hours, the bad vehicles that could not be sold at a profit, all took their toll. Whatever the reason, Robert's dad decided to go another way, a more independent path where he could use family land to make a living. He established Feld Farms.

Mike and Anne Wilson also live in our community. They're solid citizens. Salt of the earth. They're active on their farm and give to needy members of the community. The Wilsons are the kind of ordinary, middle-aged, country people who don't stand out in a crowd. But they would be among the first people I'd pick to have on my team if need be.

The Wilsons' family owns the floodplain meadows upstream of us, along Halting Creek. The creek has a tamer disposition than the big river it feeds. Although it floods less frequently than the Eden, its floodplain is also rich and fertile. The land had been a meadow, with abundant wildflowers, deer, and turkey for most of the time we'd lived on the farm, but during the previous few years, the Wilsons had rented out the fields to Robert to grow row crops.

I remembered that I'd heard the sound of Robert's tractor recently. He'd been planting in the Halting Creek fields before the flood.

I waited until well after church crowds spilled out of doors into pickup trucks and four-door sedans and people had dispersed over the local roads to give him a call.

"Hey, Robert," I greeted him, "I hope you-all are well." I went on, "I'm having a problem at my place and am hoping you can help. I heard you out on your tractor in Mike's bottom fields before the flood. What have you done so far out there for the planting season?"

"Oh, hey. We're fine, hope you are," he said. "Yeah, I burnt the field down the dry week after the rain."

Robert described "burning"—killing the plants growing on the field with the herbicide Roundup—on about April 11 to prepare the fields for planting. Then, he led me through his routine: he'd drilled corn seed into the soil on April 17 and injected nitrogen into the field four days later. The nitrogen was applied three days before the waters covered the floodplain.

"Was there anything else? Any other pesticides?" I asked. I told him about the still, dead water and the absence of frogs and insects in the swale.

"I have no idea what to tell you," he said. "The only pesticide I sprayed was the Roundup. It—"

I cut Robert off mid-sentence as I cried, "But Roundup doesn't do this!"

I wasn't afraid of Roundup. I'd used it on the farm. Roundup is an herbicide, a kind of pesticide that kills plants. And Roundup is very effective at killing plants. It's called a broad spectrum herbicide, meaning that it kills both grasses and other plants with broad leaves like poison ivy, trees, and shrubs. When we first established pastures for the horses, I'd sprayed the grass along the electric fence line multiple times with it until I realized that only wild garlic survived the spray. Then, I saw the garlic creeping inward, threatening to take over the pastures. After that experience, I used shears to control any vegetation that threatened to short the electric fence. But we continued to use Roundup to treat the freshly cut stems of invasive or unwanted woody plants: it prevents the stumps from sprouting again.

I'd never observed Roundup to have severe effects on the environment, although I was careful not to spray it near water. I knew that it was toxic to animals that live in water—there was a warning about it on the label. But Robert had not sprayed Roundup into the wetland, he had sprayed it onto fields next to Halting Creek, far uphill from the swale water.

That spring, I still believed the manufacturer's description of Roundup—for such a powerful tool, it seemed environmentally innocuous. The benign properties of Roundup were common knowledge among gardeners, landscapers, and property owners. We'd all viewed years of television and print advertisements for the Roundup products. The manufacturer had touted many reassuring attributes of its herbicide that made me comfortable using it. I was pleased to learn from those promotional materials that Roundup was "biodegradable and won't build up in the soil"; "it will not wash or leach in the soil. . . . It stays where you apply it." I was also reassured that it only harmed plants that were directly sprayed with the chemical and that it degraded quickly in the environment "into naturally occurring elements."

It was touted as having a "toxicity category rating of 'practically non-toxic' as it pertains to mammals, birds and fish." And "Roundup can be used where kids and pets'll play." The manufacturers explained that its active ingredient targeted and interrupted an enzyme in a biochemical pathway that plants and microbes use, but that animals do not. Plants use that pathway to make specific proteins—essential components for growth, defense against pathogens, and reproduction. But we were all assured that Roundup was safe for people and animals.

In 2017 I didn't understand that I was confusing clever marketing with science. Of course, now I realize that if accepted at face value, half-truths can be dangerous things.

After saying thank you and good-bye to Robert, I hung up the telephone, sat down, and put my dully aching head in my hands. Burnt bits of fatigue and toxic neural residue from a night of sleepless worry cluttered my brain. An anxious hum had settled in alongside the dull swamp of nausea. Part of me desperately wanted to sleep, but for the time being, I had to work. I had to figure out what had poisoned the water.

I'd learned of nothing different in the river, nothing important in the field next door. It made no sense. But insect bodies beside the water and the absent frogs told me that something was there.

Finally, I realized what I had to do: I needed evidence. I had to gather water samples if I was ever going to learn what had sickened the wetland and killed the wildlife.

I poured myself another cup of coffee and settled down at the computer to learn more. I knew that I should focus on chemicals in the water. I could not think of what else might kill both insects and tadpoles in the wetland while high on the hill above, we still seemed healthy. But I was stretching out beyond my professional knowledge. My environmental science work involved investigating and collecting information about the health of living animals and people, not sampling water for chemical contaminants. I'd read many reports about water contamination, but I hadn't done the fieldwork myself. But I knew that time was of the essence; chemicals can break down in the presence of microbes and sunlight. I didn't know what I was dealing with or how much time I had to collect samples.

The first thing I learned was that there was no single method for preserving evidence of contamination. Some chemicals, like volatile solvents, can escape (or volatize) out of the sample into the air; one seeks a tight lid and a completely full bottle to preserve those samples. Some, such as pesticides, usually require glass bottles, but some need added preservatives to stabilize the chemicals while in transit to the laboratory. Duplicate samples are always required as each water sample, even from the same site, may vary. I knew that an adequate sampling plan was essential, a plan that would preserve evidence of contamination. But I was at a disadvantage as I didn't know what exactly was in the water.

I couldn't send water samples to a lab and ask them, "Please tell me what's in this water." It doesn't work that way, because there are all kinds of chemicals in water. Some are naturally occurring, like the tannins that leach from submerged, decaying leaves, brown and flaccid in the bottom of the swale. Some manufactured chemicals are released into the environment and are known to flow into water, like the nitrogen Robert added to the fields upstream from the wetland. Water chemistry can differ, even among adjacent ponds, lakes, and streams. So to submit samples for analysis, I had to ask for specific tests. It was my job to identify a list of suspect chemicals so that *I* could tell the lab what to look for.

After reviewing the array of sampling procedures, I selected glass bottles with no additives and I hoped that they would suffice. Because that Sunday, it was up to me to collect water and to preserve evidence.

2

FIELDWORK

That Sunday afternoon, I walked the length of the Eden River flood-plain. Green trees, grass. Blue river. On the surface, all seemed well. But the water in the wetland was painted with gray. Still, lifeless. No frogs, no insects. The flow of my breath and the sound of my footfalls counted time.

I scouted the length of the wetland swale for the best sites to gather water samples. I looked for shaded pools with some depth—ideal places to preserve evidence of chemical contamination. I found four sites along our portion of the swale. As a control, or contrasting water sample, I marked a fifth site on the river bank. I identified each site with pink surveyor tape tied to a tree branch. I wrote the site number on each tape, then I captured pictures with my phone in case the plastic tapes were lost.

Focused work in bright sunshine replaced the sick knot of worry in my gut.

I made a second trip downhill through the forest to the floodplain. I pushed a wheelbarrow filled with sampling supplies gleaned from our pantry, home office, and medical cabinet—all sat next to a picnic cooler half-full of crushed ice. Next to the swale, I pulled on nitrile gloves, grabbed jars, and collected water samples—two full jars from each site. I marked a paper label with the sample number, site code, time, date, and my initials, and stuck it upon the dried shoulder of each jar. I copied sample information into a log I'd created in a notebook; I'd scan it later for my documentation file. Jars snuggled deep into ice chips.

When I'd collected all ten jars, I checked each lid again—tightly closed—then shut the cooler and pushed the wheelbarrow back up the hill to the house. Before storing the jars, I wrapped each one in aluminum foil to exclude light, then slid each carefully into place far back on the bottom shelf of a refrigerator along with a thermometer to monitor their temperature. Safe, secure, done.

As I sank gratefully into a chair, I was overwhelmed by the scope of the investigation before me. This was all new, all unknown, and I wanted help. But I wasn't concerned. I knew how to be persistent—I was determined to find the experts I needed.

In my mind, the perfect scenario was that a knowledgeable field scientist would visit the swale, that they'd collect water samples and quickly identify what had killed the life in the wetland. As a backup, my own samples waited—cold and dark. I needed to preserve that evidence as a kind of insurance. Because it was possible that my expectation of someone to help me find out what had destroyed our oasis, the very center of life in the meadows, was only a hopeful dream.

Monday morning dawned. I made my excuses at work—I needed some time away from the office to seek help. In the past, I'd worked with the state water quality office, so as soon as they opened, I dialed their main number.

"Hi, I have a wetland that looks like it's been poisoned. Dead insects lying beside the water. Who can come out and look?" The receptionist put me through to the field office manager, Mr. Dawson. I was unfamiliar with the field office and not sure what to expect.

"Thanks for taking my call," I said. I inhaled, willed myself to slow down and keep it simple. "I discovered our wetland damaged last Saturday. It's in the floodplain of the Eden. Thin gray scum. Brown water. Dead insects. We just recovered from a flood, so the wetland was submerged by both the Eden River and Halting Creek. I've reached out to the Eden Riverkeeper, but she didn't know of any contamination in the river. Do you know of anything?"

I had to catch my breath.

"No. Have you talked to your neighbors?"

"Yup," I said. "I spoke to the farmer who cultivates the bottom lands uphill of us along the creek. He's the only one who's been working in the floodplain as far as I know. He has no idea what's going on. That's why I called your office. I need help with this. I've never seen anything like it."

I took another deep breath. I waited.

"Hang on a second," he said. "Looks like I can send someone out there, a field investigator, to make a site visit on Wednesday."

"That would be great, thank you," I said. Maybe this would be just what I needed.

I was impatient for answers.

The next two days were a blur. Office hours were filled with me trying to concentrate on my work, while evenings were spent reading about the effects of nitrogen and Roundup on wildlife. Early in my search, I confirmed my previous understanding: one must avoid spraying Roundup on water. The Roundup spray Robert told me he used includes both an active ingredient (glyphosate) and a surfactant, or sticking agent, added to make the spray stay on plant parts. The combination of the two types of chemicals contaminates water and is toxic to many water creatures, especially amphibians.

Amphibians are sensitive. They begin their lives in water, they have tails, no legs, and use gills to breathe underwater. Adults develop legs and usually lungs, but most stay near water throughout their lives. Amphibian skin is unique—it can absorb both water and oxygen. Their unique physiology makes them extremely sensitive to toxic substances—more so than most other animals. A thriving population of amphibians is a good indicator of clean water. I'd become used to abundant frogs and salamanders in and around the swale—and I wanted them back.

Although I kept reading about the chemicals, nothing was making sense. Why were the amphibians missing? The Roundup had been sprayed in the cornfield during a dry week, almost fourteen days before the flood; it hadn't been sprayed into the swale and wetland. There was no information I could find that suggested that Roundup could kill insects. Even if somehow the nitrogen or Roundup had flowed off the fields upstream, the flood was large and lasted two days. Two days with millions of gallons of water flowing through the system—I couldn't comprehend how such highly diluted agricultural chemicals could kill wildlife.

———

On Wednesday, Johnson Bradley arrived in his work truck. He stepped out of the cab, a youngish man, tight lipped and neatly dressed in khaki field clothes and work boots.

"Hey, thanks for coming out." I pointed toward the river. "The wet-land's downhill through the woods. Once we get out onto the floodplain, it'll be pretty easy to see the layout." I turned and pointed. "Halting Creek is that way."

Johnson opened the back of the truck and revealed his tools: a large plastic bucket, sample bottles, a sample extension rod, and a water-testing sonde. A sonde is a wand-like instrument with delicate sensors at the tip. A basic sonde detects physical water qualities such as temperature, pH, dissolved oxygen, and other measurements.

"Can I help carry anything?" I asked, my right palm extended toward him.

Johnson grunted, "I got it."

He shut the door to the truck bed, turned his back to me, and strode out, bucket bristling with tools. We followed the old farm road downhill. I struggled to keep pace with him.

"I'm so glad you're here," I said. "I first saw the water on Saturday but didn't believe my eyes. I've never seen anything like it. I asked my husband to look at it because frankly, I had trouble believing what I was seeing. But he saw the same thing! No insects, no tadpoles."

I was in uncharted territory and I wanted Johnson to tell me *his* experience, what *he* was seeing. But he was silent. I heard myself filling the empty space between us. My anxiety manifested into a whirlwind of sound that I couldn't easily control.

Johnson kept walking.

"You know, we've lived here for about sixteen years," I continued, trying to catch up. "I spend a lot of time outside, and the wetland's one of my favorite places. I've seen so many tadpoles grow up and leave the wetland. You know, a few years ago I found a green frog tadpole. Have you ever seen one? They're *huge*! I thought it was a bullfrog tadpole when I first saw it. I had to look it up in my field guide or I never would have known."

I struggled to catch my breath between words, and finished. "This whole experience has been such a shock. I'm really glad you're here to help."

Johnson reached the wetland and set his bucket down. With one hand, he inserted the end of the sonde into a deep pool of water. He looked at the sonde's digital readout in his other hand, pulled the sonde tip out, walked twenty feet upstream and took another measurement. I followed behind. A few more measurements and he said over his shoulder, "The oxygen and pH values are all normal," he said. "Nothing to be concerned about here."

"But Johnson, there are no tadpoles here. This sunny pool should be teeming with animals," I said. "Look, here's another one. Dead." I pointed to a millipede lying on its side next to the water. "I've seen no living insects in the water since the flood. *That's* why I called your office. This is so strange. Really abnormal."

"Hear that?" Johnson asked. He pointed to the forested hillside. "That's a gray tree frog." He kept walking, his eyes on the water.

As we walked along the western edge of swale, a strange shadow in the water drew my eye. I stooped down and saw an Eastern box turtle suspended in the water; it was listing at a forty-five-degree angle, its head angled upward but submerged, its front legs visible about halfway down in the water column. The turtle's limbs were extended, motionless, frozen in space—like an insect trapped in amber.

That was new. Box turtles are land animals. I'd never seen one resting motionless under water before. I gazed at it for a moment, then realized that it was submerged in whatever had killed the insects. Without thinking, I plunged my hand into the water, grabbed the animal around its upper shell and lifted it to safety.

As I put the stunned animal on the bank by the water, I saw her dark eyes and realized that it was a female. I murmured a quick prayer for her survival so that she could live to reproduce again. Over the last few decades, turtles have become scarce in our area; each one is so precious. The turtle remained motionless. Her head was fixed and fully extended, limbs and tail stiff and straight with only her bottom shell plate touching the ground.

We left her on the bank of the swale and continued walking along the water. Within minutes, I felt an itching sensation on my right hand and wrist. Another hundred feet along and the itching sensation became an intense burning.

"Johnson, I made a mistake," I spoke into the silence. "I shouldn't have touched the water. My hand and arm are burning."

He kept walking.

We walked another hundred feet.

I tried again. "Will you collect water samples now?"

"There's no obvious sewage spill into the wetland," he said. "There's no smell. The sonde showed no abnormalities. There's no reason to take water samples."

We climbed the hill in silence. Johnson put his equipment in the back of the truck, climbed into the driver's seat, and drove away. He left a cloud of gravel dust in the air.

My stomach clenched; I used the pain to propel myself up the stairs and through the side door of the house.

Inside, I gently washed my burning arm at the utility sink and seethed. I was frustrated by Johnson's response and frustrated with myself. I'd not brought gloves to the field. I'd hiked down there with no intention of touching that water; I'd put myself at some unknown risk to help an animal in distress.

I felt like an idiot as I'd talked too much. Ultimately though, I was mystified as to why Johnson was so uncommunicative and had declined to collect water samples.

I settled at the computer and was glad to see a reply to my email from Dr. Jay Levine at the veterinary college. I'd hoped Jay's expertise in aquatic animal medicine would help me in my quest. I gave him a call. Although he listened carefully to my story, he had no immediate thoughts about the cause of the deaths. "I don't know, Betsy, it could be anything. So strange. But I think you're on the right track about something toxic in the water," he said. "The question is, what is it?

"You know, there's a chemist here at the university who screens environmental samples and analyzes them without needing a target analyte." Jay was describing new methods that could identify chemicals in water even without a list of target or probable contaminants.

"I don't know. Let me contact him and see if he can help you," he said.

I thanked him and hung up.

The rest of my week was spent calling county and state agriculture, wildlife, and extension personnel whenever I found time between my day job and farm chores. During each call, I settled into a loose script: "Thanks for taking my call. I have a problem. Our farm's near a wetland along the Eden. On May 6, I found the wetland water still and scummy. No amphibians where they'd been plentiful before. Dead insects lying around the water."

By this point people usually interrupted with something like, "There's natural variability among wildlife populations every year. It's hard to say if that's really abnormal."

I'd continue, "Well, there was a flood the week before. I reached out to the local farmer upstream to see if he knew of anything that could have washed off his cornfield into the wetland. The farmer said he used Roundup and nitrogen to prepare the field at planting, but I've never heard of those chemicals killing insects. What do you think? Any ideas?"

"Sorry that happened, but there isn't a connection with the cornfield," one said. Another expert said, "You describe a big flood. Sometimes floods can kill wildlife." Also: "How strange. I've never heard of such a thing!"

"Do you know of any toxic spills in the river or creek that could have damaged the wetland?" I asked.

"No spills I know of. What a mystery. Have you contacted the water quality group in Raleigh?"

"Yes."

Finally, I spoke to a specialist at the pesticide office in Raleigh.

"That's an unusual story, but we have limited resources here," he said. "We can only come out to investigate if there was intentional dumping or criminal activity involving farm chemicals. Were farm chemicals involved?"

"I don't know. The farmer told me about his normal field prep: Roundup a couple weeks before the flood and nitrogen a few days before. Of course, he didn't know the flood was coming."

"Were any domestic animals, people, or livestock hurt by this incident?" he said.

I mentioned my burning hand and arm. "Well you should talk to your doctor about that," he told me.

I learned that, in his opinion, an irritated hand did not rise to the level of injury required to start an investigation.

How frustrating. Were people not taking me seriously? They seemed to dismiss me. But I realized that I had reached out to all as a citizen, not a scientist. I know that public offices are typically short-staffed, and I presented a potentially complicated problem. Or did I experience disbelief in the face of an unusual and inconvenient request?

I heard that there should be no connection between the cornfield and the wildlife. That the sequence of events in the cornfield—Roundup for field prep, seed planting, then nitrogen—are common and routine. I was reassured that today's farm chemicals are designed to degrade quickly and are stable; they don't move around in the environment. I was told that the cornfield shouldn't be a problem for water nearby. Especially since the wetland was over fifty feet away from the edge of the field.

But if contamination didn't come from the river and didn't come from the cornfield, what was going on?

It felt as if I wasn't asking the right questions. Or that people were speaking in some sort of code—insider knowledge that wasn't part of my world of fruit orchards and environmental health science.

Indeed, the information I'd offered up was limited. All I had were my observations and the bits of information I had gleaned from the Riverkeeper and from Robert about his cornfield.

But there had to be more. What was I missing? My gut told me that I had to dig deeper.

Corn seems so familiar. For me, cornfields have always been a reassuring part of rural landscapes—productive land full of food. My experience isn't unusual. Corn is the number-one crop grown in the United States; in 2017, corn covered ninety million acres of farmland. Corn feeds animals such as cattle, chickens, and hogs. Corn products include corn meal, syrup, and starch—they're staples in our diets. Corn feeds us.

Corn is native to North and Central America, and it's sustained Americans for thousands of years. But the corn we know today is wholly a human creation. Modern corn is a product of almost ten thousand years of selective breeding. Over time, selective breeding can result in dramatic changes. This is obvious when we look at our dogs. Many of us know that our Chihuahua dogs' distant relative is the wolf, but we may be less aware of corn's distant ancestor, a wild perennial grass: teosinte.

Teosinte is uncommon today, but it's still found growing in parts of southern Mexico and Central America. Teosinte looks very different from modern corn; it has branches and produces long, thin, scant-seeded heads of grain. Each teosinte grain is small, hard, and difficult to process for food. Over thousands of years of selecting the best grain-producing teosinte plants for food, ancient (and modern) plant breeders have had to make tradeoffs to achieve the corn plant that we know today.

Modern corn is single stalked, with one or two large heads of grain. Many soft kernels burst with starch and sugar. During the selection process, we gained a delicious, versatile food. But we lost things too. We lost the perennial nature of the teosinte plant, its ability to live in waterlogged soil, and its ability to fix, or take, its own nitrogen from the air. Our loss is better appreciated now, because the ancient plant's superpowers are needed to solve many of modern corn's most challenging problems.

Modern corn needs supplemental nitrogen to produce high yields of grain. Most commonly, the nitrogen applied to cornfields across the country is made from ammonia manufactured with energy-intensive industrial processes. So nitrogen prices are volatile because they track the price of oil. In 2017, fertilizer was the most expensive of all the (operating) costs required to get a field planted in corn—more expensive than corn seed. But under ideal growing conditions of moist soil (but not too moist), warm days (but not too warm), and lots of sunshine, young corn plants respond well to nitrogen and grow rapidly.

But nitrogen has a dark side. Apply too much, or apply it at the wrong time, and high nitrogen concentrations can damage young corn. Bystanders can be harmed too—large amounts of nitrogen in the form of ammonia can kill other plant and animal life. Nitrogen application is an art, and rainfall is a wild card because nitrogen has a serious flaw: it's water soluble. Rainfall in the right amounts, at the proper time, can support a healthy harvest.

If it's too wet early in the year before nitrogen has been absorbed by the plant, money is wasted. Or worse: nitrogen moves in the rivulets of rainwater flowing over the surface of the land and through the soil. Nitrogen fertilizer is harmful when rain washes it out of the soil and it runs off the field into ditches, creeks, then rivers, and eventually into the ocean. Excess nitrogen hurts aquatic wildlife, feeds harmful algal blooms, and creates dead zones in coastal waters.

Gravity pulls nitrogen-contaminated water downward through soil into the groundwater. Today, many Americans receive tap water tainted with harmful amounts of nitrogen. And the problem is greatest in agricultural areas where people drink groundwater.

I had no evidence that nitrogen had wiped out both tadpoles and insects. There was no reason for me to believe that Robert, an experienced farmer, had wasted money by spreading too much nitrogen in the cornfield. There were other clues that argued against nitrogen toxicity:

young corn plants did not appear burned, and there were no apparent algal blooms in the warm, still water of the swale. I also realized that there had been so much floodwater flowing through and over those fields that most of the nitrogen Robert had applied that spring was most likely far downstream within days of the flood.

While it seemed remotely plausible that the recently applied Roundup could have harmed the frogs, it did not explain the insect deaths. It was not coming together as a coherent story. I still needed to find an expert to solve my mystery of the dead wetland. Ideally, a field investigator, someone who could come out, see the site, and take samples and analyze them for the toxic chemicals that had done the damage.

But I was striking out.

3

DAZED AND CONFUSED

MY FINGERS FELT ALONG the bedside table in the dark, then closed around notepad and pen.

"entomology dept NC State"

"glyphosate degradation in water"

"check ammonia vs. urea effects"

I was obsessed. Even at 3:00 AM.

During those dark, quiet hours, all was so still the scratch of my pen seemed intrusive. When I paused from writing fragments of new ideas to investigate, when my brain stopped churning out bits of information I'd gathered during the day, I could hear the normal sounds of the night: a clock ticking, the dogs snoring softly from their beds three rooms away, and coyote song that echoed and wove through the river valley. In the morning light, sometimes my scrawled notes offered illegible words, bizarre symbols, and few new leads.

Worry took its toll. One predawn morning, after hours of fractured sleep, I hauled myself out of bed and walked to the toilet. As I passed the sink, I caught a glimpse of movement and turned to face the mirror. A smudged reflection of dark shadows. A pale face looked back.

I watched the lip smudge stretch and heard, "Keep it together."

A quick internal accounting revealed no current crisis in my family that should cause such distress. Our daughter, Melissa, had finished college and was living in a distant city, self-supporting and well. My mother, Vivian, was gone. As an only child, I'd managed her final years of care; when she passed, the constant worry for her well-being had also been put to rest.

The last years with Vivian had indeed been difficult. Dementia progressively ravaged the structure of the beautiful life she'd created for herself. I'd moved her to North Carolina to oversee her care. But the move abruptly separated her from a self-made system of layered compensations for fading short-term memory. She struggled with adapting to a new home, and the transition accelerated her decline. Because here, everything essential—store locations, phone numbers, and neighborhood streets—all depended upon making and recalling new memories.

Together, we'd held hands and watched the details of her life fade in reverse order. Thankfully, her most recent memories of medical errors, painful falls, and hospitalizations were the first to go. Awareness of her violent, tumultuous marriage seemed to have vanished. She was unaware that my father had died two decades before. By the end, she lived her earliest days again accompanied by Mrs. Hole.

My mother was left at an orphanage at the age of four with one younger sister, Molly; the third and youngest sister had been torn away from the older girls and placed in a foster home. The Children's Home was managed by a small group of stout, stern matrons who acted as wardens and surrogate parents—including the kindly Mrs. Hole. My grandfather dropped the girls off in September 1929 as the Great Depression descended upon the community. So, as a preschooler, overnight, my mother was separated from her parents *and* her youngest sister. Her familiar home and family of five was abruptly replaced by an institution and a revolving horde of children in crisis.

After some time, the three sisters were rejoined in the Children's Home. But as the years passed, my grandfather never brought them home. During the Depression, he started a new family of sons with my grandmother; I imagine that the girls didn't seem to fit into their lives anymore. So the three girls spent their entire childhoods at the home. And as they matured, each of them wrestled in their own unique way with the toxic residue of long-term institutionalization and abandonment.

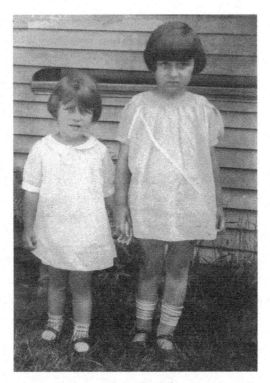

Vivian (right) and Molly (left), 1929.

I was deeply grateful when Vivian's dementia allowed her to pass beyond the exquisite pain of episodic self-awareness. She'd watched herself simplify and shed the pleasures of life: literature, choral groups, travel, and bridge games. She'd been a strong, independent woman before such behavior was somewhat accepted: in the 1950s, she worked as an insurance agent while my father attended graduate school at Duke University. He returned the favor as she earned graduate degrees in English literature after I started elementary school.

Although Vivian never spoke to me directly about life options, she never discouraged my interests. In addition to the family cats, she indulged me by allowing me to keep a series of pets in my room: hooded rats, a boa constrictor, gerbils, fish, and those poor turtles that were sold in the local Woolworth's—complete with a plastic tank and palm tree–shaded basking island.

At the age of nine I proudly declared to our family friend, Mr. Tosti, that I was going to be a veterinarian when I grew up. He laughed at me and admonished, "Girls can't be veterinarians!"

I remember that this struck me as an unusual opinion, given my open-minded family. I mentioned it to my mother the same evening and she laughed. "Do what *you* need to do. It's your life." So, despite the old man's disbelief, I worked my way to a veterinary degree and a career in environmental health science.

So I'd watched with great dismay as my intrepid, strong mother progressively lost her sense of time and direction, her former home, her independence, and the company of her best friends. By the end, she didn't recognize her family.

But I'm always grateful for a mother who fought with courage for her convictions all of her life—and I learned at her knee.

But the death in the wetland was a different kind of threat. I had no roadmap, no experience to meet the challenge. Our land and the animals I loved were in danger. But after all, I thought, I'd met challenges that seemed overwhelming before: I recalled parenting a young teen, crises at work, and my confusion at age twenty-two when I tried to make sense of my father's violent death while he was alone in another country.

If every struggle had occurred at the same time, I might have collapsed into a pile of dusty bits, immobile, gratefully at equilibrium with gravity, finally inert and unable to resist the wind or the grasp of the Eden River's current as it pushed downhill to the Atlantic.

But my eyes adjusted to the dark. The mirror reflected a resilient woman with a determined mouth. "You are strong. You can do this."

I kept moving.

The next morning, I reassessed my situation. My goal was to find the cause of the destruction or at least identify some suspect chemicals so that I could have my water samples tested. But I was hurting myself in the process. Only nervous energy kept me moving forward; I was unable to rest. I couldn't sleep, and I found that tears were coming easily when I thought about the wetland—or sometimes for unknown reasons.

I found myself drifting, wanting, needing reassurance from my family. Reassurance of life. As I passed Howard in the house, I found any reason to touch him. If he stood still, I leaned into him. Once when he paused at the kitchen counter, I ducked under an arm and rose in front of him into his surprised embrace. I found myself sitting beside the dogs on their beds, perched on one cheek. I stroked their backs and bellies. Sometimes I lay my head on a furry shoulder. I soaked up their warmth and listened for evidence of strength and vigor. I relaxed into the reassuring sounds of deep breaths and strong hearts beating.

I called my doctor's office and scheduled an appointment for later that week and wondered what I'd say to him. My primary problem was stress, my state of mind, but I was hesitant to discuss it. The unknown exposure that resulted in a burning arm seemed straightforward enough—the pain was a common symptom of exposure to an irritant or toxicant. But what about my grief about the dead wildlife and my anxiety about not knowing the cause of the destruction? After all, these were insects and frogs—creatures that most people either disregard or avoid.

Luckily, Dr. Regal and I have known each other for years, and he understands my love of animals.

"Love of animals'" may be an inadequate description. I feel grounded when I'm immersed in the vibrant community of life—it feels like a whispered conversation. An embrace. A delightful warmth. A world full of new possibilities and potential adventures. Many people love animals: cats, elephants, parrots, yes—I get it. But unlike most other people, I seem to have developed a broader fascination with all of God's creatures.

This became obvious to me when our friends Chloe and Mark joined us at home for dinner for the first time many years ago. After the meal ended, we were still at the table, talking and relaxing. Chloe sat loosely in her chair, one hand under the table petting Charlie's ear; she looked around, eyes sliding by the objects in the dining room. She suddenly sat up straighter and turned toward the corner of the room.

"What's *that*?" she asked. Her hand abruptly left the dog, and her forefinger extended toward a small stone carving atop the far corner cabinet. The rest of her body recoiled.

"Oh, this?" I jumped up and strode to the cabinet. "This is a carving of a common green snake. I love how the artist captured the texture of the scales, even the scutes on the bottom. The stone is cool, and with the texture, well, to me, it feels similar to a real snake in hand." My hand stroked the textured length of the coiled snake. "I think that's what sold me on it."

Carefully, I slid the carved stone off its wooden base and handed it to her so that she could admire the fine workmanship and the realistic feel of the object.

Chloe looked surprised but reached out tentatively and let me place the stone snake in her palm, belly up. She gazed at it thoughtfully, turned it over, then reached out and delicately dropped it back in my hastily outstretched hand.

"You're not like other girls, are you?" she asked.

At the doctor's office I was encouraged to sit down in the examination room and wait. I sat, but my knees vibrated in place as I bounced on the balls of my feet.

After about ten minutes, Dr. Regal came into the room.

"Hi, Betsy, what brings you in today?"

"Hello, John, thanks for fitting me into your schedule. I've been having a really hard time sleeping. I recently discovered a wetland near my home with dead animals. The life's gone from the water. I have no idea what's happened. I suspect some sort of chemical—I'm actively investigating it," I said. "In general, though, I'm overtired and worried because I don't know what's going on. I'm not sleeping."

"Hmmm. How long since you've had a good night's sleep?"

"About six days. The other issue is that earlier this week, I made the mistake of putting my hand in the wetland water. It itched, then burned my arm, but no lasting rash. I was able to wash it well, but only about half an hour after exposure. I have no idea what it is, but I'm concerned that I was exposed to something toxic, given the dead animals around the water."

"OK, any other symptoms?"

"A few times a day I get really dizzy and have to sit if I'm standing, but it passes after a minute or so. My major issue right now is the fatigue. I need to turn my mind off so I can get some rest."

Dr. Regal stood up. "Let's pull some blood to check your chemistry to see if there's any obvious effect from touching the water. I'll also prescribe a sedative; it should give you some relief so you can rest. Let me know if the dizziness gets worse or if anything else changes."

He gave me his best wishes. He told me to stay in touch. I could see that he was worried about me, and I was thankful that he took my problem seriously.

Sleep graced me for many uninterrupted hours that night for the first time in almost a week. And I needed it if I was going to solve the mystery of the wetland along the river.

───────────

The week after Mother's Day started warm and progressed to scorching. Together, the sun and wind conspired to dry the soil. The wetland swale was almost empty. That week in the evenings, I took photographs and videos of the remaining water. I sought to document the return of life to the shrinking puddles; my senses were fully engaged as I searched for the sight or sound of frogs or insects around the swale. Normally, low water forces the tadpoles into groups. Many times, I've gathered and raised tadpoles up in stock tanks when I found them crowded, stranded in isolated and shrinking puddles—half-exposed to air and close to death under hovering flies. But that day, there were no tadpoles to save.

One evening that week, I continued walking past the swale toward the river. The sun still covered the meadows with golden highlights. The temperature dropped back below ninety degrees, but the valley was humid and I'd already sweat through my shirt. The distinctive musk of the river rose to greet me as I neared the bank. I paused within a cluster of older riverside trees.

The rough, sturdy trunk of a massive willow oak formed a slight downstream arc after bearing decades of flood force. I settled back into the tree's embrace—relaxed, semi-reclined, feet far forward, heels planted deep in naked, sandy dune. A primordial squawk echoed down the valley, and my eyes turned to the aching beauty of a blue heron in flight. The river rolled by far below me. I saw bobbing treasures and discards treated equally—all washed downstream from manufacturers, towns, and farms upstream. From my partially hidden position, I leaned over and peered down twenty feet to the water. The appearance of my head alarmed the river turtles below. They abandoned their basking logs and slid into the turbid, brown river.

That evening, next to the water, I remember the scent of the river: a sharp, grassy note, dominated by a sweet musk that permeated far across meadows and into forest. Tight skin on my cheeks stung from light reflected off the surface of the water.

The Eden River is a powerful presence. The nature of the water itself is unchanging: heavy but yielding. Barriers only slow its inevitable course toward the ocean. Ruled by gravity, one cannot successfully argue with water. It always wins in the end.

Those living around the Eden have always depended upon it for water, food, and transportation. When the Europeans came, the colonists harnessed river power with water wheels. Settlements sprang up nearby. The ruins of water-powered mills in our oldest communities remind us of grain ground fine with millstones five feet across, of lumber cut straight and true in long, narrow rooms built to house a tangle of pulleys, rods, and gears. In those early years, sawmills never seemed to stop. River water turned tree stems into schoolhouses, farms, and churches. But the river swept away some of those wooden follies as easily as shifting a sandbank. Only hardened structures could resist for long. So the early twentieth century unfolded with the girdling of the Eden: construction of weirs, channels, and dams harnessed it in the service of commerce. But time has a way of equalizing advantage. The river will be flowing long after concrete crumbles into rubble hideaways for fish.

Although the Eden's always there, its appearance and form are mercurial. Water bottles, follies of man, are tossed in white foam. In smooth runs, reflected colors shift like moods—with the height of the sun, with passing clouds. Drought exposes rock ledges, displays sandbars, and creates eddies that only appear at low water. Rainfall upstream can make the water rage on sunny days. When water permeates the world, the river responds by rising up within its banks until it's visible from the highlands. When the water's too much for the channel to hold, the river flows out over the floodplain, and all earth-dwelling creatures run, fly, hop, and slither toward the uplands. During floods, the river creates a slowly flowing lake that can last a couple days: time enough for fish to explore the valley floor.

The river draws us in; it mirrors us back improved. It calms our minds and gives us strength. A simple arrangement: heavens on the surface, deepest dreams in the cool depths below.

Today, the powerful flow of the river and the tangle of wild vegetation around it discourage casual visitors. The river creates a corridor for life, a fixed highway. Rare animals, shy animals, eke out their existence there. Some use it for safe passage.

I thought back to when Howard and I first visited these meadows almost two decades before. Flocks of mourning doves numbered in the many dozens and dominated the canopies of riverside trees. Perched up high, they flushed together and swirled in the air when they saw us. The game birds' years of abundance here were confirmed by the many yellow and red birdshot shells we found caught in meadow thatch. I gathered and pocketed those plastic tubes as we walked.

One morning back then, the sun was still low in the east as I walked the meadows. Over the river, dozens of doves formed a loose downstream flock. I was shocked by their appearance. The early light bathed the birds, made their pink throats redder; each bird seemed slimmer and longer as it stretched out toward a shared destination. Time shifted and a remembered image of passenger pigeons arose in my mind's eye. The thought was quickly dismissed, but the momentary thrill of unfounded hope persisted.

That spring day in 2017, I realized that it had been at least a few years since I had seen any mourning doves in the meadow.

After my rest by the water, I left the shade and headed back out into the open. I made an arc to walk by the newest trees along the river. I needed to make sure they were leafing out vigorously since the flood.

I started at one end of the long row. Two-foot-high trees rested within their four-foot-high plastic tree tubes. At each tree, I stretched up on my toes to peek into each tube to see down to soil. I saw a few paper wasp nests—all empty.

This surprised me. Tree tubes are perfect shelters for paper wasps. The tubes give wasps protection from birds and from wind. Nests are built under leaves to shelter from the rain. We value the mild-mannered native red paper wasps on the farm. They gather and kill substantial numbers of insects, including garden pests, as food for their young. Paper wasps are also useful as pollinators, so we leave them alone unless the nest is in the "wrong" place. Once, I found a newly created nest dangling under a doorknob the hard way. It was removed within minutes, but the pain from the angry queen's sting lasted a bit longer.

That evening in the meadow, I was surprised that I couldn't find any active wasp nests at all among the young trees.

I left the riverside and headed toward home. I walked through the meadow with eyes down, seeking new flowers among spring-soft grasses. Colorful blooms vied for dominance in sun. Pale violets and delicate blue-eyed grass competed with purple tubes of blooming deadnettle amid flat white rosettes of blackberry flowers. I walked around the clumps of blackberries. Blackberry plants offer nectar to pollinating insects each spring but are viciously thorny. They struggle each year to overtake the meadow grasses and transform pastures into scrubland.

As I walked, I realized that there were no visible insects on the flowers around me. *How strange.* My pace slowed and I paid attention to each bloom I passed. But no bees, flies, butterflies, or moths—no flying insects at all. How could this be?

Well, what about insects below? Insects bustle along highways and thoroughfares at our feet. I knelt down and parted the grass. Fuzzy grass stems were still caked with silt from the flood. In one spot after another, I disturbed the thin tangle of leaf litter and thatch laying on the surface of the soil. In stark contrast to my years of playing and working in the meadow, there were no visible ants, spiders, crickets, velvet ants, or beetles.

A chill swept up my neck.

I stood up and walked farther into the tallest grasses. Sturdy stalks of fescue sprouted seed heads. My gaze softened and widened to detect movement. Were there grasshoppers? No. I turned over the broad leaves of forbs and examined the undersides. I inspected petioles and stems for caterpillars, spiders, or insect eggs. Barren.

An old log lay near the swale bank, unmoved by the flood. It had been there, wedged against a sweetgum trunk for some years. As I tried to lift a section of branch, a rotten portion broke off and exposed soil below. I bent down to see the animals that live beneath the wood. But there were none. No sow bugs or beetles. Using the end of the branch, I dug with difficulty. The chocolate-brown, loamy soil was strangely firm and rubbery. I found no earthworms.

The most common small animals that live in the meadows surrounding the wetland had disappeared.

4

EMPTY NEST

MIKE AND ANNE WILSON ARE down-the-road neighbors, far neighbors—in the community but not next door. Of course, no one is really "next door" here. Farms are scattered across the landscape. Front yards are divided by pastures filled with grazing animals—cows, goats, and horses—and by managed forests, hay fields, and row crops.

Here, you know that neighbors are "visiting" when you turn a bend in the road and see a car stopped ahead in the lane. A closer look reveals two neighbors in conversation, one behind the wheel and the other leaning on a shovel planted on the center line. It's common here for people to park behind the stopped car, get out, walk up, and say hello to all.

We don't see Mike and Anne often, but when we happen to meet on the road, or when we drop by their house to share information or summer produce, the conversation always revolves around family. Family is the warp and the woof of this tightly woven community. Mike and Anne occupy about the same stage of life as we do. We've watched each other's kids grow from awkward adolescents into adults. Now, we maintain empty nests with hearts full of hope. We've learned to cheer from the sidelines, hands off—but arms open and ready to slow an uncontrolled spin, to ease a stumble, to prevent a fall.

Mike's family owns the fields along the creek and many more acres of upland. In 2013, they leased their fields to Robert to grow row crops. I knew the Wilsons were trying to carry on the tradition of farming done by their ancestors at their home place, growing corn in the rich bottom lands and up in the meadows around their home.

Mike has known this area his whole life, and during phone conversations he's shared many stories. My favorites have been his tales of Halting Creek. "I spent summers as a kid roaming all over this place with my friends," he said. "It was our playground. We spent whole days outside until we were called in to dinner." He paused. "The best swimming holes were on Halting Creek. We played on the banks, swung into the water from ropes over branches. There was good fishing then, too."

Indeed, many of our neighbors still reminisce about the good fishing and happy times they spent on Halting Creek. It was a community treasure.

But we've never seen the creek that Mike and others remember.

After they built the dam upstream across Halting Creek, Mike told me that everything changed. "Those swimming holes are gone. The fish are gone, too."

We moved to the farm after the dam had starved the creek for many years. Halting Creek had become two bodies of water divided by that dam. Creek water above the dam was hoarded, carefully managed. The new reservoir stores drinking water that is piped to the community up the road. The small amount of water allowed to flow back into the creek is an afterthought in the minds of the water managers who control the dam. After the dam was erected, the vibrant creek downstream of the dam was transformed from a resource for the community and a haven for wildlife into a receptacle for unwanted water.

We never met the farmers whose family lands were snatched away to create the reservoir; never walked through their forests, now drowned. We didn't see the productive fields that became entombed deep away from air and sunlight. We never heard those family's stories, but we know the way it went. The water sealed over wooden homes built with love and care for growing families, homes built during house raisings led by young fathers with help from family, neighbors, and church members. The waters submerged big dreams and generations of hard work—triumph and tragedy.

We never knew a vibrant creek full of fish, ducks, and children's summer laughter. We first met Halting Creek as a trickle of water that doesn't reach the Eden during dry summers. A creek that flashes full to the top of eroded banks when water is released from the dam during heavy rains.

Local people here don't have access to the drinking water, but they have paid the price for it. In this part of the county, the dam is an unpopular topic.

Back in early May, when I first found the dead water in the swale, I'd called Mike to tell him about it.

"I don't know what to tell you," Mike said. "There always seem to be frogs down there in the bottoms."

Because he owned the land, I'd kept him informed about my conversations with Robert. Mike was as mystified as I was. I'd called him frequently to discuss all that I was learning (and not learning) and had recounted my saga of trying to get help from agricultural and environmental experts. I'd promised him that if I figured it all out, I'd let him know what I found.

But the dead meadow had shocked me. I'd never seen that land when it wasn't moving, singing, humming along. Maybe Mike had some insight. It was time for another telephone conversation.

"Hey, Mike, I hope you-all are well."

"We are, I hope you are."

"Do you have a minute to talk?"

"Yeah, just a minute though, we're about to sit down to dinner."

Just a minute. That would be a first. When Mike and I start talking, I look for a comfortable chair. We share stories of the plants and animals that live here. We share a love of the place and the land itself. Mike remembers how the land has been used over the years. He remembers the history of the neighborhood and tells me stories of neighbors, most of whom are gone now.

"OK, let me know when you need to go," I said. "Unfortunately, I'm calling with some bad news. Today, I walked down to the meadows to check on the trees. The swale water's pretty much the same. The scum's disappeared in some areas, but the water's still a weird brown color. No life in it. But the *new* thing is, I didn't see any insects out in the meadows today either. I turned over a log and dug—no worms. It's strange. I have no idea what happened. How are things at your place? Anything new?"

"There's not much to say. Of course, we have corn up in the yard, so it's different here now because of that."

Robert had leased almost all of Mike's land: the fields alongside Halting Creek and the fields high above. And although over the years Robert had planted different crops like soybeans and wheat, in 2017, everything was sown in corn.

"OK, well, I'm getting very concerned over here," I said. "I feel like whatever it is, it's spreading. But I have no idea why. I'll keep digging into this and let you know what I find."

"Sounds good, I'll let you know if I learn anything, too. . . . I have to go, Anne's calling me to table."

"OK. Well, have a good night. Give Anne my best."

As I hung up the phone, I felt lucky to have a neighbor who also cared about the land and about wildlife.

———————

It was new to me, that lifeless meadow. I knew those fields well, yet I'd never seen barren plants or dead soil. I didn't know what the future held for life in the meadow. The thin layer of the planet where the earth touches the sky is a fulcrum upon which life balances. So this was not a trivial finding, a curiosity.

The multitude within topsoil is an assembly of small animals and microbes like fungi, bacteria, and protozoa. They cooperate with each other. They cycle and recycle; they sequester the essential elements: nitrogen, carbon, and oxygen that define most life on earth. That layer of living topsoil—the surface of the earth—creates our world as we know it.

Topsoil cradles plants, modifies our atmosphere, and influences our water quality. The earth's surface is visible to us, but we don't *see* it. People refer to our planetary support system, this living soil community, as dirt. Dirt—the same word we use for filth.

Yet the people who lived here long before us referred to the living soil as their mother. Today, we don't understand our mother very well.

Scientists compare the completeness of our knowledge of the multitude living in the soil to our knowledge of the composition of outer space, or more aptly, to our knowledge of life in the deepest oceans.

Molecular biology, the science of genes, has opened a window for us to gaze upon the multitude of microbes within soil. The tools of molecular biology have allowed us to create catalogs of names for some members of the multitude. But we still don't have a comprehensive understanding. The microbes are different from one type of soil to another, different between elevations, between sunny and shady spots, and different between wet and dry soil. We can name members of the multitude, but we don't fully understand their jobs, or their relationships to each other or to the plants they serve. But we all depend upon that largely invisible microbial soil community to keep plants healthy by holding water and delivering nutrients straight to roots.

The animal and microbial multitude are recyclers of dead things and waste too—recyclers we depend upon. Imagine if the wastes that lay upon the ground—wood, dead animals, leaves, dung—all persisted and did not transform into rich soil. Imagine if leaves took more than a season to become loam, if dead trees and branches persisted for decades, or if kitchen scraps did not break down into compost within weeks to months.

I can imagine.

A horse produces over thirty pounds of manure each day. If the multitude disappeared, their waste would pile up in pastures, cover the grass, and foul their food. Without the multitude at work, we would all be buried in waste.

But I was still uncertain of the meaning of the barren meadows.

The next morning, I contacted the office of wildlife resources for the state of North Carolina and was transferred to Katy, the staff member on duty for general calls. She answered, "Wildlife resources, how can I help you?"

"I need help with some sort of contamination of my floodplain," I said. "It started in the wetland. The insects and frogs died or disappeared, but it's spread to the meadows around the wetland. There are no insects there at all. Do you have an expert who can come out and help me figure out what's going on?"

"We deal with hunting and fishing issues," she said. "Nongame wildlife's different. Let me see, hang on for a minute." I waited while she tapped at her keyboard.

"OK. We have a wildlife biologist on call—Stephen Lawson. He works with reptiles mostly, but he may be able to help you. I can give you his number. Are you ready?"

"Sure, thanks." I hung up and immediately dialed Stephen's number. His voice message greeted me after the phone rang.

In my message, I asked him to call as soon as possible.

I carried my phone with me that afternoon, and when Stephen's number appeared as an incoming call, I answered right away.

"What do you think? Have you dealt with anything like this?" I asked, after telling him about the dead animals around the wetland, the lack of tadpoles, and the meadow flowers without insects. I'd described the dense, rubbery soil under the rotting log. He was quiet as I spoke.

"Oh, yeah. It's probably runoff from the cornfield," Stephen said. "That happens all the time."

I was momentarily speechless. After all of the phone calls and emails; after speaking to almost a dozen water-quality, insect, and agricultural experts at all levels of government; after speaking to colleagues and friends, *no one* had suggested that the cornfield may have been the source of the problem.

The words finally came to me. "How could that be?" I asked. "I spoke to the farmer and he said that he only used nitrogen and Roundup to prepare the fields. I understand that Roundup can harm frogs, but what could have wiped out the insects?"

"In general, agricultural runoff harms wildlife," he said. "I don't know what specific chemicals could be involved. Normally, either the impacts are not so dramatic or no one notices the damage."

Well, that was unhelpful. It was true enough though, I *had* noticed. I was aware of the animals around us every day, and they were disappearing. But the fact remained: after the conversation with Stephen, I was no closer to identifying the harmful chemicals that may have poisoned the water.

Later that week, I received a message from Jay at the vet school. In the email, he introduced me to Raymond, a chemist at a local university who specialized in detecting unknown chemicals in water samples.

I replied to Raymond and once again told my story, from field location to drainage system to field prep and flood timing. I told him of the normal sonde readings that Johnson had described. I told him about my water sample collection and storage. I asked if he thought he could help.

Raymond asked me to come by his laboratory with the water samples. Eagerly, I set up a meeting for the following Friday.

I drove to the university on my lunch break with water samples in my red plastic chest cooler, the same one that had transported the jars from the wetland to my home.

But I wasn't carrying all the samples.

After Raymond's invitation, I'd discussed my good fortune with my friend Ann at work. "Raymond told me that he could analyze the samples and maybe tell me what was poisoning the water," I told her.

Ann looked at me closely. "*Maybe* he can tell you. Sounds like a long shot, Betsy. Are you sure you want to give him all of your samples? If it was me, I'd keep some jars back just in case he can't help."

As I drove to meet Raymond, I was confident that I would soon have the answers I needed. But I'd taken Ann's advice. She had a lot more experience with sample management than I did. Even I, driven by my thirst for answers, could hear the truth in her words. Shit happens, and there was *no way* to go back and replace those samples.

I drove through twisting and turning university roads, designed to accommodate large clusters of huge brick, concrete, and glass buildings. I found the back entrance to Raymond's laboratory and pulled up to a loading and unloading area. I stopped and gave him a call.

After about ten minutes, Raymond and his graduate student walked out of the glass building. The student pushed a rolling stainless steel cart before him. Raymond looked ill at ease.

We shook hands. I lifted the cooler out of the Toyota and placed it on the cart. I opened it and grabbed the plastic sheaf of chain-of-custody documents. I handed him both transit logs and a pen.

"Please initial these two copies and sign at the bottom." He hesitated but used my car roof as a desk to dash off his initials and his signature of receipt on each form.

I gestured toward the cooler, "I brought six samples from the swale." Then I pointed to two bottles marked as river water. "And here are the two controls from the river. You keep this copy with the samples and I'll keep mine. That way we can communicate about what you find, and I'll know where the sample was collected."

I closed the lid of the cooler, and the student wheeled it away toward the lab.

Raymond showed me where to park and waited for me outside the building. As I walked back, I considered my message. I didn't know Raymond, but I had a big ask: evaluating samples for an unknown chemical could require many hours of work and hundreds of dollars to accomplish. Somehow, I needed to spark his interest and to forge a personal connection. I needed him to care.

Raymond stood at the main entrance. He forced a small smile. "Come on, let's go see the department." He held the door for me and we climbed the stairs to the laboratory suite.

"So, you described wetlands near a river," Raymond said as we took seats in his office. "How are they connected to a cornfield? I don't have a good picture of it at all," he said.

"Let's pull it up," I said. I gave him my address and showed him the aerial view of the land. I traced the flow of water from the river and from the creek, and showed him where the last bit of drainage enters the swale.

"We've lived at this place for over fifteen years. I know it very well. I spend a lot of time in those meadows," I said. "I'm planting new trees down there along the Eden.

"I don't know what killed the animals, but a biologist warned me that it may have been the cornfield. That's the focus of my investigation now. But really, whatever it is may have come from the creek or the river during the flood. I just don't know," I said.

On the desk sat a picture of Raymond and his bride taken in front of a sand-colored stucco church. "Have you been at the university long?" I asked. "That doesn't look like North Carolina." I pointed to the picture.

"No," he said. "I've been here just a few years." He glanced at the picture. "That's home—New Mexico. I'm just getting the lab going."

"So, tell me about your process. Is this something I'll be able to fund?" I asked. "This is personal. I don't have a grant or anything."

"We'll have to see as we get into it," he said. "I'm OK doing it on my time and charging you for supplies. I'm not really sure of how much it'll cost. Let's keep in touch as I learn more."

"OK. Well, I have to get back to work. Can I grab my cooler before I go?"

Raymond left the room, then returned. "The samples are still in the ice; we're making room in the walk-in cooler for them. You'll have to get it later."

"OK, that works for me. Let's talk about supply costs as you move along," I said. "I'll keep digging for possible target contaminants and will let you know what I find."

Raymond walked me to the front door, and I turned to him and held out my hand. He took it and I looked him in the eye. "Thank you so much; this has been a difficult experience, and so far, I haven't made much progress," I confessed. "So, I *really* appreciate your eyes on this."

He pushed the glass door open, and I walked from the shaded lobby into the bright sun. I felt lighter, less burdened than I had in some time. The samples were safe, and they seemed to be cared for and handled properly.

Raymond lifted his hand and waved as I crossed the street to the parking deck.

I left campus hoping that I'd made a personal connection. But Raymond was hard to read. Analyzing those samples was a lot to ask, but I was no chemist. Maybe taking my water samples would help him develop his methods. His results would help me too. But time would tell.

The next weekend I busied myself in the garden, spreading straw mulch around my young tomato and pepper transplants. Early each year, tomato and pepper seeds are pressed into warm pots of soil under grow lights. As the plants mature and harden off, I can set them out in garden beds after the last frost. As I walked along, I lifted my board traps and carefully scouted for slugs. Slugs are enemy number one for young pepper plants, so I maintain vigilance in the garden. The young peppers were starting to get established and put out new growth, but due to the recent rains, they looked leggy and weak to me—they were growing into prime slug food.

Tomato stems were trained within stout circles of supportive wire in anticipation of steady growth now that they'd settled into their summer homes. I walked among the beds and surveyed the spring crops—English peas, round red beets, tender white salad turnips, and spinach. In the next bed I saw that some late-season lettuces remained. The mature head lettuce was a mess—most of the plants had rotted after the recent rains. Some of the red and green loose-leaf lettuces persisted, and I was grateful for the warm, dry week we'd just had.

Elephant garlic, red Russian kale, and Vates collards had been in place all winter; they pushed out spikes of flowers that signaled they were nearing the end of their time in the soil. I studied the kale plants' bright yellow flowers. I saw no bees, no pollinators.

The sight of those bare blooms sobered me. In normal times, kale plants are havens for pollinating insects. For many years, moths, butterflies, flies, and bees enjoyed the early spring nectar. If left standing, the fertilized blooms shriveled and fell—small pods formed that set hundreds of seeds. The seeds matured and dry pods burst open and threw them out over the soil. Animals apparently carried some seeds far from the kale plants, because I've been blessed by volunteer baby kale that grew up in summer between the peppers and tomatoes; I've picked the young leaves for summer salad.

I wondered as I stared at the bare blooms: Do the plants miss the opportunity to sweeten their flowers in response to the sound of pollinators? Do they feel the lack of their insect partners when they remain barren?

My first garden, at about age ten, was a potato patch my mother helped me start in the backyard. Our family friend, Greg, used some of his teenage energy to turn grass sod into a soft bed of black soil. To my young mind, the fact that a living plant could grow from a small chunk of potato was a miracle. I watched them grow and learned that potato plants were as vital as my pet cats. Their delicately cupped leaves, like the begging hands of a supplicant, followed the sun. Shoots stretched up skyward; they lengthened noticeably day by day. Rainfall sped that growth. Stems began translucent green and fragile but hardened with maturity. Buds formed, flowers opened, then withered.

I can't remember if we gathered many tubers from that first effort, but it started my journey. A life spent growing food.

In my teens, I learned to manage my own vegetable gardens. I remember having trouble thinning the vegetables. I was reluctant to kill plants that I'd nurtured from tiny seeds. Weeding and pruning felt like plant abuse. It took me years to mature and harden myself to perform those routine garden tasks. Even today, I extend deep gratitude to the living things that provide me food.

To me, food is a sacred gift. I eat with full knowledge that something had died so that I may live.

That sunny May day, I found weed plants, chickweed and henbit, growing among the leaf lettuces. In other places, those plants would have been welcome; I wouldn't be so eager to eliminate them. Chickweed is an early, leafy succulent and adds a juicy crunch to spring salads. Henbit's a valuable early pollinator plant—it supplies nectar and pollen to young queen bumblebees, roving honeybee workers, and growing wasp colonies as they're building their families. But there they were, threatening to overtake the lettuces.

As I pulled the unwanted plants up with their roots, I noticed the texture of the soil: fluffy and porous. Weeds were easy to pull; earth yielded and crumbled aside as weed roots erupted into air. The light texture was noticeable to me for how different it was from where I'd dug in the floodplain under the dead tree branch looking for worms. The soil there was dense and rubbery—there were no pores, no air spaces. The community in the floodplain was damaged, and the effect was obvious with soil texture like a thick, firm baked pudding.

In the floodplain below, the animals of the multitude that collaborate to maintain soil structure were missing.

Fertile soil is maintained by creatures large and small. Small creatures help to cycle nutrients from the decaying plant and animal material, making sticky clumps of organic-rich soil in the process. Larger animals such as beetles and earthworms tunnel vertically and horizontally—they break up compacted soil. Animal tunnels allow rain water to soak deep and nourish the plant roots that spread out and thrive in loose, fertile earth.

As a young gardener, I'd known none of this. I'd learned to make deep, loose soil by using the French intensive cultivation method. Each spring I double-dug each raised bed. At that time, my routine was to add a good layer of compost to add nutrients to the soil each spring before turning it over. I understood the main benefit of the compost was to raise the organic matter content of the soil.

But soil dries quickly here in North Carolina during the baking-hot summers, and heat speeds the breakdown of organic matter—it was always a challenge to keep the soil fertile. My routine *had* been to add compost and mulch to the soil surface around my plants a second time in mid-summer as heat hardened the soil.

But I don't double-dig my beds anymore. About twelve years ago, I was challenged to reexamine my gardening routine. One warm, spring day, as I finished a row of turned soil, movement caught my eye. It was a large toad in the garden bed, and she was struggling. I was shocked to see that I'd severely injured her right front leg. I'd almost severed it with a sudden stroke of my spade. Reaching down with gloved hands, I scooped her up and carried her to the house.

I cleaned her wound and settled her into a furnished terrarium. She received shelter to hide—moist, clean bedding and a low container of water for drinking and soaking. Mealworms and calcium-dusted crickets sustained her for many weeks. Gradually, the toad healed and learned to get around on three legs. I introduced her back into the garden with a cool shelter and piles of mealworms twice a day. After a few days she abandoned her shelter and struck out on her own.

She appeared occasionally in the garden for months afterward, so she survived for a bit at least. But the lesson was a valuable one: I wondered: Who else had I damaged or killed as I thrust that spade each spring?

Creatures are so small and easy to overlook. Was there another way to achieve the high-quality garden soil I needed to produce food?

The toad's injury changed my way of gardening. That was the year that I abandoned turning the garden soil and instead adopted cover cropping and mulching to suppress weeds. Soon I saw a remarkable increase in the number of earthworms, ground-nesting bees, and other beneficial insects in the garden. The system retained more moisture, and I didn't need to add compost each summer.

Although I'd never lifted my eyes beyond my own garden before, I finally understood that these were the benefits of a healthy soil community. The soil-life-focused approach I'd stumbled upon because of a toad's misfortune has a name: regenerative agriculture. That May day in the garden, I saw the soil with greater clarity. Earthworms fled as I pulled weeds. Determined beetles lumbered and tiny springtails somersaulted. Above on the hill, the soil in my garden was alive. But below in the floodplain, the soil was dead.

After noon that sunny day, I left the garden and walked to the barn to let the horses out. They needed some exercise in their dry lot, a fenced arena with no grass. They waited impatiently behind stall doors, and I met them with halters in hand. My horse, Joe, and pony, Snoopy, both pinto—mostly white with chestnut brown patches—nickered to me. Both were eager for playtime.

We walked together toward the lot. I was flanked by an animal connected to me by mutual trust and by a rope in each of my hands. That short walk was a reminder of the long journey we'd traveled together.

I thought back to the spring of 2014 when our lives were forever altered, when the horses lost their ability to safely graze out on pasture. I remembered one evening—I sat beside Joe as he lay in his dimly lit box stall. I stroked his neck and whispered in his ear. He groaned and stretched out. He laid his head in my lap. My right forearm mirrored the curve of his massive jaw, and my forefinger slipped between lips to check for moisture. Three fingertips of my left hand rested upon the

Elizabeth walking her horses. *Courtesy of House*

artery nestled along the bony ridge just below his eye. I could feel his pulse racing. The intravenous pain medicine wasn't touching the agony of his throbbing feet.

My first horse, my teacher, my friend, Joe, didn't want to stand. He'd foundered and lay in a deep bed of softwood shavings. His food and water sat six feet away, outside in his paddock. It might as well have been a mile. We sat together; the beating fan blades above kept the air moving. We breathed resinous scent of pine and listened to the pony eat his hay. At times, inspired by the forest smell, I sang our favorite trail song in a whisper, "My buddy, my buddy. Everywhere he goes, I want to go . . . " and angled my face to keep tears from falling in his ear. I massaged his head between his ears, his favorite spot to be rubbed. I told him that better days were just ahead.

During Joe's confinement, Howard had to travel away from home for a week, and our neighbor Carla pitched in to help. She walked over to the barn twice a day to steady Joe's head as I slowly injected a big syringe-full of pain medication into the large vein in his neck. I fit Joe with special orthotic rubber boots to support his fragile soles—to ease his pain and to try to heal his deformed feet. Specialists were recruited to guide his medical treatment and, after many weeks, to fit therapeutic steel horseshoes.

Snoopy had a different experience that spring. His lameness developed ten days before Joe's. There were no special boots available for such a small pony, so I cut thick pads from the soles of beach shoes. The soft rubber was duct-taped and secured under Snoopy's feet. He gained an inch in height and some relief from his pain. But Snoopy's special hell was all in his gut. He developed a diarrhea so persistent that I worked with his veterinary specialist over many months to find a solution. We tried a series of treatments, a series of feed changes to see if he responded. But nothing worked. Ultimately, I realized that he would always need special supplements and an extra fancy, leafy hay to approach normal digestion.

That summer, I didn't interpret his illness or Joe's sudden lameness a short time afterward as a warning. How could I have known?

By that sunny spring day in 2017, we'd completely settled into our new routine. I pushed the gate open wide with my foot and freed the horses. They strolled to the center of the pen and chose their spots. Joe went first. He gazed downward and pawed the surface, making hoof-sized divots in the rock dust. He sank to his knees, flexed his hind legs, and lay down on his belly. He eased onto his right side with a deep groan and rubbed his face into the stone grit. He rolled all the way over, belly up, feet in the air. By the time Joe had scrambled to his feet and shaken off dust in a big brown cloud, Snoopy had completed his roll.

Then, it was play time. Joe bucked wildly down the center of the pen, then cantered a bit in wide circles, to the right, then the left. He found a sunny spot where he stopped and relaxed. But the pony was not ready to relax. He taunted Joe—he ran in close, nipped the horse's backside, and ran away. Joe threw his head up in the air; he spun and shook his head from side to side at the pony; and he menaced Snoopy with head down, ears back. The pony ran in small circles around Joe, one direction, then the other. He stayed just beyond Joe's playful feet and teeth.

That happy May day in the sunshine ended abruptly that night. I returned to the house after giving the animals their last meal of the day and climbed the side porch steps. I opened the door, poked my head in, and called Howard out to join me. He came out onto the porch in his slippers, and I closed the door behind him. I pointed to the porch light to the left of the side door. "Look, there are only two moths around the light."

"Well how long has it been on?" Howard asked.

"About thirty minutes or so. I just finished up with the animals," I said.

He was quiet. We both knew that thirty minutes was plenty of time to attract a full eclipse of hundreds of moths of all shapes and sizes around the pale yellow porch light. We love to see them. They can be so beautiful. Although most were generally unremarkable brown moths, we frequently paused to admire iconic black-and-white giant leopard moths, the huge, green luna moths, and the small, fuzzy-bodied, pink-and-yellow rosy maple moths. All had been frequent visitors at the porch light before our strange spring.

Because of their great numbers, we'd discussed the problem of moths covering the wall of the house and the surface of our side door. The door swung inward. We'd take care to brush them away from the entrance with our hands so that we could slide sideways into the house with only a few rather than dozens of animals.

We'd been discussing what to do. We needed light to descend the stairs. The solution we'd finally settled upon was to keep the porch light next to the door switched off. But I'd neglected to switch on an alternate outdoor light when I went out to feed the horses—I'd left the light on right next to the door. That night, it was no problem getting inside by myself without any moths. I could have thrown the door wide open and walked straight in.

That Saturday was my first realization that the problem may be bigger than the death in the wetland and meadow far below.

––––––

Sleep eluded me that night. I worried that damage was spreading. That the dead area was getting bigger. It was hitting us closer to home, up on the hill, seemingly far away from the floodplain.

It had been dry all week. Could it be that in the absence of upland rain puddles, the animals had been drinking from the small pools of swale water? Those wetland waters were still and had lots of plants—rush and sedge blades to alight upon. Insects were more likely to drink from the swale than from the turbulent river or creek because of the threat of drowning or being eaten by jumping fish.

Did that mean that the swale water was still toxic? And if so, what could I do?

As the sun rose the next morning, I jumped out of bed, threw on work clothes, and walked out toward the barn. The dry lot contained the horses' water troughs, and I needed them. With difficulty, I rocked the troughs to shift the water weight until I could tip the remaining thirty gallons of water out of each shallow plastic tank. The fine gravel in the corner of the lot flooded and flowed out through the wire fence onto the grass beyond. I replaced the troughs with fresh buckets of water for the horses.

Awkwardly, I carried the newly emptied tanks to evenly spaced locations along an upland ridge near our home. Garden hoses, stretched far from house taps, half-filled each trough with water. The tanks were made insect- and bird-friendly with some partially submerged field stones and tree branches wedged between the stones and the sides of the tank.

I hoped that the animals would accept and use their new drinking water pools. It was the only way I knew to protect them.

Our neighbors' properties also contain portions of the wetland. Later that afternoon, I called Carla's number. Her husband, Edward, answered the phone.

"Edward, I have some bad news. I found the swale water below in the meadows damaged—brown and scummy. It's been a couple of weeks; I still don't see anything living in it. The meadows have no insects that I can find."

He was silent.

"Now, we have few moths at our porch light," I said. "How are things over there?"

"We're fine, thanks. We haven't noticed anything wrong," he said. "No problem about the wetland; we don't really go down there."

OK. . . . Then I remembered that Edward routinely sprayed his yard to kill ticks, chiggers, and insects. And, I reminded myself, most adults don't go tramping around through unmown floodplain meadows during their free time; most don't creep up upon wetland pools with the hope of watching tadpoles play. Most people would not be aware of the event that now cast a shadow over my waking hours.

With my second attempt, I tried a different approach for an absentee neighbor: email. "Hi Amanda, I have some bad news," I typed. "Some sort of contamination has killed most of the life in the meadow and wetland. I don't know what's happened, but I'm trying to find out. I'll let you know what I find."

Amanda replied soon afterward: "Well, that's terrible."

Yes, indeed.

––––––––––––––

Our lives are full because many of our close friends live nearby. Our neighborhood is a blend of families who've lived here for generations and also of newcomers. But in this place, if you weren't born and raised here, you are, by definition, a newcomer; never mind that you may have lived here for a majority of your life.

We live in a diverse community in some respects. Some of us can build the entire shell of a house from footings to roof, and some must hire help to hang a gate. Some of us can repair a disabled backhoe excavator, and some can't drive a stickshift. Some can design and develop a web page, and some of us don't use email. Some can feed their families from their own land, and some are dependent upon them, and those like them, for food.

We're a small community and most of us act neighborly. Here, we stop and speak to each other as we pass on the roads. We help each other out. We plow snow-covered driveways and pull vehicles out of ditches. We mow lawns for the disabled and plant vegetables to share with neighbors. We clear downed trees off roads and bring hot dishes to the sick and the grieving. We know each other's kids' names and have watched them grow. We trade labor, knowledge, food, seeds, plants, supplies, and tools. It's the way things work here.

Our community is rural but not too far from cities. Our location has made the neighborhood an attractive target because we have "undeveloped" land. This is what I imagine: somebody drives by and sees fallow crop fields, forest, or dozens of acres of uncut hay stretching to a woodland edge and thinks, *Hmmm, look at all this empty land. It would be perfect for my* fill-in-the-blank *project.* Again and again, we've been threatened with eminent domain or development that would harm the community with noise, pollution, or disruption of farm activities.

When we were facing development of an airport that would have cut our neighborhoods in half with noisy jets and ruin our drinking water with forever chemicals and jet fuel, we resisted. No one can keep babies sleeping or livestock growing near a runway buffer zone. We all know that it's not only the loss of land that's taken, it's the *use* of nearby land, and the character of the community, that's also threatened. Many members of the community remember the changes after the damming of Halting Creek. Continued threats to our land and way of life have only served to pull us together and make us stronger.

Most houses here were built during the nineteenth and twentieth centuries. The community was settled when the South was segregated. So our neighborhood was mostly White, mostly Protestant. But we know that today, members of our community, our neighbors, have different life experiences, different belief systems. Our yards are dotted with red *and* blue signs every election season. And because our neighborhood is ultimately a mix of people with differing political outlooks, education levels, and religious affiliations, we're careful in how we speak to one other. Bring up climate change, evolution, or trade unions and some might get testy. Or more likely, become stonily silent.

We talk about the things that we have in common: our health, family, weather, how crops or the kitchen garden's doing. Births, deaths, moves, and our kids' new jobs. We value our community and respect each other. Live and let live.

Sunday evening, May 21, brought heavy rain. It was forecast to continue throughout the workweek. I hoped that it might flush the poison out of the swale and into the river, where I also hoped it could be safely diluted.

As I drove home from work that Monday evening in the rain, I could hear frog song as I passed ponds in my neighborhood. I realized that I had a rough indicator of water health from the scattered ponds and ditches around the area, something that people normally notice—the sound of frogs calling. One may love them or hate them, but during springtime here, it's hard to ignore the frogs.

I spent the evenings of the following week calling around to nearby neighbors and to some who lived farther from our property, both upstream and downriver. After opening with greetings and inquiries about each family's health, I asked people if the frog song in their area was normal this year.

"Yes, things seem fine. Loud as ever!"

"No problems here."

But no frog song returned to the brimming swale in the floodplain below us that soggy week.

Evening drives became my new routine. My car rolled slowly through neighborhoods with the windows down. As I drove, I turned off radio chatter and listened for frogs.

On rainy nights, I drove like a half-blind drunk, zigging and zagging to avoid crushing frogs with my tires as they gathered on the warm, wet roads. I noticed where low land in the countryside was quiet and where frogs were partying raucously. No frogs called near my area, but their songs were heard farther away from Robert's cornfields, where he had used Roundup in the weeks before April's heavy rains.

In 2005 Rick Relyea, then at the University of Pittsburgh, reported the results of experiments he'd conducted: he exposed frogs and toads to Roundup at concentrations relevant to actual agricultural use. He found that Roundup in water killed a majority of the animals he studied. In Dr. Relyea's experiments, the tadpoles were the most affected: only 2 percent survived Roundup after three weeks of exposure to 3.8 parts per million of active ingredient. Among young frogs and toads who'd

grown legs and transformed out of the tadpole stage, only 21 percent
survived *one day* of exposure.

Well, you may ask, what is 3.8 parts per million, really? I admit, it's hard
to visualize. As I write this, the United States has a population of about 330
million people. So, 3.8 parts per million is equivalent to 1,254 people out of
the entire US population, or about four movie theaters filled with people.

But how is that experiment relevant to real-world conditions?
Roundup is advertised as staying where it's sprayed. And Roundup *does*
bind to soil after it's applied. But a report of surveys by William Battaglin and colleagues at the US Geological Survey show that Roundup
loves water. When it rains and the soil becomes heavy with water, the
herbicide is released from the soil and it moves. It runs off of fields into
ditches and flows downhill with water. Amphibians that are unlucky
enough to wander through recently sprayed fields or animals that happen to live in water downhill from places that have been sprayed are all
exposed to Roundup—sometimes with lethal results.

Evenings at the computer enlightened me that Roundup was not
just one product. There were many different combinations of herbicides
that could be sold under the name. All they had in common, apparently, was one active ingredient: glyphosate. And runoff of water-soluble
glyphosate is becoming more of a problem as episodes of rainfall have
become heavier *and* more frequent.

I emailed Raymond and copied Jay about my discoveries. Was it
possible that a combination of herbicides could harm not only the frogs
but the insects too? I wasn't sure but looked up each active ingredient
and the surfactants, or sticking chemicals, with which they were mixed.
I summarized my findings and sent the lists to the men. Jay replied with
some questions, but Raymond didn't answer.

As the rainy week came to a close and clear, dry evenings resumed
at the end of May, I realized that more than floodplain insects, frogs,
and moths were affected: the eastern phoebe nests were strangely quiet.
Tiny naked hatchlings lay abandoned in their soft, woven cradles of
horse hair and grass.

Nesting phoebes had been a fixture at the farm each year. They
colonized rafter ties on the open side of the utility barn. Each year, they

filled at least a dozen mud-fortified nests snugged up against the sturdy planks. The birds had been successful here. Eastern phoebes are insect eaters, and apparently, our farm had provided a good living. Usually, the birds produced two clutches of eggs each season. I loved seeing the fledgling birds when they ventured out of the nest—sometimes they bumbled about until they mastered flight. The phoebes instinctively time the emergence of their first set of hatchlings to coincide with the onset of abundant caterpillars, moths, and flies in mid-April. By late May 2017, the first fledglings had flown, and parents had already produced their second set of hatchlings.

It crept up on me.

Apparently I'm very aware of life around me, but I don't always notice the absence of life. So, I can't tell you the exact day the bats ceased hunting overhead in the evening sky. I can't tell you the exact day the bluebirds stopped visiting their nest boxes around the farm. Nor can I state with certainty which day I noticed that the eastern phoebes had abandoned their nests.

Disbelief and shock grew to dominate my days. I realized that my distress was not only due to the loss of wildlife that gave me so much joy to watch. It was much more than that. It was the realization that our farm, when functioning normally, was a complex system where some parts depended upon other parts to work. I'd never thought about it before. I always took those countless, moving, interdependent pieces for granted—they'd always been there.

You may ask, Why should I care that there were no moths at my door when the light was left on?

I learned a lesson that spring—moths are the winged embodiment of the myriad caterpillars that live on native trees and shrubs all over the property. Those caterpillars and other soft-bodied insects are *the* essential food for nestling birds. Almost all birds need soft insects to feed their young, even seed-eating birds like sparrows, because nestlings can't digest seeds. Without enough nutritious, digestible, soft insects like caterpillars, baby birds starve.

I think of the complex web of life that supports us as an intricate puzzle of stacked sticks. *Intricate* may not be a strong enough word—the puzzle pieces of life are not fully known. We can't name them all. We don't fully understand what they do individually or how the parts support each other to create an intact, working whole. But in the spring of 2017, too many sticks had been removed. The baby phoebes bore witness that at our farm, the system had broken.

One evening soon after my discovery of the dead birds, I was outside the barn pulling Japanese honeysuckle vines from the flower beds. The horses heard me and called to remind me it was time for dinner. I pulled off my work gloves, dropped them near the bed, and headed to the pole barn to fetch hay. I carried big armfuls of hay to the horse and a large handful for the pony. I checked their water buckets, removed a few piles of manure, then returned to my weeding. As I worked, I made my way toward the dark blue flowered salvia beds that form a border around the horse paddocks. Their tube-shaped flowers attract hummingbirds all summer long. Although I hadn't seen the birds recently, I kept the plants weeded, watered, and ready for their return.

My work was interrupted again by Joe nickering a greeting to an approaching vehicle. I wondered, *Who could that be?*

A well-used Carolina-blue pickup truck rounded the drive toward us. My neighbor Bill, a relative of the Wilsons, pulled up and opened the door. Bill climbed out of the truck, looking a bit stiff in the legs as he walked toward me. Bill's thinning blond hair and neat casual clothes did not telegraph his life of hard physical work, but his calloused hands did.

Tucking work gloves in my left pocket, I greeted him with a hand outstretched. "Hey, Bill, how're you doing?"

"Oh, fine. How are you-all? I thought I'd stop by with the Lazy Wife bean seeds," he said. "I was hoping you had some of those hazelnut seedlings handy."

Bill and I share a love of food plants and gardening. We visit each other's gardens. Like me, he's always trying out new plants. Over the years, we've traded food, animals, seeds, and seedlings. We've gifted each other small tools, surprising anecdotes, and helpful gardening tips. I've called Bill when I had questions about local conditions, when I needed help to guide my plant selections, when I needed an authentic recipe for Brunswick stew. I've learned a lot from him—not just about farming but about joining the community. Bill never stops by empty-handed. Small gifts are a social currency here.

"Oh, we're OK," I said. "Yeah, I can lift those seedlings now. We're recovering from that big flood. What a mess."

"It *was* a big flood. Because of all that rain . . . " he paused. "We had over five inches in two days at the house. They had to release water from the dam. Robert's tractor was down in the bottoms and got caught up in it."

My head snapped up. "What? That's horrible. Was it submerged?"

"Yeah, it was pretty bad. I don't know if it can be fixed," he said.

"Wow. I hope that he can recover. That's a big setback . . . right at the beginning of the season too."

"Yeah, there was no warning about the water release. He got caught too low."

We were silent. A tractor is so valuable. Hard to afford—hard to replace.

Finally, Bill broke the somber mood. "How's your garden doing this year?"

"OK in general, but it's been suffering. From the rain, I think," I said. "There are few tomatoes, and they seem to rot before they ripen. Come have a look. I've been trialing a new Japanese cucumber the last couple of years. I *really* like it."

"I think that it may be the only variety I'll grow from now on," I continued. "They look funny, because they're not straight, but they're tender and don't get bitter in the heat." I led Bill to the cucumber patch.

I showed him baby fruit forming on the vine. "If I let them go too big, I can still use them as cooked vegetables too. I have some seed left from last year's crop if you want to try it," I said.

Later, as the back of Bill's truck disappeared around the bend, I thought about what he'd told me. My heart was heavy for Robert and his family. Farming can be a struggle. But Robert and his father had an advantage: the men had developed mechanical expertise and nego- tiating skills from their years in the retail business. It set them up for success in the heavy equipment auction world. They knew their way around a used machine *and* a greedy man. And those big machines could generate farm income too. Over many years, the family had acquired a mixed fleet of dump trucks, roll-backs, high-powered tractor cabs, agricultural tractors, backhoes, utility loaders, and trailers. The Felds could haul loads for others, seed a new hayfield for hire, or brush hog and then spray a customer's overgrown field right down to bare soil.

In fact, in the early days at our farm, Robert had helped us out. In the years before contamination prevented me from using the floodplain meadows for pasture, the horses were led downhill each morning to graze. Then, before dark each evening, I led them back up. It was a long walk around and down the old farm road. I wanted a way that led directly to the pastures. Frequently, the horses were frisky; I needed a path with good footing. We hired Robert. He had the knowledge and the equipment for the job.

Robert had arrived with his compact utility loader with a front bucket and his chainsaw. He cut trees and pushed over stumps; he smoothed and finished a seven-foot-wide trail. He left me a path through the forest broad enough to accommodate a horse in each hand for the walk to the floodplain.

I respected the effort that Robert made to keep the family farming business afloat. Over the years, the Feld family tried their hand with meat goats, row crops, and hay, trying to find that sweet spot of profit that's so elusive for a small family farm.

I imagine it was slow going at first. It was all new; they leased land to grow row crops, and every field was different. Maybe they sought guidance from their farmer neighbors, from county extension agents, but most probably from local seed distributors. Farmers find collegial company and very specific guidance for how to farm a row crop at seed stores.

Seed consultants help farmers by analyzing field locations to estimate growing conditions. Each farmer is presented with a contract of how the patented seed can be used—a contract that prohibits seed sharing or seed saving. A contract sometimes details the exclusive locations where the seed can be planted—with GPS references. For beginning farmers, there's more. Each farmer is supplied with a kind of "cookbook" of when to spray or turn the soil, what the crop needs for protection against potential pests, and when to harvest for optimum yield and quality.

It was probably a daunting task for the Felds as they began to farm row crops. There is upfront investment in agricultural tractors, farm implements, seed, fertilizer, and chemicals, as well as building storage for grain and figuring out that whole process. Banks lend money for those kinds of investments. The Felds had their home and land as collateral. But to have people like those seed consultants? Experts at the ready with confident answers and full technical support? Well, that can make all the difference to someone learning a new job.

Maybe the men didn't fully appreciate that the detailed advice they received came from employees of the seed manufacturers themselves, not from independent advisers whose goal was to serve the farmer's best interest. Maybe they didn't know that over the last decades, consolidation in crop seeds, chemicals, and markets; the rise of agribusiness and the loss of much publicly funded agricultural research and development; and the decline in the number of seed companies had reduced farmers' options. In total, the changes have diminished farmers' freedom to farm and their freedom to choose the best options for their financial well-being and for the long-term health of their land.

In 2021, President Biden issued an executive order to reduce corporate consolidation in multiple sectors, including agriculture. It's about time. Josh Sosland reported in *World Grain* in 2021: "The markets for seeds, equipment, feed, and fertilizer are now dominated by just a few large companies, meaning family farmers and ranchers now have to pay more for these inputs. For example, just four companies control most of the world's seeds, and corn seed prices have gone up as much as 30% annually."

Consolidation does not benefit the farmer or the long-term health of our farmland. Mary Hendrickson and Harvey James describe the effects of industrial agriculture on farmers: "As the structure of the marketplace has changed for farmers, the decisions they *can* make about what plants and animals to use in their farming operation are being severely constrained." The result is that "many farmers find themselves in economically marginal jobs."

Later that evening, after Bill stopped by, I thought more about Robert's tractor. Maybe this was a clue as to the source of the contamination in the swale. But what kind of contamination? I'd not seen the rainbow sheen of hydrocarbons on the water, so I didn't suspect diesel fuel was the problem. Maybe something else was in or near the tractor that got caught in the floodwaters. That would certainly explain why the damage seemed to be fairly local in nature.

So after dinner, I called Robert. "Robert, how are you-all doing? Bill told me the news about your tractor. I am *so sorry*. I had no idea."

"Yeah, it was pretty bad," he said. "The creek jumped right out of its banks. They called some people about the water release from the dam, but they didn't call us. We had no warning at all. We didn't learn about it until the flood was fully up."

"Can it be repaired? Do you have another tractor to use?"

"No, our old tractor's much smaller and can't do for us. The new one can't be repaired—it's a total loss."

I murmured my condolences again. The news was hard to hear. "Robert, you know that I've been trying to figure out what's killed the animals. It's getting worse. We have no moths around our lights at night now, and the birds are leaving their nests and their babies. I was thinking, after Bill told me about the tractor—I was wondering if the events were related. Was your spray tank full when the creek flooded?"

"No, we didn't have the spray tank on the tractor."

"Was there anything else stored near the tractor on the ground, or on the tractor somehow? What was it being used for?"

"We'd just finished planting, so the seed hopper and drill was on it. There was nothing else down there," he said.

"The seed hopper?"

My voice trailed off. I couldn't think of what else to ask. How could this be relevant at all to the dead and missing animals?

Finally, I asked, "Well, what was in the hopper?"

"Just the corn seed that we hadn't planted yet, about twenty-five to fifty pounds of it, I reckon."

Just corn seed. Another dead end. I was left with no more information than when I started.

5

RED ZONE

My joy was gone.

I cared for the animals, prepared meals, and drove to work. I went through the motions, but my heart was hollow. Sunlight didn't warm me, nor did blue skies penetrate the gray. Over time, I felt as if the natural world had receded.

Was it some kind of barrier that I could fight through, or had I folded into myself and withdrawn from nature? Maybe retreat was my ultimate defense against the pain of loss. Loss of the animals, sure, but it was more than that. It was the loss of my relationship with them.

Some wild animals were accustomed to me as I worked outside the house, and many, such as birds, deer, rabbits, and amphibians, tolerated me.

Change had arrived swiftly that spring. Familiar companions at the barn were gone. Where were the barn toads? American toads, the large gray and the smaller brown, had claimed a corner of the barn's wash stall as their cool daytime haven. They dispersed each evening to hunt insects around the farm. Where was the cheeky hermit thrush who used to hop toward me from under his American holly tree? He alerted me each time the water dish needed to be refilled. I missed the moment at twilight when chimney swifts were suddenly replaced by big brown bats. Neither remained in the empty skies.

The familiar sounds of summer had stilled. Where were the wood thrushes with their brilliantly improvised water-flute phrasing? Where were the bluebirds' conversational warbles and the phoebes' raspy whistles?

In the past, wild animals sometimes chose to interact with us. Years ago, on a late winter morning, I chased after my semi-trained Great Pyrenees pup, Charlie. I turned the corner of the house to find an eight-point buck stomping and challenging the young dog at his feet. Charlie was oblivious: puppy crouching, tongue lolling, and tail wagging. My eyes locked onto the deer's as he lifted his head to my presence. Fortunately, the buck did not linger. Maybe it was the protective-mother sound that poured from my throat. Or it could have been my vector-straight sprint (with arms wide) toward those wild eyes.

With wildlife disrupted at the farm, I'd lost a regular means of interacting with other creatures in my daily life. Yes, there were the family dogs and horses, but wild animals are different; they're independent. Each wild creature possessed its own agency, its own purpose, most of which were mysteries to me. Wildlife around the farm was always surprising me, and I frequently learned new things when I spent time with wild animals.

Before that most unusual year, I'd been delighted many times by some new observation at the farm:

- **Mid-morning, late winter:** A tight cluster of dark-eyed junco birds, a gray blur of terror, sped by my head. I turned to their tails. Scant feet behind, a sharp-shinned hawk pursued—focused and hungry.
- **Afternoon, springtime:** A horse in each hand, we walked along the road. Honeybees swarmed in a loose brown cloud low over our heads. Each bee held its relative position, and all together they formed a small school—like forage fish in the air.
- **Midnight, late summer in lamp light:** A constellation of keen yellow-green-blue diamonds glittered from the forest floor, reflections from hundreds of tiny wolf spider eyes.
- **Dark evening, September:** Raccoon family bounced among limbs in the crown of a wild cherry tree. Yellow eyes kept watch,

glowed in my headlamp. Each jostled for space; pulled at grape vines to reach the sweet-ripe fruit.

- **Night, autumn:** Barred owl flew so close to my head that I stilled my breath in anticipation of hearing wing whisper. But of course, heard nothing.

In late May 2017, I watched my outdoor community fragment and disappear, and I was unmoored. For years, while working outside, I'd been able to fully relax, to daydream, to lose my protective social boundaries and to spread out comfortably into the place. In contrast to the performances of public life, my time at the farm felt like the comfort of easing into deep warm water after being exposed to wind and chill. But that spring at the farm, there was no respite. I kept my edges fortified, my mind disciplined. My goal was to be objective, to watch, to record. But I felt weirdly homesick—I missed my interactions with wildlife, with being a member of the unpredictable, dynamic mix of animals that used to define my time outside at the farm.

I was grounded in place and knew my part by heart. But that spring, I walked through an altered, alien landscape. When the wind died, all was still. There was no background hum of bees gathering. There were no gnats or flies in the air. No butterflies and few pollinators on my flowering plants. The porch light was left alone at night; no moths could be seen in its wide, diffuse yellow glow.

There were happy exceptions upon which I focused with great intensity. There were still some eastern carpenter bees—big loud bees with shiny black abdomens. Although they're pollinators, I don't generally greet them with unclouded joy as they drill into any bare-wood rafters they can find. But by this point, in this most distressing year, I was ridiculously grateful to see them. As evening fell and the distant tree line faded to a deep charcoal gray, I sometimes saw fireflies flickering their love signals along the upland meadow at the far forest edge. I fancied them as little flames of hope—hope for some insects to survive.

I ponder the seeming relative nature of human happiness, health, and well-being. The loss of animals changed my life. But everyone has a unique point of view, each colored by our own experiences and circumstances. As the naturalist Aldo Leopold wisely noted in *A Sand County Almanac*: "We grieve only for what we know."

Each of us makes an attachment of some kind with other life. It could be a familiar street tree, a pet, or a flowering houseplant on the windowsill. And there's increasing evidence that many of us are deeply affected by loss in the natural world. For example, those who work or play in the same place over time and then find damage may grieve for the loss. I know that Mike feels the loss of Halting Creek. Naturalists certainly feel it. Recently, coral researchers discovered their familiar study site—the biodiverse reefs of Guam—bleached white and newly barren. Ecologist Laurie Raymundo described crying into her dive mask as she surveyed the damage.

But what about people who are not routinely immersed in nature? Do we grieve in some way as the members of the natural world are diminished to include only those few animals tolerant of human development? Do we grieve as biodiversity and animal abundance fade? Could our increasing separation from the multitude of living creatures that sustains us be part of the total burden of stress and anxiety afflicting modern Americans?

It appears so. Even among people I know who do not study nature or live in the countryside, I frequently hear sad voices complain about the decline of the beautiful creatures that they knew and loved—birds, butterflies, and fireflies. They notice the animals are disappearing. As author and naturalist Margaret Renkl wrote in 2021: "I grieve what is happening to the natural world, and I understand perfectly well that my own efforts to help are far from enough. But when I watch a bluebird introducing his mate to the nest box I've installed for them, it's impossible to give up. When the tiny hummingbirds make it back from far across the Gulf of Mexico, it's impossible to give up."

An underlying grief for the loss of nature runs deep among many of us. But this feeling of "ecologic grief" after the loss of animals and places we love is a natural and a healthy response. As Neville Ellis and

Ashlee Cunsolo put it in their 2018 article in the *Conversation*: "Just as grief over the loss of a loved person puts into perspective what matters in our lives, collective experiences of ecological grief may coalesce into a strengthened sense of love and commitment to the places, ecosystems and species that inspire, nurture and sustain us."

Consider why we suffer. In less than one human lifetime, so much has gone. Since 1970, an estimated three billion birds, or about 30 percent of the total population, have disappeared in the United States. Birds are easier to count than some other wild creatures, but there are also a few good studies of insect populations over time. In one of these, Caspar Hallmann and colleagues report the results of their work to capture flying insects and measure total weights (biomass) at protected natural areas in Germany each warm season for twenty-seven years. Over that time period, they discovered a loss of over 80 percent of insect biomass during mid-summers, when populations peak. And as I have learned, the effects of insect loss ripple through the biosphere like a seismic wave, destroying dependent animal communities.

The tiny creatures of our world may not be so small after all.

Meanwhile, my hopes for progress in Raymond's lab were fading. In mid-May he sent a message that he was having difficulty with his lab equipment. He'd let me know when the lab was up and running again. And although I contacted him regularly during the weeks that followed, I received no reply.

Another blow to my best efforts. But really, what had I expected? In those early days after the flood, it appears that I'd been blindly optimistic. In reality, Raymond had only recently established his lab at the university. He worked under constant pressure to develop difficult methods to use in his research, methods that would attract large grants to support him and his students. I had come with a request, but my needs were not his priority. I'd not paid him to do the work.

Over those next weeks, in the face of Raymond's continued silence, my greatest consolation was that I'd not given him all of my water samples. Two bottles of the ten I had collected remained, and my hope for answers rested upon them.

One May evening, I stood over the stove tending a stockpot of simmering chili. I realized that tears were running down my cheeks.

Howard came into the kitchen to get some water. He filled the glass from the kitchen tap and must have seen my wet face. "What's going on, Bets?"

I turned the heat down and turned to him, "I'm so sad, sweetie. The animals. They're dying or gone." I took a breath and swallowed, but the tears welled again. "I've been so happy here. So close to life. Every day. Our animals, sure. But wildlife are so special. Now they're disappearing. Everything's *different* outside. I feel like it's not my home anymore."

Leaning back against the counter, the knot in my stomach clenched tighter. "Howie, I think that we need to move away, I can't take this."

Living on the farm, working outside every day in the emptying landscape was increasingly hard to bear, to see. Daily life among familiar animals had contributed to my well-being, to my joy in life. The living community had been part of my support system, and I struggled with the fact of their loss.

"You're going to have to keep it together, to manage this stress better," Howard said, facing me. "Regardless of how long we stay, we're going to be here for a while. We can't just run away. It's obvious the situation's getting worse. You're going to have to find a way to deal with it." His shoulders softened and his fists hung helplessly at his sides. I could see that he struggled to distance himself from the death. To be the strong one.

That wasn't what I wanted to hear. But I recognized the truth of his words. Running away was not the answer.

And hope waited for me in the fridge: the last two jars of water. Potential evidence. I *had* to figure it out. By myself, apparently. But I knew that once I understood what had killed so much of the life in the place we loved, I was going to do everything in my power to prevent it from happening again.

———————

The week of May 22 was rainy, with enough rain to keep the swale full. I continued to visit the water regularly in the evenings as I watched for tadpoles and frogs to return to the warm nursery waters. But the wetland continued to look like an uninviting place to live. The water was brown and still. In some areas the surface scum had reformed. But this warm evening was different. I thought I detected movement.

To get a closer look, I leaned in and crouched down. As I peered at the water, I was irritated by small bites on my forearms and neck. Bites? What was happening?

Mosquitoes were bombarding me. Small, fast ones. They attacked the bare skin on my arms, face, and neck. The movement that had attracted me was not so delightful after all. It was something foreboding. It was the repeated rise to the surface and fall back into the depths of the swale of thousands of wiggling mosquito larvae.

I stood up abruptly, stumbling a bit backward in my haste. My hands kept moving as I brushed my arms to ward off the biting insects. I walked briskly, intending to finish my rounds, only to realize that the swarm around me was not only matching my speed but becoming more intense. The crescendo of attacks persuaded me to change direction and head straight uphill. The mosquitoes stayed with me through the still air in the forest and did not fall away until I reached the open, breezy upland meadows.

The intensity and size of the mosquito swarm was new to me. It made no sense. The water was apparently toxic. How could the mosquitoes live where other insects could not?

Mosquito larvae are tiny, wormlike wigglers—active water creatures that don't know that they're destined for the air. When they mature, they rest just under the water surface as pupae. When it's time, they split their skins, unfold their wings, and dry them in the sun. Then they take to the sky.

Many water creatures eat mosquito larvae or compete with them for food. Those active diving beetles, the dragonfly and damselfly babies that were missing from the swale, were all voracious predators of mosquitoes. The creatures that had lived in clean swale waters had helped protect us from mosquitoes. An intact, healthy wetland with a diversity of animals kept mosquito numbers under control. But that spring, many of the creatures that would have controlled mosquitoes in water and air had disappeared.

The mosquitoes changed our lives—they made us miserable. For all the years that we'd lived at the farm, we'd not been bothered much by mosquitoes. They'd been around in the summer, but in low numbers. Neither we nor the horses needed insect repellent when outdoors. We could sit out in the evenings and enjoy sunsets; the horses had been able to rest with relaxed, quiet tails.

Those clouds of mosquitoes were the beginning of a new kind of torment for all of us at the farm. There was no more standing, sitting, or relaxing outdoors in evenings—even in the uplands. We started using insect repellent if we had to be outside for any length of time; it became a routine to spray the horses before they were turned out of their stalls to go play. When in their stalls, I kept high-velocity fans on them to prevent mosquitoes from attacking. Even the dogs did not linger during their necessary time outdoors.

Down in the floodplain, the mosquitoes were especially active. I quickly learned to protect myself with the equipment I use to inspect honeybee colonies: the screened hood and thick jacket I wore to minimize bee stings. The clothing was much more effective than insect repellent and long sleeves alone. I was able to focus on my work rather than constantly trying to brush biting insects off my face, neck, and hairline. The jacket hood featured a large mesh porthole through which to peer upon the outside world. In the middle of the buzzing, aggressive swarm, I often felt like I was viewing mosquitoes in an aquarium, but I was the one contained.

In late May, I received helpful information. I got a call from David Reston from a local water quality group.

"Thanks for calling, David." I searched my memory for when we'd last spoken. The weeks of frantic calls after I discovered the dead animals had faded into a blur of names, of offices.

"I've been thinking of your situation," he said. "I found a wetland assessment group that may be able to help you with your contamination issue."

"Let me give you Will Gustafson's number," he continued. "I'm not sure, but he may be able to help you figure out what happened down in the floodplain. Are you ready?"

Was I ever.

The first week of June was ushered in by more rainy days. Every time it rained, I imagined toxic chemicals flushing out of the swale into the river. The weather gave me hope that the wetland would soon recover. Corn in the Halting Creek fields was almost knee high and growing well in most areas. But some bare soil remained under puddles that had persisted for most of the spring. The second batch of corn seed that Robert replanted during a dry week in mid-May did not grow—the fields were too wet.

Will and his wetland assessment team planned to visit Monday, but heavy rain was forecast for the day. I hoped that the rain would hold off until after the visit as the river needed to stay in its banks for the scientists to see the swale water.

Will and his colleagues Andrew and Jamie pulled up in their work truck promptly as promised. The dogs had sounded an early warning of truck rumble, so I was ready. I stood in the yard in my bee jacket, looking from afar like a big puffy marshmallow perched upon blue-jeaned legs and knee-high white rubber shrimp boots. As they emerged from the truck, Will introduced them all.

"Thanks for coming out," I said. "The mosquitoes are fierce. You may want some of this." I tried to share my high-potency repellent, but apparently they'd come prepared.

Andrew was the wetland specialist, and he unloaded his shovel and plastic buckets from the back of the truck. Will grabbed a sonde and more buckets. Jamie's background was in the study of water systems and the life within them. I hoped to talk with her, as I had so many questions about what I was seeing in the wetland and meadows.

With the team members fully laden and me emptyhanded, we started downhill through the forest picking our way through brush and downed wood. As we approached the meadows, the mosquitoes thickened. Zipper in hand, I lifted, then secured the mesh hood of the bee jacket over my head. We stopped low on the hill above the floodplain. While we stared at the water bisecting the meadow below, I took the opportunity to describe the system.

"The water you see is the drainage swale that forms a seasonal wetland," I said. "Water flows out of the crop fields along the creek, then overland into the swale. The system was designed that way, and it's still working. I think it's been almost a century since it was built. The swale's where I first noticed the frogs had gone and saw the dead insects."

We resumed our descent, reaching swale water near the middle of soggy fields. Then we split up. Will, Andrew, and I turned right, and Jamie crossed the water, headed toward the river. Andrew strode ahead toward the cornfield. Will walked slowly westward, sloshing through the swale ahead of him. He suddenly bent down and pointed.

"Look. That looks like a crawfish eating a partially decayed bullfrog tadpole," he said.

I stooped, squinted, and peered at the water. "A tadpole," I exclaimed, "that's really good news!"

Will said, "Well, it is a *dead* tadpole."

I silently reminded myself to rein in my enthusiasm. We continued walking slowly through the water. Will told me that he saw no living tadpoles in the area, no insects. Will took sonde measurements, pausing periodically as he slowly splashed upstream in the swale water.

"Will, look here. This pool keeps its water even when other parts of the swale have dried. The southern exposure keeps it sunny. In the past, this has been one of the most productive breeding sites for the amphibians," I said. "Here's another one." I pointed. "I've been monitoring during evenings. I keep looking in the swale, especially in these pools to see if tadpoles are returning to the water here."

Will kept walking, watching the readout on his sonde display. I bubbled inside with hope that Will would find living amphibians.

Meanwhile, Andrew had found rain-filled pools of water that collect at the base of the forested hill, separate from the swale. In previous years, these ephemeral pools had been prime salamander breeding areas. He dug a foot-deep hole next to the water. As I stood next to him, watching, he explained that there was no black band visible below the surface, which meant oxygen *did* reach deep down through layers of brown soil.

"Even though water collects here sometimes, this is not technically considered a wetland. It doesn't support amphibians all year long because it dries out sometimes," he said. Andrew continued his walk downstream alongside the water, periodically digging.

Jamie had headed west along the river, and I hurried over across the meadow to reach her.

"Hey, what are you seeing?" I asked.

"Not much. The river looks OK. I saw some turtles basking on logs," she said.

"Yeah, the turtles are reassuring," I said. "When this thing first happened it was so dramatic I thought there might have been a big industrial spill in the river." I went on to describe my nighttime frog song survey in May. "So, my conclusion was that it's more local. But I still have no idea what happened.

"Speaking of turtles," I said. "A few days after I found the dead water, I saw a box turtle hanging underwater in the swale. It was weird. She looked stunned. I'd never seen that before. Totally motionless."

"Yeah, sometimes they do go in the water. We've seen them swimming in rivers before," she said. "They like to eat tadpoles too!"

"Well that day there were no tadpoles in the water. She shouldn't have been in there. I made the mistake of lifting her out bare-handed. My arm was burning for a few hours even after I washed it."

"Yikes!"

"I know, right? It was a reflex," I said.

Meanwhile, Will had disappeared toward the upper part of the drainage system within the Wilsons' cornfield. After twenty minutes or so, he walked back toward us. When he was within earshot, he called out, "I found tadpoles in the cornfield."

I excused myself from Jamie and followed Will up to the field-side ditch he'd visited. Some adult frogs leapt into the water as I approached. I instinctively slowed down and scanned the banks to see which frogs had returned. I could see they were small, but they were way too fast for me to tell what kind they were. Sure enough, there were tadpoles in the water! They were very young. A few days old. I was so happy to see them.

Will and I walked back downstream in silence. Will led the way beyond the edge of the cornfield and stopped. We were in a shaded spot on our land where the deep part of the swale begins. The mosquitoes were thick and I was grateful for the jacket. The mosquitoes made a constant high-pitched drone in the background as our conversation resumed.

"What's all this straw stuff?" Will pointed to deep piles of partially decayed wheat straw sitting in and around the water.

"In fall 2015, we had a flood," I explained. "Robert, the guy who farms those fields, had harvested wheat that year. The straw washed off the fields and floated downstream when the creek flooded. The wheat straw made huge drifts where it was strained out of the water by trees, by the pasture fence. It was a mess. It completely buried our wire fences. I had to get Robert out here to clear my land. It was so deep the horses could have walked on the straw piles right out of the pastures."

I poked at the wheat straw pile with the toe of my boot. I remembered that after months of requests, I'd finally succeeded in convincing Robert and his dad to come out to fix the mess. There'd been way too much for me to clear with my digging fork. They were surprised when they saw that straw drifts completely buried the land in places. They did not seem to know that farming is less predictable when practiced in a floodplain.

Will remained for a while in the damaged swale. He checked the water with his sonde. He moved close to the submerged piles of straw and then away from them. He walked around the northern part of the swale, dense with river oats, where they thrive in the moist areas of land around the swale.

Taz investigating wheat straw on the horse pasture, January 2016.

"Come, look over here," Will said. "I'm getting very different readings here. The pH of the water changes between the area with the straw and the area free of straw."

"What does that mean?" I asked.

Will didn't answer at first; he was still looking around. "Look," he said. "The river oats are damaged and shorter here near the wheat straw. If you move away from the straw, the plants are taller and green all the way down their stems. But look at these near the straw—their lower leaves are all brown and dead."

Once he pointed it out, I could definitely see it. There was a gradient of plant vigor, with sick-looking plants near the swale and healthy, green ones farthest from the wheat straw.

"Weird. What does that?" I asked.

"I'm not sure, but the sonde shows the water quality's different in this area as well. I'll take some water samples and we can check them out."

How I wish I'd found this group weeks before, during the first days of the discovery. They saw things that I'd looked at but had not clearly seen. They had experience with wetlands. I was so grateful they understood the plants, animals, and insects.

"I didn't see many insects out in the fields," Jamie said as she walked up.

"No, the insects are sparse, except for these mosquitoes," Will said. "We'll touch base with our insect specialist. He may have something to add."

Andrew joined the rest of us near the opening of the farm road that led back up the hill. "This part here is not a true wetland; it dries out sometimes," he said. "I'd call it a floodplain-associated wetland. But I walked the length of the system to where the swale drains into the Eden. The end of the system *is* a true wetland. And I saw tadpoles in the water there."

We walked as a loose group in silence to the top of the hill where the work truck was parked. I was so confused. The team had found tadpoles returning to the cornfield *and* to the deep water farthest from the cornfield. That left the middle of the system, including our land, still damaged. If Roundup was hurting the frogs, how could they be breeding successfully in the cornfield swale where the land had been sprayed with Roundup two months before? But frogs were absent in the unsprayed areas in most of the middle of the system. It made no sense to me.

"Thank you guys so much!" I said. I shook hands with Will as Jamie and Andrew stashed tools in the truck.

Howard walked out of the house to see them off. "Howie, they found tadpoles!" I said. "At the ends of the water up in the Wilsons' fields and down near the end at the Eden."

"Really? That's great. So it's all better?" he asked.

I tried to explain, "The water in the middle still has no animals. Few insects, no frogs. But this is what's weird—the pH in the western pools near the old wheat straw are different than other parts."

I looked to Will. "I'm not telling this right, am I? Was it higher or lower around the straw?"

Will smiled. "Yeah, something's going on in that part of the swale. Not sure what. We'll be in touch."

As they drove away, I waved at the truck. I was so grateful for the new information. But I had no idea what it meant for my investigation or for the health of the water on our land.

The second week of June started fine and dry. A particularly lovely, warm day inspired me to take a walk outside of my office in town. Nearby, an older neighborhood with lush landscaping was the perfect place for a stroll. As I walked down the quiet streets, I admired flowering tulip trees, lindens, and some bright-red peonies. A crape myrtle showed an early glimpse of pale lavender-pink blooms.

But it was the sight of a gaudy, multicolored bed of flowers that stopped me in my tracks; they covered almost half of a sunny, sloping yard. Native orange butterfly weed near the road, followed by new purple-pink coneflowers, backed with purple and red bee balm. Bees— honeybees and native bees alike—covered ripe blossoms. The still air was perfumed by bee balm, and a low, soothing buzz arose from the multitude in the yard. A car passed behind me, almost unnoticed. I was mesmerized by the bees as they worked the flowers.

With cell phone in hand, I stood quietly and watched the pollinators moving among the blooms. Although I was patient, the bees were fast and I couldn't capture good images on the phone's camera. It was a lovely break that reminded me of the beauty of wildlife—wildlife that had been common at our farm.

But things were not well at home. The lights of the fireflies had disappeared from the forest edge, and I found myself walking through a landscape of small deaths.

One morning at the barn, I dropped a running water hose into a bucket to top up the pony's drinking water. The drone of the spigot buried an announcer's words from the radio down the aisle, eclipsed the reassuring sound of horses chewing breakfast hay. Bright sun streamed through the eastern door of the barn, and a beam illuminated a strip of concrete floor beneath my feet. Green summer lawn next to concrete teased with the illusion of vibrant life.

Small movement caught my eye. Lying upon the concrete next to the threshold, a brilliant blue damselfly lay on her side. She was alive. Barely.

She rhythmically extended and contracted her long abdomen. Her gossamer wings trembled, useless for flight. She lay recumbent, struggling, constantly moving. Contractions were sporadically interrupted by convulsions. With unsteady hands, I recorded her suffering with my phone.

The phone became my companion outside. I tried to take videos, but my technique was poor and some were not fully in focus. I was probably too close to the animals. I regretted that my inexperienced recordings let the poor creatures down. What will be the final record of this event and all these deaths? My life had not prepared me to be an adequate historian. The weight of the event humbled me, as did my inability to stop it.

The following weekend, I made the mistake of showing that video to my friend Emily when we met at a local café. We'd been discussing the decline of animals at the farm, and I mentioned the damselfly as an example of what I was seeing. I started the video and handed the phone to Emily across the table.

She started watching, then averted her eyes. "That's horrible!" She pushed the phone aside.

As I reclaimed the phone, I apologized to her. Emily's reaction made me sorry that I'd shared my discovery and my burden. I hadn't anticipated the effect upon her. Apparently, I was becoming accustomed to sad discoveries, hardened to the parade of horrors at the farm.

A wood thrush lay still and lifeless in the horses' dry lot. Swallowtail butterflies twitched and struggled impotently on their sides, seeking to right themselves upon the grass. Eastern carpenter bees, the largest and last bees to fall at my place, were failing. But in contrast to the other bees, they didn't just disappear. Instead, I witnessed their decline.

Some carpenter bees I discovered lying dead on the ground. Others lay there alive but not moving. Of the stricken, I thought that if they had some nutrition, some energy, they might survive. I collected, then spread, ripe blossoms full of sweet nectar and small piles of pollen around their heads. When I returned, sometimes they were gone, and I hoped the bees lived. Sometimes they were dead, still lying in the semicircle of blooms around their heads, appearing to me like Millais's *Ophelia*, accompanied by her drifting garland of flowers as she eased into the next world.

Some carpenter bees were found frozen in place, clinging to flower spikes in the heat of the afternoon. They were so still, I stroked their fuzzy backs with little response.

Wood thrush lay dead.

Sometimes, I found living carpenter bees manically moving—uncoordinated, unpredictable. They climbed plants, trembling limbs outstretched attempting to grasp a leaf for support as a base for the next faltering step. The creatures' neurologic systems were overloaded, fully in the red. Every synapse was firing, every muscle twitched. They couldn't fly, and they couldn't control their movement, not even to extend a tongue into blooms to reach the sugary, life-giving nectar. But they continued, unable to replenish precious energy reserves, unable to stop moving.

I wanted to help the bees, to spend time with them, to support them in their time of crisis. But then I thought about what a dying animal needs. It needs solitude and it needs to feel secure. Bees don't seek out human company. When content, they ignore us; when hungry and irritable, they actively move away from us. Even pets, the largest animals most intimately connected to us, seek solitude at the end of life. Finally, I realized the best way to honor the bees was to just leave them alone.

Mid-June brought an inch of rain, and it came down hard. The gray sky was thick with mist and larger drops formed on my glasses. The air softened edges of backlit oak leaf and pine needle. It was a pastel landscape carelessly handled, colors smeared. Rainwater flowed over the surface of the land so forcefully that small rocks were pushed downhill, creating clay gullies on the gravel road. The horses huddled within shelter, ears at half-mast.

But Howard was out in the rain with a worn shovel. He worked to stave off a minor disaster. Rainwater flowed over a speed bump midway down the long slope of the drive. He pushed loose stone up on the mound and deepened the upstream trench. He worked to fortify it in the deluge. If he failed, he knew that instead of water flowing off into the forest, it would flow along our gravel driveway and wash it out.

The weather service issued flash flood warnings, so I took a hike downslope to check on the floodplain. I saw green meadow grasses rather than gray water, so I proceeded to cross the brimming swale. I approached the river, watchful for sudden erosion—I didn't want to fall into the rushing water. As I walked, the sweet, musky smell of the river enveloped me like a cloud. Down below in the water, random items large and small were caught in the flow and hurtled by me: coolers, children's balls, plastic bottles, all bobbing and dipping in the waves.

I watched the river consume the exposed earthen face of the unstable bank. The water submerged the turtles' sunbathing rocks, submerged downed timber. Inch by inch, water ascended the formerly mighty trunks that had come to rest at unnatural angles in the river. I watched an ancient green ash close to me progressively disappear. Water had concealed its branches, lapped at the dark crevice that was the entrance to a bird's abandoned nesting cavity, a shining gray finger stretched into the hole. I watched it fill and it was gone. Water covered an old scar edged by healing cambium. The bark had been chewed away, made bare by a beaver's attempt to girdle the mighty tree. The tree had won the battle with beavers only to succumb to unstable soil and gravity. I watched until all I saw was a tangle of broken roots reaching toward the sky like the last hopeful finger-stretch of a drowning man's hand.

It was loud by the river. Raindrops bounced off my jacket hood and tree leaves above; the foamy water raged below. Wind rustled leaves, branches rubbed and screeched. I disturbed a blue heron, and its sharp cry pierced the din. The bird escaped upstream, belly low over the turbulent water. It had been such a wet year that the soil had never dried out. I expected this relatively small amount of rain to cause the river to flood. It did.

Sunday morning dawned bright and sunny. I caught glimpses of the floodplain through the forest. Strong light reflected off the flooded meadows that overnight had transformed into a slowly moving, newly born lake. I remember thinking, *Surely these new, cleansing floodwaters will bring life back to the floodplain.*

By late morning, foliage had dried with the help of warm sun and light breezes. The humidity dropped. It was a lovely day, and I planned to spend it in the garden. It was a bit early for the rabbiteye blueberries, a southern specialty, but I could see that many of the berries had lost their grass-green tone and trended decidedly toward blue. It was time to protect them with the shade cloth covers we'd made to keep the berries out of the birds. Years ago, we learned that a flock of American robins could strip all of the fruit—blue and green berries alike—from the bushes within a scant span of hours. But if protected, we could pick blueberries from late June through Labor Day.

I toured the long, straight garden aisles. I straightened tomato cages and bean poles as the soft, rain-soaked soil yielded to my insistent pressure. As I moved along the rows of plants, I surveyed their health and needs with a critical eye. The peppers had escaped major slug damage and were getting tall. Some listed to the side as they grew, so I collected shorter remnants of bamboo stakes, pushed the stakes into the soil, and tied the peppers upright. The rich smell of black earth rose from the beds as I disturbed the soil, and I paused to appreciate it all—the warm day, the sunshine, aromatic soil, and healthy food plants.

In the next bed, the tomatoes were in a growth spurt and had started to produce flowers—the promise of future fruit. But I needed to control that growth. As I straightened each tomato cage, I pinched side shoots that threatened to make plants top-heavy and fruits small. With tomato-leaf-scented fingers and brown-stained nails, I continued my tour.

At the back of the garden, I ambled among the early fruiting shrubs and trees scouting for ripe fruit. I stopped to rest under the mulberry tree: our tree of life. That day, red-bellied woodpeckers trilled from the canopy. In better years, shy summer tanagers would flit among branches, gathering fruit for themselves and caterpillars for their nestlings. Below the tree, bushes offered candy-red goumi berries and pale yellow Nanking cherries, ready to pick. Low tree branches dripped with purple-black mulberries, soft and ripe. I gathered handfuls of fruits to nibble as I walked. Nibble fruit are the garden equivalent of cooks' treats. I sighed as the sublime taste of a perfect Illinois Everbearing mulberry exploded in my mouth. The sweet-bright flavor of ripe fruit eased grief's grip on my heart.

6

MOVING WATER

I CARRIED MORNING HAY in a large tub as I walked behind the barn, but my stride broke, the tub tumbled—I caught my balance before the fall.

I'd almost stepped on a box turtle.

I stooped down to examine it. The seven-inch-long cryptic-patterned shell and brown eyes meant it was a female. She looked back at me. She didn't withdraw into her shell, nor did she move. Knees on the wet grass next to her, I reached out and gathered the spilled hay. I knew what she needed in this mid-June sun: water and sugar. I had plenty in the form of mulberries. The horses nickered at me through the paddock fence as I jogged by. "Just a minute, boys." It was breakfast time, but they'd have to wait.

At the mulberry tree, ten minutes of picking yielded half a pint of fruit; I returned to the barn with mulberries cupped in both purple-stained hands. I gave some to each horse as I passed. They wanted hay, but berries would do for the moment.

Around the corner at the back of the barn, the turtle sat in the same spot. She looked up at me as I approached. I dropped fruit in front of her face and wished her well on her journey.

But the turtle was in the same place when I returned after an hour of chores. I stilled. The mulberries lay before her untouched, and she was digging with her hind claws. Shredded grass leaves, roots, and small clumps of clay were slowly, steadily pushed aside. I crept backward into the barn.

When I returned to her spot a few hours later, I saw that the mulberries were gone and that a bare patch of packed earth had appeared. I knelt down beside it. What was this? It was then that I realized that I'd become the custodian of a nest of box turtle eggs.

Over the weeks that followed, our uplands hosted a parade of turtles.

A few nights later, returning home, I slammed on my brakes—back tires skidded on the driveway to avoid a large olive-gray river turtle as it slowly marched across the gravel. Phone in hand, I got out of the car and took pictures and video. The turtle turned its head to watch me but didn't slow or alter course. Its low-domed, smooth, gray-brown shell, slightly flared at the edges, was just over a foot in length. This was an unusual sight: I'd never seen a river turtle up close before—not on land. Down at the river, they're wary. If they see you, they slide off their logs into the water. But here was one on our road, three feet from me. The turtle looked back at me again suspiciously before it entered the forest.

Once inside the house, weaving past the welcoming dogs, I made my way to the laptop and searched the North Carolina herpetology site to try to identify the visitor. Satisfied that I'd exhausted my limited skills and picture angles, I texted the picture to Stephen. "Is this a river cooter?"

"Yes, definitely a river cooter, very nice," he replied.

She was probably a female, because at over a foot long, she was much bigger than the smaller males. A river cooter almost half a mile from the river had entered the upland forest. Why would she leave the lowlands? Maybe searching for a spot to nest?

About two weeks later, while pulling out of our drive to go to work, I did a double take: a large river turtle was in our front yard, digging. She was slightly smaller than the river cooter, a dark slate gray with a bit of yellow plastron visible under her chin. I got out of the car with my phone and took a picture from far away as I didn't wish to disturb her. If she needed to nest there, she was welcome to do so. When I returned that evening, I stopped and looked for evidence. A large bare spot showed me where she had firmly packed and smoothed the clay.

Later, Stephen confirmed by text that I'd seen a yellow-bellied slider.

The next day, I asked Howard to walk with me to the front yard. I pointed to the bare spot of clay where the yellow-bellied slider had nested. "This is where the big river turtle was digging. That's *two* turtle nests now, where I've seen a female digging. And two river turtle sightings in one year. How unusual."

I walked a few feet to the west. "Look here. I think this is another smaller nest near the river turtle's nest. This bare spot in the grass." I crouched down. "Here. Does that look like one to you?"

Howard walked over to examine the ground beneath my outstretched finger. "Yeah. Much smaller, so probably another box turtle. Crazy!"

"I know, right? I've never seen *one* before, now we have three turtle nests in our yard."

It's still a mystery as to why so many eastern box turtles nested in our yard, why the large river turtles visited the uplands at the farm. We've not seen them nesting here before, or since 2017. The year ultimately proved to be unremarkable for the amount of rain that fell or for the number of floods. I've learned that turtles can migrate from rivers to uplands to nest, but why not during other years?

Could a lack of insects in the floodplain have prompted the animals to roam farther afield than normal? I've found little information about the travel habits of river turtles. So I may never know.

Over the following weeks, we found four more box turtle nests scattered around the property in the grassy uplands, and I became an attentive caretaker. I covered a few nests near the house with large wire baskets weighted with a rock to prevent egg raids by raccoons. Or more likely, I feared, by our own dogs. When outside with the hose, when watering plants during long dry spells, I also watered the nests. Howard was careful to check them for activity before mowing nearby.

As time passed, it became more difficult to see the nests. Grass and weeds grew into the bare spots and helped to hide them. If I'd not known where they were, I would have missed them.

The turtles were a welcome distraction from the loss of other animals at the farm. After dinner each night, I continued to read widely about insect losses. I wanted to know if this had happened to other

Female eastern box turtle.

people and if so, why. A report captured my attention—it was a recent *Audubon* magazine article by Elizabeth Royte: "The Same Pesticides Linked to Bee Declines Might Also Threaten Birds." Elizabeth wrote about a Canadian researcher who studies insect-eating birds in the prairie pothole region of Saskatchewan, Christy Morrissey. A professor at the University of Saskatchewan, Morrissey conducts studies to learn if bird health is impacted in areas where row crop agriculture has altered insect populations.

Dr. Morrissey had studied the effects of agriculture on wildlife for years. Maybe she'd have some insight into why our insects and birds were dying. So, I sent her an email. With a few sentences, I summarized my situation: I described the cornfield and mentioned that the farmer reported using Roundup and nitrogen to prepare the fields for the new planting year. Remembering Stephen's comment, I asked, "Could the cornfield somehow be responsible for the insect deaths at our farm?"

To my relief, Christy responded within days. She suggested that another group of chemicals could be involved: neonicotinoids. Corn seed is typically coated with neonicotinoid insecticides and other pesticides such as fungicides. However, a farmer may not know that they're applying pesticides when they plant the coated seed. She wrote that the corn seed coating is water soluble and can be carried from the field in runoff into nearby waterways during heavy rains.

I straightened up in the chair as I read her message. Not only had we had heavy rains, we had a flood. Robert had said that his tractor contained corn seed waiting to be planted. Both tractor and seed were submerged in the floodwaters.

Neonicotinoid, or "neonic," insecticides were somewhat known to me. Neonics are an important group of insect poisons—the most commonly used insecticides in the world today. Although they're toxic to helpful insects and pests alike, neonics are probably most infamous because they've been implicated in honeybee colony losses and wild bee deaths.

Beekeepers and scientists report that honeybees and native bees suffer great harm from the potent neonics. (Neonicotinoid active ingredients include acetamiprid, clothianidin, dinotefuran, imidacloprid, nitenpyram, thiacloprid, and thiamethoxam.)

The insecticides can kill bees outright. A high dose can kill rapidly—this can happen if bees fly through neonic seed dust or spray. But it's more common for animals to be poisoned but not to die right away. Damage varies: young bees may not develop normally and may die before their wings dry; bees who initially survive may die young, before they've fully contributed to survival of the next generation. Some bees suffer immune system damage and can't resist infection or parasite infestation. Others can't learn to do bee work properly; they lose their sense of direction, and when they go out to gather food, they can't find their way back home. Queens may lose their ability to lay eggs—a serious situation when a colony depends on a constant supply of new bees to work throughout the summer. Exposed solitary bees may have smaller families and fewer descendants. The result is that pollinator populations are damaged, they decline, and they may be destroyed.

But I hadn't known that neonics were used as a coating on corn seed.

Since the 1990s, when neonics were developed, their use has grown rapidly. Today, the insecticides are used by homeowners to treat landscape plants and by farmers to grow fruits and vegetables. They are used in greenhouses to protect nursery plants. But I learned that day that, by far, the largest use of neonics is to coat the seed of field crops like soybeans, cotton, and corn.

My previous knowledge of neonics was confined to their use on fruit trees and nursery plants. I was aware that many plant growers use the insecticides in their greenhouses. So when I bought plants, I always asked if they were treated with neonics before I purchased them for my pollinator garden. I didn't want toxic pollen and nectar to poison the butterflies and bees that I hoped to support. I didn't wish to poison the pollinators that gave me apples.

For fruit and vegetable growers, neonics have become an effective way to produce blemish-free food. But there's a substantial price to pay for that perfect piece of produce. Neonics are called systemic insecticides because they're distributed within all parts of a plant. Neonics are inside the food and can't "be removed from fruits or vegetables by peeling or washing."

Neonics are sucked up by the plant when it draws contaminated water up from treated soil. The insecticides can also be sprayed onto or injected into plants. Whatever form of application is used, the entire plant becomes toxic to insects; the leaves, flowers, fruits, and guttation drops—the sugary, mineral-rich liquid that plants exude at night and that insects love to drink in the mornings. Exposures add up. If a bee survives the first dose of a neonic, a second exposure may kill it. Among insects, the damage is cumulative and irreversible.

So, although I knew something about neonics, I didn't give them much thought because I didn't use them. I didn't apply neonics to my plants and avoided buying new plants if I knew they were treated. I'd felt in control of my little part of the world.

I provided healthy plants to support the bumblebees that pollinated my cucumbers, tomatoes, peppers, beans, and okra—the southeastern blueberry bees that gave us blueberries. Blue orchard bees emerged early each spring to pollinate the apples, pears, and cherries. I thought I could protect them all. I kept my garden and orchard a clean place for them to carry out their work in the fresh air and sunlight as they foraged, drank nectar, and gathered pollen for their offspring.

But neonics on seed were a different kind of threat. Especially if that seed coating could wash off into waterways. Everything drinks water.

It was time for another call to Robert.

"Hey, Robert, me again. I have a new lead: I was wondering if you used coated corn seed?"

"Sure. And that flood made a mess of that coating. Green residue was crusted all over the seed hopper."

"I'm hoping to learn which chemicals were used on the seed," I said. "I want to get my water samples tested, but I still need a list of what to test for."

"I don't know what chemicals were in there. I work with my seed distributor, and he gives me the seed that will work best for each field I farm. I have no idea what to tell you. I have the seed company name, but that's it. That won't tell you anything about the chemicals."

"Do you have any of that green residue left that I can get tested?"

"No, that's gone. It took a long time, but we cleaned that hopper out."

"What about a lot number? Do you keep tags from the bags?"

"I don't know. It's been a long time. I'll send you a picture if I have it."

"OK, thanks. Let me know if you find anything that can help. If I can figure this out, I'll let you know."

The call ended and I sat back down at the computer. The pieces seemed to be falling into place—or were they? I didn't understand. How could twenty-five to fifty pounds of seed do so much damage? A disabled wetland, dead meadows, empty nests, and dying creatures? It was hard for me to imagine.

The damage was widespread. Some of the dying animals lived far above the floodplain in the uplands, about a quarter mile away from the tractor accident.

I looked at an aerial photograph of the floodplain online. Floodwaters had submerged all the crop fields and meadows for at least two full days in April: the twenty-fourth through the twenty-sixth. Tons of moving water would have dissolved some of the pesticide coating off the seed stored in Robert's tractor. The diluted seed coating chemicals would have spread widely over the land.

But *not that much* coating. Small amounts of pesticides. I struggled with the mismatch between the small amount of seed and the large area of damage.

I saw how Halting Creek flows into Eden River. The Halting Creek fields are uphill from our wetland. My finger traced the lines onscreen of old drainage swales cut into the fields.

The lower part of the drainage system for the Halting Creek fields emptied directly into the wetland around the swale cut into our flood-plain meadows. If more water flowed into the system than the wetland and swale could hold, the water continued to flow through the old drainage system until it finally reached the Eden River almost half a mile downstream. So, the last bit of concentrated drainage, the final water coming from the Halting Creek fields, was water flowing from the many acres of cornfield and from the seed hopper. That contaminated drainage topped off the water already sitting in our wetland.

It started making some sense to me. Neonics are extremely potent. Neonics can poison insects in the part-per-billion concentration range. But how can I truly understand a small number like parts per billion? I looked it up. A useful way to visualize one part per billion is to think of one penny out of $10 million, or one second out of thirty-two years.

What amount of neonic is used to coat a single kernel of corn seed? About a milligram. Thankfully, Erin Hodgson, a professor at Iowa State, did the math for me. In the April 6, 2012, report from Iowa State's Integrated Crop Management News, she wrote: "a single corn kernel with a 1,250 rate [1.25 mg] of neonicotinoid seed treatment contains enough active ingredient to kill over 80,000 honey bees."

And an acre of corn starts with about thirty thousand seeds.

I finally understood how a small amount of seed coating drainage might have poisoned insects living in the wetland, may have poisoned animals that drank the water. But I thought about the loss of animals in the meadow—bare plants and bare soil far from the swale. Was it possible that the meadow plants also absorbed the chemicals from the corn seed and became sources of neonic exposure for other insects? Or was the floodwater so toxic that it killed or repelled everything it had touched?

The day after our conversation, I received a text from Robert. It was a picture of part of a white piece of paper—with a lot number.

I spent the next few mornings on the phone. With seed brand, name, and lot number in hand, I called local seed distributors to find a representative who worked with Robert's brand of corn seed. After a few conversations with hesitant seed company representatives, I pieced together that corn seed was routinely coated with a palette of pesticides, a mixture containing neonic insecticides, meant to kill anything that wants to eat corn plants, and fungicides, chemicals meant to protect corn from harmful fungi.

But the actual chemicals used to coat each lot of seed can vary. Different coating formulations may be "prescribed" for each area a farmer cultivates. Different chemical mixtures are used for each soil type, each field condition, and weather conditions anticipated for the coming year. For example, as I understood it, if a cold, wet spring is anticipated, a mixture with more fungicide may be recommended.

There were so many conversations, and I can't remember all the details of specific discussions with each representative. But as I paced around the kitchen early mornings with phone pressed to my ear, I quickly learned that mine was an unusual request.

"Thanks for taking my call. I'm trying to find out the chemicals used in the coating mixture used on a specific lot of corn seed. I have the lot number. Can you help me?" When asked why I was interested, I described the flood and the fact that the tractor was submerged.

"We had an accident at our place and the coating washed into our wetland. Our insects down there and up above at my orchard are dead or dying. I'm trying to figure out what it means for our farm."

After that, my questions were met with tightly guarded answers. I remember fragments from some discussions.

- Some representatives shut me down immediately:
  "Unless that's *your* seed tag, I can't talk to you about company business."
  "No, ma'am. I can't help you."
  "That's need-to-know information."
  But I need to know!

- Some people wanted me to give Robert up:

  "If you give me the name of the farmer, I'll look into this for you."

  "Where exactly did this happen?"

  "How did you get that seed number?"

- More than one sought to deflect my request:

  "Don't worry about that small amount of seed. It won't do nothing."

  "How much seed? Why, that's nothin' at all." I clearly heard *little lady*, but I don't think he actually spoke the words out loud.

After the first calls, I learned to leave dead wildlife out of my opening. The fact of the dead animals only provoked irritation from the man on the other end of the phone. They were all men. Or was it anger I heard?

I shifted to focus upon the possible impacts to our family: "We had an accident at our place, and corn seed coating dissolved into our wetland. Our drinking water well extends below the level of that water. I'm concerned because those seed coating chemicals can seep into the groundwater," I said. "I need to find out what the coating chemicals are so I can get my water samples tested."

Luckily, I finally found a seed representative willing to talk with me. When I spoke to Josh, I sketched out the problem and sequence of events. Then, I added a detail to support my concern. "I think there *was* something in the water, 'cause when I touched it, it burnt my hand," I said. "That's why I'm trying to chase this down."

"How deep did you say your well was?" Josh asked.

"I didn't. It's about six hundred feet," I said. "It's a pretty deep well, but that floodplain is sandy loam. Our groundwater seeps down through rock fractures. To the best of my knowledge, the well doesn't draw from an aquifer. So I have no idea where the stuff from the floodplain may travel below ground."

"I don't know if your well could be affected either," he said. "What was that lot number again? I can look and let you know if I have it.

"What's your email address?" he asked.

Within days, I received Josh's email. He included a list of pesticides used to coat the specific lot of seed that Robert had sown in the Halting

Creek fields. The pesticides that left the bright green goo that fouled Robert's equipment.

The list of chemicals that I'd sought for so long was finally revealed to me. The corn seed was coated with four pesticides: a neonic insecticide, clothianidin, and three fungicides—trifloxystrobin, metalaxyl, and ipconazole.

List of pesticides in hand, my next task was to find a laboratory that could detect them. The last two water samples still waited in the back of the fridge.

My first call was to the state, but I was told that the state water laboratory didn't have the proper instruments to do the analyses. Well that seemed strange. I pushed a little more and was finally connected to the senior chemist. He explained that the water-soluble pesticides, the neonics and glyphosate from Roundup, required different, more sensitive equipment to detect them in water samples. Their lab instruments could only be used for the older classes of pesticides that didn't dissolve in water so easily. They couldn't test my samples.

I received suggestions for analytic labs from state and local government chemists. But when I called those labs and asked if they would test my water samples from the floodplain, I found that they, too, were unable to detect the chemicals on my list.

My next idea was to find a private environmental laboratory on my own. Many are scattered throughout the Southeast. I made a list. Labs that advertised the ability to perform multiple tests *and* those located within a three-hour drive of my home were prioritized with bold text. I knew that sending water samples is risky. I wanted to hand-carry my precious samples. So much can go wrong in a shipment: delays that allow samples to warm, damaged or illegible water-soaked paperwork, or broken sample jars.

My mornings were again dominated by a series of telephone calls to inquire about each lab's specific capabilities. "I'm looking to analyze water samples for neonicotinoids, fungicides, and glyphosate. Can you do any or all of these? The samples were collected from surface water, not drinking water."

My calls were usually greeted by a voice message, and I responded by leaving my name and phone number. In each call, I'd carefully say, then spell, each chemical group I wished to evaluate. Sometimes, a receptionist answered. When I had the opportunity to speak with someone, I unfailingly learned that they weren't able to test for the neonics or for glyphosate. It was such a common response. I learned to save time during precious morning hours by leaving voice messages at labs in the evenings. Although I left my telephone number, most of the time I received no reply. A few courteous folks called back to tell me that they couldn't analyze my target pesticides.

So, although there were multiple analytic labs that advertised as environmental laboratories, I found none that were able to test water samples for the pesticides on my list. Most labs tested samples of drinking water from wells for evidence of bacteria. Some could also evaluate samples of the most common of the chemicals regulated in drinking water. Those water tests—nitrate, arsenic, chromium—are typically performed at the request of vigilant homeowners or during the discovery period of a home sale. Apparently, there was little demand for the tests I was requesting. The number of labs crossed from my list was growing. After a week of calls, it felt like another dead end.

It made me wonder how, or even if, anyone is tracking these pesticides in the environment. These two groups of chemicals, glyphosate herbicides and neonic insecticides, are the most commonly used pesticides worldwide. Is it truly this difficult to get water tested? It was for me. I can only hope that the situation is improving.

One challenge is that the active ingredient of Roundup, glyphosate, is difficult for some laboratories to measure in water. Over time, glyphosate degrades into a related chemical, AMPA. Both chemicals are typically found together in samples. After water becomes contaminated with Roundup, the glyphosate concentration decreases and AMPA increases. Both chemicals are water soluble and assume different forms depending upon the acidity of the water; in this way, they can evade easy analysis. They're shapeshifters.

Yet when people are prepared and plan to analyze samples for glyphosate, when they have the right laboratory equipment, when they collect the proper samples in the proper volume, glyphosate is detected in water where people live and work. Because we use so much of it. Agriculture uses the most. In the years 2012 to 2016, on average, about a pound of glyphosate was applied to each acre of US cropland. But that's a historical average; usage has increased over time. As Pat Dempsey wrote for the Midwest Center for Investigative Reporting, some states in the middle third of the country use three times that amount.

But it's not only used on cropland. Glyphosate is the most popular herbicide for home use; about five million pounds were purchased by consumers in 2011. Close to another five million pounds were applied by professionals in yards and gardens, on walkways and patios, in parks, on school grounds, golf courses, and upon the expansive, manicured landscapes surrounding commercial and government buildings. When rain falls, the glyphosate dissolves off of the soil or plant material and flows off the site in water. Glyphosate is found in field-side ditches and in surface and ground water used for drinking water, and it is discharged into rivers from our treated waste water. Glyphosate has been incorporated in the earth's hydrological cycle—it's now found in rain as it falls from the sky.

———————

As I continued reading about chemicals used in modern farming, I realized that wildlife were not the only creatures who might potentially be harmed by the crop chemicals. In the summer of 2017, controversy swirled in the United States and European Union news media about potential health effects associated with exposure to Roundup. In 2015, the World Health Organization's International Agency for Research on Cancer's analysis of toxicology studies prompted them to declare that glyphosate, the active ingredient in Roundup, was a probable carcinogen, or cancer-causing chemical.

The resulting controversy over glyphosate use stemmed from the fact that the developed world's industrial agricultural practices and genetically modified seed markets were so dependent upon its continued use. So proposed restrictions on glyphosate were a serious financial threat to agribusiness. The potential for health risks such as cancer was of great concern to me, given that glyphosate is frequently detected in water and as a residue in human and animal food.

Presumably, Robert was at highest risk of pesticide exposure because he worked directly with the chemicals. But what are the consequences for people who live near farm fields but don't mix or spray pesticides? Contaminated soil blows around in the wind; neonics and glyphosate can leach into ground water. What were the consequences for people who eat food or drink water contaminated with these water-soluble chemicals? After all, pesticide residues are commonly found in samples of food and water.

Paul Mills at the University of California at San Diego has reported that urinary concentrations of glyphosate, a marker of exposure, have increased among the people he's studied over the last two decades. A recent report from Jean-Marc Bonmatin from the French National Centre for Scientific Research found neonics in hair samples from people who lived near agricultural areas. The highest concentrations in hair were gathered from townspeople who lived near areas with the most neonic soil contamination. The scientists reported hair contamination in samples collected from citizens, not just from farmers. They concluded that multiple routes of exposure such as soil dust, contaminated water, and food may have contributed to people's neonic exposure. Recently, the Centers for Disease Control and Prevention (CDC) found that about 50 percent of people in a nationally representative survey had evidence of at least one type of neonic in their urine. Each chemical was measured separately. But we are not exposed to just one pesticide—most of us are exposed every day to mixtures or combinations of toxic chemicals.

We don't know the effects of all the pesticides to which we are exposed. We don't know the potential effects of occasional larger exposures or small exposures every day.

Our drinking water well stretched far below the level of the swale in the meadows below. If the pesticides in Roundup and in the corn seed coating were all water soluble, what was *our* risk of exposure?

That Thursday, I stopped by the grocery store after work to do my weekly shopping. Spooked by my recent reading, I added six two-gallon plastic totes of drinking water to my cart.

When I got home, I climbed the side steps and poked my head in the door. "Howie, can you help me unload the car? I bought water."

Howard walked into the utility room from his office; he looked at me strangely. "Water, why?"

We walked to the car together, and I considered how to frame my unexpected purchase as we unloaded groceries. "I told you about those agricultural chemicals being water soluble, how they moved off the fields and into the swale. Well it turns out they can leach into ground water too," I said as I staggered up the steps, my arms draped with bags. I clutched a two-gallon tote to my chest.

"But our well is so deep, do you really think it's an issue?" he asked.

"I have no idea, honey," I sighed, and sat down. "It all depends upon how fast water flows down from the surface, where it flows through fractured rock, our soil type, how much it rains. It's a guessing game."

That was the beginning of drinking and cooking with store-bought water. Next to our kitchen sink, a series of two-gallon plastic totes occupied prime counter space. They had flimsy plastic spigots built into the side that seemed to leak if you looked at them wrong. We became aware of how much water we used every day.

The water tasted like plastic and was fully flat, a big change from the cold, mineral-rich well water to which we'd become accustomed. We could afford to share the "safe" water with the dogs. But they looked disgusted after drinking from their bowl; they seemed to question why their water tasted differently too. The horses were a different story; an animal could drink up to ten gallons of water per day. There was no way for us to provide them with store-bought water.

I wanted to defend our health, to defend my farm. But so far, I was not totally sure of the enemy I faced. It was clear that I had to keep pushing to find out what was in the water. Those test results were the only sure way forward.

One of the puzzling facts that still confused me was where the frogs *had* returned to the wetland. Tadpoles swam in the pools of the cornfield swale and in pools far downstream near the river. If the chemicals had come from the cornfield, why had frogs returned there but the entire upper and middle sections of the swale were still without tadpoles?

One evening I found a possible reason. Maybe it was the break-through I'd been seeking. Laure Mamy and her colleagues from France's National Institute of Agricultural Research studied how glyphosate persists in dead plant material long after plants have been sprayed. They reported that plant residues still contained glyphosate for months afterward.

Normally, after Roundup is applied, the glyphosate is broken down by bacteria in the soil. Bacteria break down the glyphosate most quickly on bare soils, such as the soil between the rows of corn in the cornfield. But glyphosate-sprayed crop residue retains the herbicide, keeping glyphosate active in the environment much longer than if the soil were bare.

The Halting Creek field was sown in a wheat crop in 2015. I learned that herbicides, including glyphosate, are sprayed on some crop plants just before harvest. Crops of wheat, corn, oats, other grains, potatoes, sugar beets, peas, and beans can be treated this way. But why would someone spray herbicide on their living crop at the end of the growing season?

Spraying herbicide on a crop before harvest accomplishes two things that are useful to farmers. First: dying plants quickly ripen their seeds, the ones that are close but not yet quite ready to leave the plants' protective cradle. In this way, a dying plant produces more seeds. You may have observed this effect as a tree fails—a pine tree becomes damaged or infected, and during its last few years, it produces bumper crops of pine cones. The plant uses its last energies to reproduce. Life force in action. But row crops only live one year. They have the one set of seed. As crop plants are dying from herbicide exposure, they rapidly ripen that remaining seed, and this can increase a farmer's yield.

Second: the chemicals can be drying agents. When the plant dies from herbicide exposure, the vegetation withers and it loses moisture. The grain or bean also dries—an essential step for harvest. Storing a wet crop is a recipe for fungal growth, with money lost if the crop can't be sold. If a farmer harvests a wet, juicy crop of grain or beans, they may have to pay to have the crop dried; more expense, less profit.

Will's observation of the damaged river oats at the upper part of the swale suddenly made sense. The two-year-old wheat straw that buried the swale was apparently still releasing glyphosate into the water as it slowly decayed. The plants in and around the water appeared burned as if herbicide had been applied to them. Maybe the frogs couldn't tolerate that area because a damaging concentration of glyphosate was still leaching from the crop residue. It became clear that I needed to gather some of that straw and send it to a lab along with the water samples for analysis.

At home, we were still drinking the plastic-flavored water from the grocery store. If glyphosate was still leaching from straw into the wetland, was it more likely to be in our groundwater? Our county conducts water testing, but in my many conversations with receptionists, I was still unsure what they could actually do.

During a conversation with Elena, who greeted the public at the county environmental health office, I learned something new: our county laboratory had the capability to analyze drinking water samples for one of the chemicals on my list—glyphosate.

The progress encouraged me. Howard and I discussed the testing as an opportunity to check for other potential contaminants in our well water. We'd never had a problem, but it had been a while since we had it tested—"a while" being since the discovery period during our home purchase. We prepared our list of tests.

Later in the week, I called Elena back to inquire about which forms to use, which boxes to check. "You can fill out the boxes of the individual tests you want, but I recommend the screening panels; they'll save you money. There's a bacteria screen and an inorganic chemical screen," she said. "Be sure and check the pesticide screening box too, but my understanding is that the equipment's not working right now for the glyphosate test."

"Oh. Well that's the main reason we're getting our water tested. Can you let me know when the equipment's up and running again?" I asked.

Within two days, I received a call from a laboratory manager, Joe.

"I understand that you want to test your drinking water for glyphosate?" he asked.

"Yes, but I was told that your equipment was down."

"Well, it's up and running now," he said.

"Can you test for AMPA too? I understand that as glyphosate degrades, it breaks down into AMPA. With both results, I can get a better idea of our total level of exposure to the toxic chemicals."

"No, we don't do that test. Do you have a shallow well? An older hand-dug well? We don't get many requests for glyphosate testing," he said.

"No, our well's quite deep, but it stretches below a wetland that we suspect was contaminated with Roundup. I'm trying to figure out if our well water's contaminated too."

"I have some experience with this chemical," he said. "You should know that one negative test will not tell you much about your future risk for contamination. It can take months for glyphosate to leach through the soil and be detected in your water. If you really think it's a potential problem, I recommend repeated water tests over months to years."

"I need to look. This testing is pricy. If it's negative, I guess we'll figure that out as we go," I said.

Joe transferred my call back to Elena. She took my credit card number to pay for basic panels of water tests: bacteria, nitrate, metals, and minerals, plus the glyphosate analysis. Within a short week, a technician visited to collect most samples directly from our well; the test for lead was collected from our home taps.

Within a month I received an email with the results of the water screening tests, but not the glyphosate. I was told that would come later.

A month went by before the second email arrived. In it, I read that they couldn't perform the test for glyphosate after all. No explanation. Just a blank where the results would be.

I was disgusted. It's not easy for people who wish to know if our most commonly used agricultural chemicals are in their water—even their drinking water.

What about family farms? Families can be exposed to these chemicals year after year. Water-soluble chemicals leach from fields and can contaminate the groundwater beneath their homes. Probable carcinogens like glyphosate. Chemicals toxic to the nervous system like neonics that are known to persist in soil and groundwater for years. A study of one neonic and its breakdown products revealed "detections in groundwater . . . started after 500 days from application and continued five years after application." But that groundwater is the water rural families use for their animals, water to irrigate home gardens, the source of drinking water that is pumped up and served to their loved ones.

I was shocked to learn not only that it is hard for someone to test their water for the most commonly used pesticides, but that there *is no tracking system* to understand if there are any harmful effects of pesticides once they're approved and released into the world. No system to investigate if the new pesticide poisons other animals like birds or mammals. No system to find out if a new pesticide is contaminating people's property or their well water. No system to find out if it hurts people.

In the United States, manufacturers of drugs and pesticides must receive government approval before they can bring a new product to market. But pesticide safety is handled very differently than the drug safety procedures most familiar to me. It makes sense: drugs are chemicals *meant* to go into people's bodies. Pesticides are meant to control pests. But now we know from CDC tests of blood and urine from a representative sample of US residents that pesticides frequently end up in our bodies too.

Drugs undergo extensive testing for safety before they're approved for the general public. After approval, they're monitored for potential harm by the Food and Drug Administration (FDA). Because although hundreds or thousands of people may participate in the tests, or clinical trials, to determine if a new drug is safe and effective, the study size may be too small to detect uncommon problems. That's why tracking, or post-marketing surveillance, is so important. Even with care and attention, sometimes dangerous drugs make it to the market.

From the FDA's Center for Drug Evaluation and Research, FDA-TRACK: "Even the best clinical trials cannot ensure a drug is completely safe and effective. Trials are often conducted on relatively small populations of test patients. After a drug is approved, that same drug can be taken by thousands or even millions of patients. With this large-scale use, new risks and new information about the drug's effectiveness are often found. FDA maintains a system of postmarketing surveillance and risk assessment programs to identify adverse events that did not appear during the drug approval process."

In other words, the real world is messy and always more complicated than early studies may suggest. Sometimes monitoring reveals previously unrecognized threats. These discoveries are possible due to manufacturer-independent monitoring programs. Independent monitoring is important because the manufacturer has an inherent conflict of interest: unless required to do so, few manufacturers will voluntarily withdraw a profitable product.

As with drugs, pesticide safety studies are required to be submitted for government evaluation before the chemicals are approved or registered for use. As with drugs, studies are conducted on a very simplified model of the world. But the pesticide registration process is less comprehensive than the drug trials. In the registration process, the health of laboratory animals is examined.

But during tests, animals aren't typically exposed to the final pesticide formula. Tests are conducted on the active ingredients alone. And that really matters. Robin Mesnage from King's College, London, and other colleagues report how in the final pesticide, active ingredients are mixed with other inactive ingredients, such as surfactants, that allow easy mixing and sticking of the product to plants. These final mixtures can be much more toxic than the active ingredient alone.

Nor are test animals exposed to the complex mixtures of chemicals typically used on a single crop field. But in the real world, after pesticide approval, many kinds of wild animals (and people) are exposed to complex mixtures of agricultural chemicals in their food, water, and air.

Our daughter, Melissa, spent her early adulthood working with people who'd been diagnosed with intellectual and developmental disabilities (IDD). There's a spectrum of disability among those with IDD: attention-deficit/hyperactivity disorder, learning disabilities, conduct disorders, low IQ, and autism. Melissa worked with severely affected individuals who received full-time assistance with daily activities such as eating, dressing, bathing, and other support. She learned that most of the people she worked with will be dependent upon others for their entire lives. Her work made me more aware of the needs of the over seven million Americans living with IDD.

Over the last fifty years, IDD has become increasingly common in the United States, and most of the people living today with IDD are children. A CDC-led study published in the journal *Pediatrics* reported that since 1997, developmental disabilities have steadily increased and by 2017 were reported among almost one in five children in the United States.

Although causes of IDD vary—genetic abnormalities, accidents such as oxygen starvation at birth, and traumatic brain injuries—IDD is also associated with exposure to neurotoxins: chemicals toxic to the nervous system. Many modern insecticides are neurotoxins, but there are others: mercury, lead, alcohol, nicotine, and so on. Major public health initiatives to reduce exposure to neurotoxins have included eliminating lead in homes where young children live and discouraging smoking and drinking among pregnant women—because the age at which people are exposed to neurotoxins really matters.

Adults are less likely to be severely damaged from exposure to low doses of neurotoxins than children are. Adults have more resistance as we've established most of the structure and function of our brains and nervous systems. Young children are especially vulnerable because they're still forming, growing; our brains and nervous systems largely develop in the womb and during early childhood. Exposure to neurotoxins early in life is linked to a range of developmental disorders and disabilities.

But as a society we don't always act to prioritize children's health. A product strongly suspected or known to be neurotoxic can be on the market for decades before it's possible to withdraw it. In 2015, over forty health and environmental scientists came together to publish a warning: "We assert that the current system in the United States for evaluating scientific evidence and making health-based decisions about environmental chemicals is fundamentally broken." Because sometimes, hazardous products are only removed long after the damage to people's health has occurred. As Bruce Lanphear, a professor of health sciences at Simon Fraser University, put it: "Unfortunately, industries are allowed to market a product until it is repeatedly shown to be toxic in both human and laboratory studies."

One problem is that once pesticides are approved, there's no monitoring to track potential harm. They're free to be applied as registered: to food crops, to fields, in public parks, around schools, and in homes. Once a harmful pesticide is on the market, it can take years for independent research to be conducted, years before the number of reports of harm become too big to ignore. And many more years to achieve the political will to act.

A recent example in the news involves a common group of insecticides, the organophosphates. They are registered for multiple uses including to protect food plants and ornamental plants, and to serve as bait for termites in buildings. High-quality scientific reports were published in the first decade of the twenty-first century that alerted us of potential damage to children's learning abilities, IQs, and nervous system development associated with exposure to organophosphates. But a commonly used organophosphate, chlorpyrifos, continued to be approved for use on food crops until it was withdrawn in 2021. Kids were exposed to food residues of chlorpyrifos for over fifty years. More than a dozen other organophosphates are still registered for use.

There are increasing calls from scientists in Europe for post-approval monitoring so that any environmental damage can be detected rapidly after a pesticide has been introduced to the marketplace. But the United States' steadily rising rates of IDD suggest that post-approval monitoring for health problems associated with pesticide use may also be warranted. Monitoring may have detected the risks of neurotoxic chemicals like organophosphates earlier, and may have reduced exposure earlier. The results of monitoring could be used to protect the health of millions of babies and children.

I became so discouraged in my search for a laboratory to test my water samples. But I had an idea. I shifted from searching the Internet for laboratories and started scouring other people's published scientific reports. The reports always include the methods used to detect pesticides. Sometimes reports identify the labs used for pesticide analyses. I found that most reports were not helpful for my purposes; they described using academic labs that participated as collaborators in the research effort.

But I needed an accredited lab that performs these tests as part of their daily business. A lab that undergoes rigorous procedures to calibrate instruments and to test known quantities of chemicals. A lab that ensures its activities are correct, precise, and reproducible. A lab that could test my samples—one where I could trust the results.

In a report about glyphosate in water, I discovered what I needed: the authors described using a public laboratory that specializes in testing for agricultural chemicals. I searched for its name and learned that it is accredited, with a strict quality-control program. The location was not ideal as it was many hundreds of miles away, and I had hoped to drive my samples to a lab.

But I didn't see that I had a choice.

The next morning, I gave the laboratory a call and was able to talk with the director, Jessica Walker.

"Dr. Walker? Thanks for taking my call. I have a few questions. Apparently, a wetland near my home was impacted by agricultural runoff. I have water samples and a list of target analytes: Roundup and corn seed–coating pesticides, neonicotinoids, and fungicides. I need to know the most cost-effective way to find out if the water's contaminated with those chemicals."

"The most cost-effective way is a screen," she said. "We can test the water for classes of related chemicals, like neonicotinoids, then list the specific ones we find. That may be your best bet."

"Great! My other issue is potentially more serious. I only have a subset of the samples I collected, slightly under one liter total if we combine samples. My control samples are gone. Can you still do an analysis?"

"We can, but with the smaller amount of water, the limit of detection will be higher. So, we won't be able to detect the lowest levels of contamination. It's OK about your controls. We can backfill with local surface water controls," she said.

"But you should know that your experience is not unusual," she continued. "In the time I've worked here, the problem of pesticides in water's gotten worse. Now we're having trouble finding surface water samples here that are *not* contaminated."

That was hard to hear. The lab is located in an agricultural area and it analyzes many water samples each week for the commonly used pesticides on my list; much of that work is local. Apparently, crop farming was contaminating water in places far from our farm.

The next morning, I talked to the lab receptionist to make sure I filled out the paperwork correctly. I clipped my check to the forms. I needed to send the samples overnight, and they needed to stay very cold. I settled the foil-covered glass jars of water into a sturdy Styrofoam-lined cardboard box. I added gallon-sized freezer bags of wheat straw and many ice packs. By wrapping bubble wrap around each jar multiple times, I made airy nests within the plastic wrap and ice packs so that the samples would stay cold and protected in the center of the box during their journey. The ziplock bags of wheat straw fit nicely between the bubble-wrapped jars and the sides of the box.

I knew that if I failed and the jars broke in transit, I would never know the truth of what contaminated the water. I closed the box with my documentation inside a waterproof ziplock bag and sealed it with way too much packing tape.

Once inside at the delivery service office, the box slid easily across the counter to the clerk, where she weighed it.

I hesitated for a heartbeat as I learned the cost of shipping the large, heavy, insulated box overnight, but remembered that I was not the only one in the United States with contaminated water. It was worth the cost to make sure I knew what had happened. I handed over my credit card and hoped for the best.

7

BEES PLEASE
(QUEEN'S DANCE)

I WATCHED BEHIND CLOSED EYELIDS as my insulated cardboard box hurtled through space—eight hundred miles in one night. The box moved from loading dock worker gloves to transport truck, from cargo handlers to airplane, from conveyor belt to handcart to truck. The complicated journey of my precious water samples dominated my dreams.

The next morning, a check of the tracking number on the shipper's website informed me of the expected time of delivery—11:00 AM. I called the lab midday to check on the samples.

"We received them, logged them in at 11:20," said the lab's receiving clerk. "The jars were fine, no breakage. All nice and cold. No problems," she said.

The best possible outcome. The tension drained out of my shoulders as I received the good news. I prepared myself to wait two weeks for the results.

Days at the office were a blur of constant activity. But at the farm, life moved slowly, strangely. When I worked in the garden or with the animals, I felt off-balance. I acted out life on the set of a movie about a farm. The quality of light cast on the foliage around me was bizarre, as if we'd flipped into another hemisphere. Sunlight seemed refracted through crystal. Rainbows of abnormal brightness reflected from grass blades at my feet and forced me to squint. Shifting shadows of trees formed stark contrast between gray and green.

And as if visiting a strange new place, my mind was wide open and ready for just about anything. I'm not sure I would have been surprised if a meteorite struck the earth beside me as I walked, or if from the forest behind the house a tiger emerged.

The familiar thrum of life that had always enveloped me while outside was gone. Yet individual sounds gained more significance. I startled when a barred owl called from distant forest in the middle of the day.

Funny how the mind fills in what "should" be there. In the past while by myself far from home, after some time I found myself "recognizing" faces of passersby—all complete strangers. At the farm, I would catch small movement in my periphery, then turn and find that it was only a trick of my eye.

I counted the days, waiting for the results of the water tests. My time spent at work was busy, too busy to obsess about the samples. At home, I found respite in a place of comfort and security: my kitchen. Cooking connects me with the food plants we nurture, with the sensual pleasures of umami from concentrated flavors and the aromatic scents of fresh herbs. Cooking connects me with the women who came before me and the inescapable memories evoked by a kitchen filled with inherited objects.

One evening, I prepared a pepper and tortilla casserole. Corn tortillas browned in a cast-iron pan on the stove top. I flipped them with a spatula with insistently burning hands. Pepper hands. I'd spent a good twenty minutes cleaning seeds and placental membranes from Anaheim and poblano peppers and had not worn gloves.

Sliced pepper strips roasted on a sheet pan in the oven. I started to smell them; I'd have to check them soon. Tortillas rested cooling upon paper. I checked the peppers and turned the heat off to slow their progress; they were almost there. I scooped up a serving spoon and turned my attention to my faded red Pyrex mixing bowl.

The squared bowl was a remnant of a set my mother received as a wedding gift. She was able to keep it through all of her moves—all of her kitchens in modest apartments and in big houses. I thought of her as I mixed cream cheese, crushed cumin seed, garlic, and shredded Oaxaca cheese in the bowl. My mother, Vivian, loved to cook, and one of her first gifts to me as an independent adult was a cookbook, *The Joy of Cooking*. The book sat on a shelf in the room next to me, crammed with scraps of paper—other recipes she had copied for me in her elegant, slanted cursive.

I folded some chopped sweet onion into the cheese mixture. In a large glass casserole, I layered tortillas, tomatillo salsa, roasted peppers, and cheese. I'd just slid it into the oven when the phone rang. Mike's number was displayed, so I grabbed the phone and sat down.

"Thanks for checking in, Mike," I said. "I'm feeling a little better this week about everything, I hope to have an answer soon. Did I tell you that I found a laboratory to test the water?"

"No, you didn't. That's progress."

"Yes, I'm so happy. It took for*ever* to find one that actually tests for the corn seed–coating chemicals. Apparently, most labs can't test for glyphosate either."

"Gly-what? Don't start with the chemical names," Mike said.

"Oh, I'm sorry. I've been diving so deep into this stuff for so long. It's part of my everyday now. Glyphosate is the active ingredient in Roundup. Now, you can get other kinds of Roundup with other herbicides added too, but as I understand it, that's still the main ingredient."

Mike dropped his tone and spoke slowly, "I can't understand why crop production is so chemical-heavy now. My grandfather grew crops. He ran cattle for years. We never had problems like this."

I thought about how I may have missed the destruction of the wetland if I'd not been looking for tadpoles. "Well, is it possible that you were a kid and didn't notice?"

"*Because* I was a kid, I would have noticed," Mike said. "We were all over those creeks, catching crawdads, playing and fishing. Halting Creek's really changed since the dam was built. . . . You would have loved it here back then. There were more ducks then too. Lots of wood ducks that used to nest in trees above the creek. Now the frogs are disappearing, the whip-poor-wills and crawdads. The place is poorer in my opinion."

Mike's words resonated. When we first moved to the farm, I saw a wood duck on the creek. I'd been shocked to see it fly up and perch high in a tree when it saw me. I'd never seen a wood duck off the water. But that was my only sighting.

"Yeah, when we first moved here, I could hear the whip-poor-wills at night, but it's been years since I've heard them. What about mourning doves? There used to be huge flocks all summer in the meadows along the river. Now, I rarely even hear them."

Mike was silent for a moment. "Well, I'm not sure about the doves, but I do know that we're not going in the right direction with our crops. Be sure and let me know what you find in the water."

"Will do, Mike. Have a good night."

As I turned my attention back to dinner, I thought about how short term my perspective was compared to Mike's. He'd known and loved this place his whole life.

———————

On the last day of June, I received an email from the wetland assessment team. Will wrote (I'm paraphrasing), "We're still working to finalize results, but our lab tested samples of both sediment and water. No detections of anything yet. We also conducted aquatic toxicology testing with daphnia. Our technician is writing up the results. Those should come to you next week."

The next email I received from the wetland group was from the technician who conducted the aquatic toxicology tests. She'd exposed three generations of water fleas to samples of swale water the field team had collected in early June. Water fleas, or daphnia, are small aquatic animals used in toxicity tests of water. Daphnia were placed into two different groups of water samples: water from the upstream swale where no tadpoles lived and water from the far end of the swale where tadpoles had returned.

The technician explained that although there was 19 percent less reproduction in the daphnia from the upstream sample compared to the downstream sample, it did not quite meet the state-defined threshold of 20 percent that was considered a "significant toxic effect."

I was surprised. The damage was so dramatic. But maybe, like the mosquitoes, could the water fleas survive where other creatures could not? Or could the toxicity have declined since I first found the damage in May compared to when the wetland team had visited?

There had been inches of rain and days of sun since I first found the damage. Time for toxic chemicals to degrade, to be diluted by rainfall and destroyed by sunlight—all could change the toxicity of the water. But maybe that meant the wetland was healing. Maybe the toxic chemicals were fading.

But the lack of statistically significant damage to the water fleas could have been that water fleas are less affected by the clothianidin I suspected was in the water. Eventually, in 2020, I learned from an Environmental Protection Agency review of the insecticide that "clothianidin is practically non-toxic to water fleas (Daphnia magna), but is very highly toxic to other taxa, including shrimp and aquatic insects."

In a separate email, Will sent the chemical test results. They detected no chemicals. But I noticed that they didn't test for any of the chemicals that Robert had told me he used on the field. Will wrote that they didn't have the equipment to test water or sediment for the chemicals on my list: not glyphosate from Roundup nor the neonics and fungicides on the corn seed.

So the state lab was unable to test for the most common agricultural pesticides currently used on most every cornfield in the United States.

My hope for answers rested upon the far-away lab that *could* test for the chemicals. And I was impatient to learn what the water and straw samples contained. But I had to wait.

What could I do to learn more? I had no more of the water I'd collected in May, but there were piles of wheat straw lying in the fields. Maybe I could figure out if the old wheat straw was still toxic. If so, that could explain the lack of tadpoles. Could the straw still be releasing glyphosate after two years out in the environment? It was obvious that I needed to test the straw in water. But I required something in the water that would change if exposed to the herbicide—something that I could easily see.

Most natural waters contain green algae. Green algae coat the rocks at the stream bottom, float on the surface near lakeshores, and grow on branches that dip low into meandering creek water. Green algae are a basic and abundant food source for many creatures, including tadpoles. Whenever I rescue tadpoles from drying pools and raise them in a stock tank, I have to feed them until the nutrient levels in the water increase enough to start algae growth in the tank. Then I can relax, as the green algae feeds and supports the tadpoles' long, perilous journey toward legs and land. The algae grows on every surface of the tank and can form mats on top of the water. That protective cover, along with rocks piled below and tree limbs over the tank, give tadpoles shelter from predators.

When I learned that Roundup can kill green algae, I realized that I had my perfect test subjects nearby.

There are always empty containers around the farm from horse supplements that arrive in food-grade plastic buckets. As I washed the buckets, I designed my study. At least four buckets would be required to see any noticeable toxic effect from the old wheat straw. The first one was filled with water from a stock tank I had in waiting. It had no animals in it yet, nor any visible algae, only a mixture of rainwater and well water. Bucket number one was my reference water, my "control."

Buckets numbered two, three, and four were filled with water from the upper, damaged portion of the swale near the dying river oats. All four buckets were set on a stand inside the eastern door of the barn. They would all receive the same morning light but were protected from weather and the summer heat.

Next, I gathered green algae from a pool at the far end of the swale system near the river, where tadpoles were still playing. I carried it up the hill and put about half of the algae in the stock tank in case I needed it later. A compressed quarter cup of algae was slid slowly into each test bucket. Then to each bucket, I added four tadpoles.

For two days, all the buckets sat. The tadpoles swam and grazed, the green algae grew. On the third day, I added a handful of the wheat straw collected from the upper swale into bucket number four.

Then, I watched and waited.

Sunday dawned clear and warm. Early July heat built rapidly while I gave the dogs their morning walk. But it was a short walk. Midsummer weekends were devoted to processing blueberries and vegetables, and for serious cooking. Work starts early to escape the punishing heat. I grabbed the orchard gate and leaned backward. It opened slowly as the heavy bottom wire rubbed and caught upon tufts of grass. Blueberry hedges were lined up west of the gate, and I turned toward them with anticipation of sweet, ripe fruit.

Rabbiteye blueberries are adapted to the South, and blueberries have their own native pollinators here. Each spring, southeastern blueberry bees covered the bushes. Their long tongues reach deep into tubular flowers. Their diligent work gave us gallons of big berries each year. I slipped under the protective shade cloth and spent a relaxing hour filling two sacks with blueberries while listening to distant birdsong. Then, it was time for vegetable harvest. There would be no more shade for me. I replaced my sun hat, grabbed my basket, and turned my attention to the raised beds of beans, tomatoes, cucumbers, okra, and finally the peppers—shining like bright jewels among fragile stems.

Every July, the dining room table disappears under large platters upon which tomatoes of all sizes are laid out. Each day, I touch and turn the tomatoes, looking for signs of ripe perfection or declining quality. That bounty of crimson, gold, and wine-colored fruits is never wasted. Some tomatoes regularly find their way into my mouth throughout the day. Tomatoes are used fresh, sliced, and dried. Some are reduced down for sauces and coulis, a thick, almost paste-like tomato jam. Stovetop alchemy reduces gallons of pureed tomatoes into scant cups of coulis.

One summer past, we had our friends Emily and George over for dinner. We started with an appetizer of crostini spread with tomato coulis with herbs, and finished with wedges of fresh local chevre, oven-browned just before serving.

"What a treat!" Emily said. "We never have enough tomatoes to make this dish."

Indeed. Over a thousand tomatoes flow through our kitchen each year. The ability to make tomato coulis is one of the perks of life on the farm. The vines we plant each spring keep us in sauce, dried tomatoes, and coulis all winter. The bounty is courtesy of our native bumblebees—bees that nest in the ground within our flower borders and in fallow areas of the raised beds.

Bumblebees are expert pollinators of tomatoes, peppers, and egg-plants. Those plants' flowers hang downward, and bumblebees have a trick: they grasp the petals with strong feet and, while hanging upside down, put their faces in the flowers and buzz. As they vibrate their wings, they vibrate the flower. Pollen rains down upon their fuzzy bellies. When they seek pollen from the next flower, they fertilize that flower with the gift of their belly-pollen. Bumblebee pollination is the secret to big tomatoes, fruitful vines, and abundant pepper harvests.

The garden provides much more than tomatoes. Over the years, a variety of peppers have occupied more and more space in the raised beds as our palates now demand them. Raised with sweet green bell peppers in New England, we entered adulthood in this new place and promptly started challenging our acquired tastes. We experimented with more spice, more variety. We started sampling poblanos, then jalapeños, serranos, and finally habaneros. It's been a journey, but peppers have become a main crop in the garden, and we enjoy our store of them from the freezer all winter. The majority of that bounty enters our kitchen during July and August.

But that July day in the garden, the vegetables were sparse; the basket on my arm was not even half full. The cucumbers were especially disappointing: there were few fruits on the vines, and the ones that remained were small. The runted fruits were weird shapes—many ended with a tiny rat-tail twist.

During the previous few years, there were so many vigorous, healthy cucumbers that I gave armloads of them away to anyone who visited the farm. This was different. Very different. Close examination revealed nothing that alarmed me: the vines looked good. I couldn't find insect or fungal damage, and water had been more than adequate to produce a good crop.

Much earlier than anticipated, I collected bags and basket and headed back inside. In the kitchen, I dropped the bags of berries into the cool depths of the refrigerator and sat down at the computer.

A quick search confirmed the reason for my lack of cucumbers—lack of pollinators. The cucumbers in my garden looked exactly like images of inadequately pollinated cucumbers.

Cucumbers grown outdoors have both male and female flowers. Quarter-sized cucumber flowers are bright yellow and wide open to attract insect pollinators. The plant needs insects to move pollen from the male to the female flower. The grains of pollen, if successful, produce seeds; our cucumber fruits don't develop normally unless they contain ripening seeds.

That day, I learned that a total lack of insect pollination is obvious—there are no fruits at all. Poor pollination creates stunted fruit.

Pollination suffers if the weather's so bad that pollinators are not flying, or if there's a lack of insects. In our case, although we'd had many rainy days in the past month, they were interspersed with fine days. The cucumbers were in bad shape most likely because we had fewer pollinating insects.

When we developed the farm, we unknowingly set the stage for years of vegetable-growing success. One night, in our early years at the farm, I learned to appreciate the diversity of the multitude of small life from a lesson delivered by a peach tree in full bloom on a fine spring night. As I approached the tree, I found it altered—the deep pink blossoms appeared pearly white under a full moon. Peach flowers shimmered with the fluttering of hundreds of moths—so many shapes and sizes. Backlit wings glowed in moonlight. The moths fed silently upon the peach blossom nectar and pollinated the tree in the process.

During those early years, I didn't understand or appreciate the breadth of the work that insects do to provide us food, but now I know.

I realize how precious our remaining native animals, our wild creatures, are and how essential they've been to the abundance we've enjoyed here. During the previous two decades, generations of birds, bees, flies, beetles, wasps, moths, and butterflies have lived with us—and have helped us. They've made our garden and orchard a success.

We unwittingly helped ourselves too. We worked hard to support the wildlife that lived here before us, to add to their numbers and diversity. We left some areas wild and encouraged flowering plants. Mowed less. We planted native plants that bore food for wild creatures so that every season would yield fruits, nuts, seeds, and berries. The yaupon, Juneberry, possum haw, and hackberry fed animals in summer. Acorns, hickories, beechnuts, and persimmons fattened them in autumn. Birds feasted upon flower seed heads and the berries of wax myrtle and holly in winter. We removed invasive vines and autumn olive shrubs that threatened to smother anything neglected.

We'd laid out raised beds for vegetables with sparse grass in the walkways between. The edges of the orchard were planted in colorful native flowers: coneflowers, butterfly weed, anise hyssop, brown-eyed Susans, sedum, and asters. Flowering trees like tulip poplar, redbud, and black cherry grow wild around the property.

In return, we'd been blessed with abundant pollinators. We commonly saw the anthill-like mounds of ground-nesting miner bees among clumps of grass in the walkways. Sometimes, bumblebee nest mounds appeared in garden beds in spring, which, when discovered, were marked off and left alone until autumn. The wild bees, along with flies, wasps, and the blue orchard bees we supported, had always ensured a bountiful harvest of fruits and vegetables.

But in summer 2017, the air was still, the ground was quiet, and the nests were gone.

Yet two full bags of blueberries sat on the lowest shelf of the refrigerator. There were plenty of berries still on the bushes. Puzzled, I thought, *But they need pollinators too. Why do we have so many blueberries but the vegetables are doing poorly?*

I thought about the timing of the damaged wetland. It occurred after the flood in late April. By then, the apples, pears, and blueberries had all flowered and been pollinated. The fruit had started to form. But the cucumbers and other vegetables developed and flowered in May and June—I was seeing the results of insect loss *after* the flood.

Poor pollination is a problem far beyond our garden. Wild pollinators are in trouble nationwide. I found that it's common for extension services to publish warnings for home gardeners about the need to hand-pollinate squash, melon, and cucumber plants in backyard plots. Plants in the squash family are especially sensitive to insect loss as they can't reproduce without help. Large commercial growers can buy pollinators, either by keeping honeybees at their farms or renting honeybee colonies to come to the farm and pollinate their crops.

But I know that keeping colonies and renting honeybees can be expensive. It struck me that the loss of wild pollinators is yet another financial burden piled onto today's farmers.

Consider the cost of food if we had to pay to replace all wild pollinators. In 2006, John Losey and Mace Vaughn estimated that wild bees contribute about $3 billion worth of value each year to fruit and vegetable production in the United States. After I shut the laptop cover, I rested my chin in my hands. Joni Mitchell's refrain from her song "Big Yellow Taxi" echoed in my head: *"You don't know what you've got 'til it's gone . . . "*

Pollinating insects have been so precious at the farm. They were a major reason that we've been able to grow so much of our own food. Although we've always recognized that we needed pollinators, could we have done more to support them? More flowers to feed them? More hollow-stemmed plants left standing, more piles of leaves, downed brush, and dead wood? More scattered patches of sunny bare ground to house them?

I continued reading to learn more about the pesticides on Robert's corn seed. Many reports agreed that neonics by themselves are potent insecticides and kill insects at low doses. But another group of reports caught my attention. They showed that when two different classes of pesticides are mixed together on seeds—fungicides such as the ipconazole and neonics such as clothianidin, both used on Robert's seed—the combination can be more lethal to bees than either one alone.

Specific effects depend upon the exact chemicals and concentrations applied, but studies have shown this type of enhanced toxicity among different combinations of fungicides and neonics. The effects of the two together are often more than additive, they are synergistic. The end result is that two plus two does not equal four in the amount of harm inflicted—two plus two can equal twelve or more.

This was alarming to me. If the combined effects of the pesticides that flowed into the wetland are poorly understood, what are the long-term impacts on the pollinators? This could be disastrous for farmers—and for our food supply.

Another report stood out from the others—a review: "How Neonicotinoids Can Kill Bees" by the Xerces Society. Xerces is a non-profit, and its mission is to conserve invertebrate life—animals like mussels, bees, and fireflies. They have extensive experience with bees and neonics, and I hoped they could give me information on how to help the bees and other insects at the farm. I searched their website for contact information.

In my first email, I sketched out an overview of the situation and asked for guidance. After a few messages back and forth, I was able to talk to Aimée Code, an expert on neonics. I started with a bit more detail about the corn seed accident.

But my basic question was: Given the apparent exposure to seed-coating chemicals and glyphosate in the wetland, how could I get my pollinators back?

"Aimée, I've placed stock tanks full of water along the hill above the wetland. I've left more flowering plants, even weeds, around the garden to provide more forage for bees. I'm not sure what else to do."

"Do you have many flowering plants and trees?" she asked. "Pollinators need pollen and nectar to survive."

"Yeah, I have the fruit trees and garden plants. I keep pollinators fed during summer with native flower beds, plantain, and clover in the lawn. We have lots of mixed forest around. Good nectar trees," I said. "Our local garden store used to stock only neonic-free nursery plants.

Mostly, I've bought those for the farm. But Aimée, I think that they're expanding their stock, and I'm not sure anymore if the plants are neonic free. In the cases where they can't tell me for sure, I pick the flowers off for a couple of years until I think the plant may be free of the insecticides. Is that a way forward?"

Aimée laughed. "Yeah, I've been there. I pick the flowers off mine for three years. But really, it's a guess. We don't know how long it takes for plants to clear. Each plant retains the toxic chemicals differently. So for sure, if you can get the neonic-free plants, they're the safest way to go."

Her mood sobered. "You should know that this kind of thing is common," she said. "People call us to ask what to do after neighbors spray for mosquitoes and then all their bees and butterflies are gone. It's not unusual for us to hear of damage to land near crop fields. What does the neighborhood around your farm look like?" she asked.

"We live far out in the country," I said. "We're in a neighborhood of big lots and small farms. Most people just have vegetable and flower gardens, woodlots. But there are some farms with livestock, and some grow row crops."

"Where you live really matters," she said. "Your farm is just part of the whole picture. If you're surrounded by farm fields, or developed neighborhoods with lawns, your farm is more likely to stay barren. But if you're surrounded by good insect habitat, with trees, flowering plants, and lots of healthy insects nearby, then natural migration of animals may repopulate your farm," she said. "Over time, six to seven years or so, the insects may return."

"Six to seven years!" I was shocked.

"Yes, these are persistent insecticides. They contaminate the soil and water for years, especially the clothianidin that you say was on the seed next to your property. It has a long half-life," she said. "Elizabeth, you should be prepared. The bees may never return."

The next week at work, I met with my supervisor, Henry, late in the afternoon. We discussed a field project and last-minute details about travel scheduled for the upcoming week.

We finished the meeting, and I walked toward the door. As I was about to leave his office, he asked, "How are things going at the farm?"

I turned to face him. After a moment, all I could say was, "I feel like I'm seeing the future."

Indeed, I've learned that life without pollinators is not a future prospect but a current reality in many places. From California to Alabama, across the United States, gardeners struggle to produce cucumbers and other vegetables in the squash family. In eastern Kenya, farmers are forced to hand-pollinate fruit and vegetable crops as insect pollinators are absent. Farmer Joseph Mbithi explained, "We are mostly affected by pesticides because they have killed most pollinators which pollinate our crops—this has affected our food production compared to previous years."

In the apple and pear orchards of Sichuan province in Southwestern China, people have replaced insect pollinators. Each spring, lightweight men and women climb high into the tree branches, carrying tufted brushes and vials of pollen. They spend long hours moving pollen to each receptive flower, over and over, during the crucial few days during which pollination will be successful.

It was not always that way. For most of the twentieth century, wild bees and other insects pollinated the apple and pear trees, and villagers harvested the fruit. But throughout the 1970s and 1980s, Sichuan's orchards expanded. Wild bee habitat, the space insects need to eat and nest, diminished as land was converted to fruit orchards. Wild bees and other pollinators disappeared, and honeybees were used to pollinate the trees. "New, improved" methods of fruit production were promoted by the government—methods that depended heavily on pesticide use. A lot of pesticides: "Pear trees are sprayed once each week to 10 days. The kinds of pesticides/insecticides are recommended by the sale agents. But usually around 5–10 different kinds of pesticides/insecticides are used during the course of pear production." Honeybee colonies dwindled as even they were unable to survive the poisons. By the mid-1980s, pear and apple harvests had plummeted, and human pollinators were required to replace the labor of insects.

Pollinator loss is a problem in the United States too, due to the familiar one-two punch of habitat loss and pesticide poisoning. Consider

California's Central Valley: a fertile expanse of prime farmland that stretches four hundred miles from Bakersfield in the south to Red Bluff in the north. Diverse natural areas of vegetation provided habitat for native pollinators. But as demand for crops such as almonds increased, more land was transitioned into orchards. Since 1990, almond acreage has more than doubled and now occupies over one million acres of prime valley farmland. Trees are grown in bare fields stripped of insect habitat, and native pollinators have declined.

Today, almond farmers replace the formerly free pollination services of wild bees by renting honeybee colonies each spring—at an increasingly steep price. Consider: two honeybee colonies are needed to pollinate an acre of almond trees during the six-week bloom season. In 2022, the fee to rent one colony of honeybees was just under $200.

But honeybees are facing their own challenges. About 40 percent of colonies are lost each year in the United States. The almond industry cannot survive without pollination services, and there are too many trees to hand-pollinate.

Although work is underway to develop high-bearing self-fruitful almonds that do not require insect pollinators, so far nut yields from the new trees have been somewhat disappointing. But there's been about two decades of work spent to develop and refine the performance of robotic drone pollinators. Many see it as an obvious market opportunity as the demand for food plant pollination is high and growing rapidly. But consider the eventual cost of these patented devices. Will they be less expensive for a farmer than honeybees? Less expensive than the free services wild bees provide?

Southern magnolia trees opened waxy, white, nine-inch-wide blooms every few days during the first week of July. On my way to the barn one afternoon, I paused at a tree to inhale a magnolia flower's crisp, lemony perfume. Then, I looked for small visitors. During normal years, the wide-open magnolia blooms were a reliable source of delight. Then, tiny tumbling flower beetles and flower flies covered with large yellow grains of pollen would stagger around in the depths of deeply cupped petals, tuck up their legs, and roll among shed stamens like sugared-up preschoolers in a ball pit. Dignified bees would wobble slowly under their loads of pollen, grasping the edges of the bloom as they walked to avoid a slide down the smooth white petal into the pollen pit with the little ones.

But I saw only bare white, beautifully scented flowers. The only movement was prompted by my fingertip: I stirred tiny stamens where they lay in the base of the bloom like fallen cream-and-red-colored candlepins.

An email arrived from the analytic laboratory with the water sample report attached. As I waited for the file to open, I felt some trepidation and thought, *If the analyses showed no evidence of contamination, where do I go from here?*

The results confirmed some of my suspicions, but raised more questions: there were herbicides other than glyphosate in the water. I knew little about those. Could they have been included in the type of Roundup Robert had used?

I returned to the computer each evening, perched on my chair at the head of the dining room table while the television droned and burbled from the next room. The sound was punctuated by Howard's hopeful-sounding laughter, as if to advertise the irresistible programming that would surely lure me away from my work and over to the couch close to him.

But I had to make sense of the lab's test results. Over the next few weeks, I carefully considered how to frame the information that I'd promised to share with neighbors. Robert, Mike, and Bill had all helped me. Robert had walked me through his field preparation with Roundup and how he planted corn seed. He gave me the seed tag that was eventually translated into the list of chemicals that washed into the swale. Mike had listened and asked good questions as I was struggling with the situation over the previous months. He gave me access to his property to investigate the life there. Bill had told me about the flooded tractor.

I wanted to be complete but not overwhelming. That was a trick. Because *I* was overwhelmed by the implications of what I'd learned. The wetland down below was not the only victim of Roundup and the corn seed chemicals. I found more and more reports about how these common seed-coating pesticides were contributing to a rapid loss of birds and to an "insect apocalypse."

I was given a front-row seat to witness the destruction—from a cornfield! It was still hard for me to believe.

Finally, I prepared a packet of materials that included the water sample analysis report and my attempts to put the results into context. Then, I drafted summary letters to Mike, Bill, and Robert. I gave my drafts to Howard—I needed some feedback about my tone and my message.

Eager for an escape from troubles at the farm, early on a Saturday in mid-July, I drove to the mountains high above the Blue Ridge Parkway. I traveled northwest through the Piedmont's agricultural heartland and marveled at the diversity of farms and farmers. Farming's hard work, and many small farmers seek to find a niche that will give them financial freedom. During the nearly four-hour drive, I passed bison ranches, ostrich farms, dairies, crop fields, cattle ranches, tree farms, horse stables, goat operations, pastured hogs, and poultry houses.

But those farms were far away from salaried jobs. Some operations obviously struggled. Evidence of distress caught my eye: ponds and creeks filled with algae blooms; bare, rutted slopes; soil washed onto the road; and overgrazed fields dotted with cattle clustered around rotting bales of hay. Some farmers live so close to the bone that they're not able to divert yearly gains (if any) to maintaining their land. Money is used up buying the necessities of life and, in many cases, servicing debt to keep the farm itself. And in 2017, the financial outlook was not favorable: farm debt was higher and income lower than in 2012, just five years earlier.

As I approached the mountains, the lanes narrowed and I slowed down. I entered a series of switchback roads and was lifted out of the Piedmont toward forest-cloaked mountains that seemed to touch the sky. At the top, the road straightened and widened. I looked for the first entrance onto the Blue Ridge Parkway. Needing to consult my map, I followed the parkway north until I found a parking space in a picnic area with a view—an overlook. Stepping out of the car, I turned east to a spectacular panorama, a checkered landscape of farms and villages almost two thousand feet below. From that distance, I could not see the eroded fields or the runty, rough-coated calves. Buildings rested in a mosaic of velvety green and brown patches that stretched far to the horizon. From that height, all the farms looked prosperous and thriving.

My afternoon was spent hiking on the side of a mountain in a grassy meadow filled with wildflowers: milkweed, mountain mint, and yellow thistle. Grass-seed awns caught at my jeans, then released with a sigh as I wandered through hip-high vegetation. The smell of sun-warmed herbs infused the air. An almost imperceptible breeze made flowers nod.

Butterflies covered the pink milkweed and purple thistle flowers in full bloom, and I stopped to watch them. My eyes closed and body stilled. Strong rays warmed my back and my neck. Birdsong and the hum of working bees filled my ears. I imagined the planet spinning steadily upon its axis, with all life moving over, under, and through the earth, each creature doing its own special work, every organism contributing to the bright, shining mosaic of a living planet. Each creature fulfilling its life's purpose with grace—in perfect balance.

When I opened my eyes, I saw the bees move around me, disregarding but yielding if I moved toward them. My presence among them was meaningless. They were engaged in an ancient dance—a dance refined over at least 100 million years of coevolution with flowering plants. The dance involves details more intricate than the rites of ancient Eleusis—more precise than rituals among standing stones. The calculus is complex. On a fine day with calm air after a certain number of hours of chill over the past winter, when the sun is at the right angle, the day length is correct, and the soil has warmed to the proper temperature— the dance of the bumblebee queens begins.

During a few weeks in spring, the fate of a future colony fully depends upon the efforts and success of a single bumblebee queen. She emerges from hibernation ready to start a new family. She finds

Great spangled fritillary butterfly
nectaring on thistle.

flower nectar and pollen to gather strength. She selects an attractive underground burrow and collects materials for a nest; she stores food to sustain herself there with her new brood. The queen does all the work until her first daughters emerge from their cradles. Then her daughters become the food foragers and the babysitters. As the colony grows, in time, the queen's only job is to lay eggs.

Bumblebee sister foragers work tirelessly for their colonies. They work collecting plant materials: pollen, nectar, saps, and resins. They work to make sure that their mother is fed and their sisters have the resources they need to care for the family. They work to keep their colony strong. The following summer, their sisters and nieces will work just as hard to sustain life in those bountiful meadows.

The plants the bees visit are active partners, and they receive ministrations gratefully (if plants can be so). About 85 percent of flowering plants on earth require animal pollinators such as bees to reproduce. If one considers our global dependence upon these plants for food, fiber, beauty, construction materials, pharmaceuticals, and wildlife habitat, the relationship between bee and flower is sacred indeed.

That short vacation reacquainted me with some of the multitude from which I gain strength. It gave me hope. For weeks afterward, back home at the farm, I used the memory of the warm, scented breeze and the bees' deep hum to remind myself of what "normal" can be. I was determined to experience "normal" at the farm once again.

I just wasn't sure how I'd get there.

───────────

"I'm meeting with Mike and Bill today," I told Howard on a Saturday morning in late July. I sipped coffee and leaned against his office door frame as he worked. "I want to strike the right tone when I share the results. Do you have any advice on how to present this stuff? How hands-on should I be? Should I walk them through each page, or have a general conversation and just hand over the documents?"

Howard didn't look up from the screen. "Mmm, not sure. I'd play it by ear."

Easy for him to say. It's not that I am *totally* unperceptive. My timing is rock-solid for the moment the horse has settled, and I can throw my leg over his back, or for that teachable moment during dog training. I'm patient when, belly on the ground, I watch my wind tape and distant tree leaves for the momentary lull that will let me achieve a precise hundred-yard shot. I'm aware—I can row in a double shell without ending up in the water. I watch wildlife and know how close I can edge before the animal bolts, when to reach out, and where to hold. But body language, subtle cues on human faces, inflections in people's voices? Not so much.

After I finished farm chores, I donned clean clothes and washed my face. Not sure how long I'd be or where we'd talk, I layered sunscreen on my face and arms. I grabbed the folders of documents and my sun hat on my way out the door and headed for the Toyota. The car was hot and I resented the short drive to Mike's place, but the alternative was a long walk in the heat. I opened the windows. The drive down the dirt road was slow, yet a dust plume arched high into the air behind my wheels. By the time I reached the main road, sweat trickled down my lower back.

Sun glare made me squint as I turned onto the road to Mike's place; I steered carefully through the curves. As I turned onto Mike's drive, more dust billowed behind me. Near the end, I spotted Mike and Bill in their work clothes. They stood in the shade near the entrance to the garden. As I pulled up and stopped, I ducked my head under the visor to turn the car off and had a clear view: they'd blocked the gate with the big John Deere tractor. Both men were leaning, backs against the steel. They faced me with arms tightly crossed.

8

HARVEST

I CLIMBED OUT OF THE DRIVER'S SEAT and greeted Mike and Bill with a smile. My stomach fluttered as I walked toward the men standing tall in the shade of a big tree by the garden gate. It was clear that they had come prepared for some sort of confrontation.

"Hey, folks, thanks for coming out today. Mike, how's Anne doing these days?"

Mike muttered that she was well. I smiled at him again.

I worked to ease the tension in the air with a pleasant face, open arms. My friendly, easygoing neighbors held their bodies tightly, faces blank and still. They waited.

I turned to Bill. "And how's your mama?"

"She's fine," Bill said. Mike's arms unlocked. Bill met my eye. I took this as a cue to start the meeting and handed over my folders of carefully assembled documents. A breeze ruffled edges of the papers. I wondered if the loose pages would be helpful or would end up scattered, blown against the garden fence.

"Folks, before we start, I want to say . . . " I ventured a step closer. The men didn't move. "This has been quite the learning experience for me. I've been reading, searching, and trying to make sense of all that's been going on in the meadows and above. A lot of this information is new to me, and I don't have all the answers. In fact, many things I partially figured out ended up raising more questions. You let me know if what I say doesn't make sense with what you know too. Y'all have been farming much longer and know this land better than I do." I tilted my head so that my hat brim shaded my eyes. I faced into the sun and needed to see clearly.

I looked Mike in the eye. "But at this point, now, after all these months of studying, the chemical names make sense, they mean something to me and I can mostly pronounce them. You have to promise to stop me as we talk, make me slow down, back up, whatever you need. Y'all have helped me in this whole process and I just want to share what I've figured out so far."

I added, "Because this affects all of us."

Opening the folder, I started at the first page. I pointed at an aerial map of the neighborhood along the river to trace the history that everybody knows, the history I'd been hearing ever since we arrived. History I'd learned from Bill and from another farming neighbor, Morris.

Starting from a familiar place framed the issue and gave me time to settle. "When we first moved here, Morris showed me the bottoms. He showed how years of plowing had made a berm at the bottom of the hill. How the fields had stayed so fertile all these years from the floods. He showed me this swale in the Halting Creek fields. He showed me how water flows from your fields through mine and the whole length of the Eden floodplain, then out into the river." My finger pointed to the end of the system where field water drops into the river.

"He told me that after a flood, the swale channels water off the fields and can keep crops from drowning," I said. "But this year, I learned that when it rains or floods, the ditch delivers whatever's applied to your creek-side fields straight into our wetland swale."

The men shifted their attention from the map to my face.

"I'll tell you, there were some challenges living downstream from Robert's operation even before this year," I said. "The first spring Robert cultivated those fields, he apparently decided to add nitrogen before planting by spreading liquid manure. It smelled to high heaven even from the house." I wrinkled my nose with the memory of the overwhelming, acrid stench. "Heavy rain that evening was enough to raise the river to flood level. The flood got rid of the manure all right—it ended up in Tompkin Lake downstream."

I knew something about liquid animal waste because North Carolina is infamous for hog waste pollution. In the 1990s, there were many fish kills on the Neuse River traced back to waste ponds that overflowed their banks. Manure flowed into nearby creeks, then the river. Since the days of headlines and widespread public outcry over dead fish, awareness among hog farmers has increased. Now, most seek to avoid killing fish by managing the amount of waste on their farms. Liquid waste is a valuable source of nutrients, but the large hog farms to the east make too much of it for their own fields to absorb.

"There's a reason they give the stuff away for free right before a big rain," I said.

With the aerial map balanced on my forearm, I pointed out the drifts of wheat straw that had buried our fences in the fall of 2015. At the time, I saw the straw as a heavy load of mulch—material that needed to be moved off fences and pastures but not something that had the potential for damage.

"You folks probably use straw," I said, looking up from the map. I do too. I use it to cover bare ground after I seed new grass. Straw that I get from the feed store doesn't last more than a season or two when I spread it on the ground. But this straw, sitting in water, has shown me something different, and it surprised me.

"Wetland experts came out in June to see the situation in the meadows," I continued. "They showed me that where the straw lay in the water, the frogs were gone and the river oats growing near the water looked burned. That's why I sent a sample of straw with the water samples, because I wondered, what's in there that's so toxic? As you can see in the report, the straw, after sitting outside since 2015, still has high levels of the Roundup chemical, glyphosate. That 'AMPA' stuff is what forms when glyphosate breaks down. That's why it's in the straw."

They both looked at me as I spoke.

"I was skeptical about it. *Two years.* So before I got these results, I tried an experiment at my place with buckets of water, algae, and tadpoles. I could not keep algae alive for more than a couple days in the bucket containing the old wheat straw. I had to keep replacing algae so the tadpoles could feed. Even so, after ten days, I'd lost half the tadpoles in the bucket with wheat straw, but no problems with the other buckets.

"So I guess the wetland folks were on to something. I sure couldn't see it until they pointed out how the straw burned the plants," I said. I closed the folder and held it at my hip.

"Did you folks know about Roundup lasting in straw?"

Mike and Bill looked at each other, then me.

Bill spoke first, "I can't say I ever noticed. I've never heard of anything like that."

"No, it's supposed to go away after a few days," Mike added.

"Yes, exactly! That's what I understood. Like I said, I'd never had problems with wheat straw on land. I had no idea that it could last so long in water," I said. "This was a big surprise for me."

"After the wetland folks left, I searched to try to make sense of it all," I said. "I read reports that described glyphosate staying in sprayed plants until they fully decay—even roots in the ground can hold it. This one piece of information, that straw was still releasing glyphosate while it sat in water, was my key to understanding why frogs are returning above in your fields, and far downstream near the Eden, but not where straw covers the swale at my place in between."

Mike and Bill looked at each other. Mike stared across the field as Bill refocused on the paper before him.

"I learned that Roundup is really toxic to frogs and tadpoles—their skin's wide open to whatever's around," I said. "It turns out the Roundup itself is even more toxic than glyphosate, as it has chemicals that let it stick on the leaf and go into the plants. Those sticking chemicals are pretty toxic on their own. That's why they say on the label to wear protective clothes and to take them off if they get wet with Roundup."

Mike was nodding as I spoke. "We knew a farmer not too far from here who spilled Roundup while filling a spray tank," he said. "He doused himself and his workers. The workers changed out of their wet clothes, but the farmer didn't. He died not too long after that. That stuff was probably what killed him."

"Wow." I didn't know how to respond. But I thought about how recently I'd seen so many news reports about Roundup: reasonable-sounding experts cautioned that Roundup might harm people's health, but confident voices countered that the product was harmless. I'd never heard that, unless you drank the stuff on purpose, it could kill someone so quickly.

"Well," I continued, "there *is* a lot of talk right now that Roundup can harm us. A big health agency that evaluates chemical safety has declared it a probable human carcinogen, or cancer-causing chemical. There's a lot of controversy about it now because so many people use it."

Mike's jaw tightened as his gaze returned to a distant spot across the field.

"I've been getting quite an education," I said. "It seems that most everything I thought I knew about Roundup is not quite right. One thing that scared me, let me share with you as you may be interested too. But I don't know what to do about it. . . . Roundup dissolves in water, and then moves with the water. So even some time after a field is sprayed, if there's a heavy rain, the Roundup can flow off the field downstream—but also *through* the soil to groundwater. People have found Roundup in their well water. I tried to get my water tested by the county—they said they could do it and collected a sample. But they didn't give me any results. I got my money back, but no answers."

"I didn't know it could get in well water," Mike said. He looked at me closely.

"Neither did I before all this." I thought for a moment. "The part that's confusing to me is how to deal with it. The supervisor at the county lab told me that it takes time to seep down through the soil into the water. How much time, no one can say. So if I'd gotten those test results, and they were negative, he said that's not the end of it. The test could be positive in a few weeks or in months or not at all."

I stopped talking and thought about our well. I was still unsure how to manage our water sampling. The test was expensive, and we didn't have unlimited resources.

"So how do you manage that?" I said. My face flushed. "It costs a lot of money for that test. What do you do? Test every week, every month? Who can afford that?"

I took a deep breath and regrouped. I was not there to complain about our county lab. "But Roundup didn't kill the insects down below and up on our farm," I said. "When I first told Robert about the water looking sick, he told me that the only chemicals he used were fertilizer and Roundup. Maybe he didn't know that the most toxic chemicals he applied were already on his corn seed. Toxic corn seed! I had no idea."

Both Bill and Mike stared at me. I had their full attention.

"Now those corn seed chemicals are a mix of pesticides: fungicides and an insecticide. Maybe they didn't kill the frogs, but they're *really* good at killing insects. Almost all the insects. I found out those corn seed chemicals dissolve in water. Well, those chemicals can seep down into our groundwater too." Then I asked, "Bill, remember you told me about Robert's tractor and the flood?"

"Sure," he said. "He didn't park it high enough, and it was caught in the water."

"Well, that turned out to be a big problem," I said. "The seed hopper was partially full, and it was caught in the flood too. So as the floodwaters went down, the chemicals from the seed continued to flow with the last of the floodwater out of your fields, and they ended up in the swale. But it did more damage than just the swale. The floodplain meadows had no insects in them, even the worms were gone from the soil. Then the insects in our uplands started dying."

I pulled my phone from my purse, started the video of the convulsing damselfly I'd shown Emily. I handed the phone to Bill; he squinted at it in the dappled sunlight.

Mike was looking elsewhere. Was he listening? I wasn't sure, but I ploughed ahead.

"The bees and moths disappeared, then the birds and bats did too. I think that there wasn't much for them to eat anymore. The chemical that I blame for this is largely the insecticide clothianidin that was on the corn seed." I pointed to the lab report. "It's an extremely potent chemical that kills insects in very small amounts. This spring, a week after the flood, the water I collected showed slightly over one hundred parts per trillion of clothianidin. I know, parts per trillion—that's a really small amount. One way to think about it is less than two minutes within a total of thirty-two thousand years."

At this point both Bill and Mike put their polite faces on. I struggled with how to communicate the extreme toxicity and persistence of the corn seed coating. "Look at this chart I made . . . " I pointed to a page halfway through the packet. It displayed a spreadsheet I'd prepared that showed the build-up of clothianidin applications year after year until the concentration leveled out at about 350 parts per trillion by the sixth year.

"Unfortunately for me, this chemical has a long half-life—that's the time it takes for the concentration to drop by half—of up to *four* years," I said. "But like the Roundup chemical, the soil matters for how long the chemical lasts. I didn't know how long it would take to break down in the meadows, so, for this chart, I used a number from the middle of the range of breakdown times: seven hundred days. In the wetland, it can take a shorter time or a longer time. I just don't know."

Bill peered at the chart under my fingertip. Mike looked at his fingernails. I knew this was a lot. But so much was at stake.

"The point is, the concentration in the water increases every time the corn seed–coating chemical is used," I said. "*For years*, it will build up higher than the amount that killed the insects this spring. It will continue to kill wildlife on our land. And at higher concentrations, it will kill more wildlife. I think that's why the insect specialist told me that the bees may never come back. I hope she was wrong . . . "

It was uncomfortable and strange to *tell* my neighbors all of this stuff. But I'd promised to follow up. I had to communicate successfully because I needed my bees back, but also, I'd realized this wasn't just about my wetland. This problem was bigger—much bigger.

The long-term health of our ecosystem was at risk, but so were farmers' livelihoods. I learned that after planting, the potent neonic insecticides in coated seeds can flow off water-saturated crop fields. Not just here, but all over the country. All over the world, wherever the neonic-coated seeds were planted. Because the neonics in seed coating are known to leach out away from the seeds into farmland, year after year, where the insecticides can accumulate and each year become more poisonous to life in the soil and in the water. Because I learned from Dr. Morrissey's work that neonics are found in surface water all over the world at levels similar to the concentrations I'd found in our wetland. Over the last twenty years, agriculture had fundamentally changed. All while we weren't looking.

I also knew that it was urgent; once bird or insect populations have crashed, there's no guarantee that they'll recover.

That afternoon by the gate, in the face of my neighbors' silence, I wasn't sure if I had made my point. I started again. "The thing that frightens me about the seed is that I learned from scientific reports that it releases the pesticides out into the soil and water even if there *is* no flood. Even when the seed is planted correctly, rain will wash the pesticides away from the seed and into water running off the field," I said, recalling a recent study from Purdue University scientists. "So planting more toxic coated seed in the Halting Creek fields will continue to poison the animals in our wetland."

They were both looking at me.

I tried again: "Mike, you gave me permission to check water on other parts of your land, so I walked along the small creek that drains your upland cornfields." I held my folder at my hip and looked Mike in the eye. "It's a pretty creek. I'd never seen it before. I searched multiple pools between little waterfalls. I could see where crawfish used to live back in the day. I looked in the deep pools. I looked in areas of shallow water near the banks. I didn't see any insects, Mike. The water looked clear and pretty, not like the swale at all. But I saw nothing living in it."

I turned to Bill. "So, I asked our neighbors if I could visit their pond far uphill from Robert's fields. It looked totally normal there. There were lots of frogs and dragonflies. Water striders skittered around. It was good to see them—but it was *very* different than here."

Finally, Mike spoke. "This does not make sense to me," he said in a tight, clipped voice. "I don't understand how corn seed could be so poisonous. I spent time here on this land as a kid. When we came here it was full of crops, and the creeks were full of life."

"It was a big surprise to me too, Mike." I kept his eye. "I played on a friend's farm when I was young. They grew corn for the animals, but their water was full of life too. This group of chemicals, neonics like clothianidin, are pretty new. They started using them in the 1990s and coating crop seeds with them in the early 2000s. Now, most every cornfield is full of neonic-coated seed. Some people say that it's a main reason why we're losing our bees. These chemicals are nervous system poisons, and they're really powerful."

I thought about how Mike and Bill may notice insects. "Remember taking car rides at night years ago? The grill and lights would be covered with dead insects afterward? When's the last time that happened to you?"

"It's been a while," Bill said.

"Yeah, for me too," I said. "People who study this say that these neonic insecticides are a major reason we've lost so many insects and birds over the last thirty years. That seed coating is a major culprit."

They were silent. Mike looked at his shoes.

"Well, I hope that water clears up soon," Mike said. "It's a shame about the wildlife."

Bill said, "Yeah, no one wants to hurt the animals."

"Thanks for meeting with me and for being so helpful with all my questions over the past few months," I said. "I'm not sure I could have figured it out without your help."

"Well, that was a strange thi—" Bill began.

"Look! A hummingbird." My gaze snapped to a ruby-throated hummingbird as it flew close over my head. I pointed to the bird's tail feathers as it flew off to the west. I hadn't seen one for months, and it made me so happy. But I dropped my hand. I realized that I'd interrupted. And I feared that it made me look loopy at the end of a serious discussion.

As I drove home, I thought that it had gone as well as I could have expected. It was uncomfortable for everyone, but I left with hope and the understanding that the creek-side fields would not be planted back in 2018 with toxic coated seed. I smiled with the hope that I would soon have bees back in my garden and frogs back in the wetland.

Mike called me soon after the meeting. "I'm not sure which crops to turn to now that the row crops are so contaminated," he said. "Is there seed that can be planted that's not covered with the poisons?"

"Well, I know they sell uncoated seed because people use it to grow organic crops. I think it's available locally, but I've never tried to get some," I said. I added that I ordered uncoated vegetable seeds from seed companies in Maine and Virginia. "I'm not sure if they have crop seed."

"Maybe we can grow hay. I don't know . . . " Mike said. "That creek makes hay difficult. Bill and I agree on that. When it floods, the hay gets knocked down and then it's ruined."

"I buy unsprayed hay for my horses because I use their manure for compost in my garden," I said. "I know there's a market for it. People pay extra for hay without the chemical spray."

"I don't know. I'd have to buy equipment to make hay," Mike said. "I like cattle. My grandfather used to run cattle," he said. "But I just don't have the time he did."

"Mike, thanks for thinking about it. I don't have an answer for you. I know people grow crops without using those chemicals, but I don't know how to do it. Teachers at the community college do though. They teach those methods. Maybe somebody there can help. Do you want me to check?"

"Sure. See what they say," Mike said.

I was silent for a minute.

"Hey, I have an idea. What about tree crops or wildlife habitat?" I asked. "There are government programs that'll pay you to plant your fields with trees or wildflowers to protect the water quality," I said. I'd heard about those programs at a meeting and thought that it was a solution for both of us. The Halting Creek fields flood so much that they're a risky place to plant crops.

"No trees. I worked way too hard to remove trees that had grown up on that land," Mike said.

"Yeah, I remember you doing that. OK, well let me know if I can help gathering information. I'm happy to dig. I have a strong interest in the outcome. You know that I'd like to see something down there that doesn't poison the wetland."

I knew that as much as my neighbors and I were different, we all wanted the same thing. Clean, healthy land that would benefit us and the next generations too.

"Mike, I appreciate you thinking about this. It was a shock to me too, to find out about all this."

After speaking to Mike and Bill, I texted Robert with the news that I had results to share, that I wanted to meet. He didn't reply. But I'd promised to share the results, and Robert had helped me with the investigation.

I'd known the Felds for a long time. Over twenty years before their cornfield upended my life, I'd witnessed early progress at the fledgling Feld Farms. When Melissa was about four years old, she and I visited Robert's property as we waited for Howard to finish business nearby. The Feld family had recently received a delivery of about six Black Angus heifers for their new beef cattle operation. They held the animals in a temporary pen of metal fence panels near the driveway where we walked.

Melissa made a beeline for the babies, all of which were about the same height as she. As she reached her hand through the fence, a curious heifer stepped forward and stretched her raspy black tongue out to lick sticky fingers. Melissa squealed with delight. But the heifer remained calm and moved closer, pressed her broad, wet nose through an open square of wire. As I kept a watchful eye on the young ones, I spoke with Robert's father about his plans for their new cattle business.

So in the summer of 2017, when Robert stopped responding to my messages, I still needed to fulfill my promise to share results. I decided to mail a letter and a packet of information to Robert and his father. Robert's packet was slightly different than the one I'd given Mike and Bill; both included a copy of the water test results and an explanation of what they meant. But for the Felds, I included more information about the farm chemicals they used.

When I prepared Robert's packet, I tried to summarize health information about Roundup. I turned to scientific reports and to trusted news sources such as Reuters, but I was so confused by what I read. I was buffeted by a maelstrom of opposing voices vying for dominance. Strong, confident voices reaffirmed the message: Roundup is safe. Yet the declaration of Roundup having a probable association with cancer from such an authoritative body as the International Agency for Research on Cancer (IARC) could not easily be dismissed.

American households and landscapers commonly use Roundup. Many soybean and corn farmers rely upon it to clear fields of new growth each spring in preparation for planting. So the possibility of getting cancer from using Roundup drew a lot of concerned attention.

Was Roundup harmless? Were the allegations that the IARC had been corrupted true? Or was it indeed a probable carcinogen? It wasn't clear to me. Scientists reported study results that showed toxic effects. Other reports countered that the product was safe and that the scientists were incompetent, or worse, falsifying their reports.

Christopher Wild, director for the IARC, was quoted in *Le Monde* in June 2017 (translated by machine and author): "We have been attacked in the past, we have already suffered smear campaigns, but this time we are the target of an orchestrated campaign of unprecedented scale and duration."

When I prepared the summary, I had to include information about the herbicide, because I knew the Felds used it to prepare every field they planted. I wrote, "There is currently concern that Roundup may be associated with kidney damage and with blood cancers such as non-Hodgkin's lymphoma. This is very controversial and there are lawsuits: from Monsanto to states and organizations claiming harm, and from people to Monsanto who have blood cancer and who have worked with Roundup. It is hard to know the 'truth' through all the shouting right now, but I believe current evidence suggests that it is prudent to use personal protection while using the stuff until the science is settled."

The Felds used coated seeds too. My searches at the time had turned up little information about the risks to human health from the pesticides used in seed coating. I included, "The human health effects of the insecticide and the fungicides on this seed coating are less studied (mostly unknown) . . . In general, studies of farmers exposed to pesticide mixtures over years of farming are reported at higher risk for some nervous system diseases and some cancers."

As I wrote the letter, I believed that farmers' exposure were much higher than we'd experienced. I saw the effects on our farm from chemicals after they were diluted in water. Robert and his family were exposed to undiluted chemicals; they filled hoppers with dusty seed and filled spray tanks with Roundup. I didn't know what kind of protective equipment they used—gloves, goggles, respirator . . . I wasn't sure. So I included a general caution: "Farmers are exposed to pesticides from seed coating while filling the hopper and during planting, and spraying. The seed coating spreads through the air during seed drilling. Everything I have read recommends farmers using these [pesticides] wear coveralls, gloves, and a chemical protective respirator while handling these materials and while using the tractor to drill or spray."

Yet I knew that farmers were not the only ones exposed. People use pesticides in their home and garden. Pesticides move through air and water from crop fields to neighboring homes. Pesticides are in our food and beverages—our drinking water. Residues of neonic insecticides can be found in fruits, vegetables, tea, and honey. Glyphosate is found in soy, grains, beans, and honey. Both groups of pesticides are commonly detected in food and in our bodies.

Eventually I learned that people and animals *have* been poisoned from neonics. Neonics are neurotoxins, nervous system poisons, and in high doses can kill rapidly. But people are not as vulnerable to low concentrations of neonics as insects are. We don't know what the health risks may be from exposure to small amounts of these chemicals over a lifetime. Consider—we eat mixtures of foods with mixtures of pesticides. And we start early; neonics have been reported in samples of baby food.

Although there are few studies of neonic exposures and harmful effects among children, the small amount of information we have indicates that early exposure to insecticides *can* change how children's brains develop. Because neonics are the most commonly used insecticides in the world today, there's an urgent need for a better understanding of how they may affect human health.

I found comfort in information about how people can reduce their total exposure to pesticides by reducing the amount of foods they eat known to have high pesticide residues. Or by eating organically grown foods.

After the information was delivered to Robert, the weight of obligation was lifted from my shoulders. Bill, Robert, and Mike had all helped me with essential information. And I kept my end of the deal: I'd prepared information and tried to organize it so that it was clear and to the point. Handouts were there for everyone's reference. I'd offered to answer questions and, if needed, to chase down new information.

I hoped that by showing them the evidence for contamination of our water in the lab report, my descriptions of the harm from the pesticides to our land and our animals, that my neighbors would understand more about potential risks to themselves as well.

One evening early in the second week of September, I pulled on my bee jacket and headed for the floodplain. I expected the swale would be full as we'd received two inches of rain in just one hour the previous Friday. Water flowed over the surface of the ground and filled the normally dry gullies that crisscross the wooded slope, temporarily turning them into miniature world-class whitewater runs complete with foot-high waterfalls dropping into turbulent trap holes. That Tuesday, I stepped over the wet gullies as I made my way downhill, taking care not to slide on slick clay or on wet tree branches lying hidden beneath leaf litter.

Evidence of the heavy rain persisted throughout the land. Hollows in the base of tree boles were full of water, and I peered inside to see who may be enjoying the most private of baths. Mosquito larvae rose and fell in their tiny pools, taking advantage of the protection from hungry predators that the trees offered. In places, the forest floor was scoured bare of leaves and small branches as the force of flowing water had swept the ground clean of detritus. The odor of leaf mold and wet earth hung in the cool, moist air.

River musk crept up the hill to greet me. As I neared the floodplain, I strained to see green grass through the trees, but it eluded me. Once I emerged from the forest, I could see why: fog ascended out of the river and crept across the meadow like a rising tide. It submerged grasses and flowering plants beneath a soft, quiet gray blanket. Clumps of milkweed and yellow crownbeard were indistinguishable from the scattered groups of deer frozen by my sudden presence. I was only able to discern plant from animal if, while I watched, a doe happened to twitch an ear.

Despite the cover of fog, the faint sound of my slow, uncertain steps disturbed a belted kingfisher, and its cry echoed through the bottomland as it flew upriver. The fog erased landmarks and blocked my vision. I stared at the ground as I walked, looked for edges of the swale to appear. But my next step was into shallow water. Water had filled the swale and extended far beyond it, making the banks soggy and soft. I crossed with the help of rush tufts and fallen branches. I clung to trees for support. Glad for my knee-high boots, I found myself splashing through shallow pools in areas that had been solid land the week before. I peered through a droplet-beaded bee hood at the swale water.

The water's color approached normal. No scum, but no life other than mosquitoes. I followed the water upstream toward the cornfield to scout for other animals. I found none.

During late September, the sun shone brightly one weekend afternoon; the soil had dried a bit and the humidity had finally dropped. I walked to the barn and let the horses out to play, and then gathered my tools. I carried buckets, pruners, and a ladder to the orchard—the trees were overdue for harvest. Dwarf apple trees grew low in an espalier, and I harvested ripe apples as I stood on the ground—I filled one bucket to the brim. I climbed the aluminum tripod ladder and reached to grasp the highest apples and pears in the taller trees. Boughs bent low with their burden of ripe fruit. I seized pruners from the scabbard on my belt and trimmed groaning branches as some had splintered with the weight of large pears. Fruit was abundant, borne of blossoms that had opened in mid-April and were tended by the pollinators that thrived before the flood. Fallen fruit littered the grass at my feet and fed wildlife of all sizes. A half-eaten russet apple sat in a crotch of the mulberry tree, saved for later by a squirrel.

As I picked, I found myself thinking back to April 2017, when the orchard was in full bloom. During those sunny days, I'd spent hours outside with my camera capturing the incredible diversity of pollinating insects that, unbeknownst to me, were soon to disappear.

Given the timing, I reflected on the irony of the corn seed contamination in the wetland. That April, I was taking photographs of pollinators so that I could learn more about them. I'd recently started my first clinical veterinary practice, a part-time venture devoted to honeybees.

The United States is one of the last countries in the developed world to include veterinarians in honeybee medicine. Our veterinary class had no training about insects like social bees with complex communication and behavior. We learned about insect pests that afflicted our patients: fleas among cats and dogs, face flies among cattle, and Cuterebra flies among rabbits. I knew that my new business would be a challenge; beekeepers were not used to working with veterinarians. Beekeepers worked with apiary inspectors, state-employed honeybee specialists. The apiary inspectors had decades of honeybee experience and a depth of bee knowledge. Most veterinarians, including me, had a lot to learn.

With fond memories of moonlit moths on the peach tree, my curiosity about native pollinators prompted me to learn about other pollinating insects. Now I know that there are more species of bees on Earth than birds: over twenty thousand different kinds. I knew that insects supported my ability to grow food, but as individuals, they were largely unknown to me when I'd captured their images in April. The still photos preserved images of the reflected light from a multitude of bees, flies, and butterflies that I hoped I might someday see again at the farm.

That evening, I showed some of the photos to Howard. "Look at this teddy bear of a fly, all covered with golden hair. It's called a bee fly. When I took these pictures, I remember that it was really difficult to get a good shot. He moved constantly, kind of like a hummingbird." I found another photo. "This glossy blue-black bee is a blue orchard bee. These are the bees I support with the nesting straws. They haven't nested this year, I'm afraid that they were killed off by the poisoned water too."

Howard put his hand on my shoulder. "They'll come back."

I turned and hugged him. "I hope so. I miss the animals. The only bright spot this year has been the turtles, but they—I . . . I don't even know *what* to think of them. They're just acting *weird*," I said. "I'm worried about next year's garden without pollinators. I can compensate a bit by planting more tomatoes and peppers than normal, but we may not get any squash or cucumbers. I hope we can grow enough. I resent having to buy somebody else's peppers."

Looking at those sunny April photographs of pollinating insects, all shapes, colors, and sizes, gave me hope for the future.

As autumn settled in, I looked forward to the year ahead in the garden and was happy to put 2017 behind me. I looked over my garden notes to decide which vegetables I'd plant again. Some are never in question. A select few have stood the test of many years and risen to the status of vegetables I always grow from my saved seeds: sweet basil, Thai basil,

A bumble bee queen (above) and a honeybee worker (below) pollinating apple blossoms, early April 2017.

Clemson Spineless okra, Red Russian kale, Suyo Long cucumbers, and Rattlesnake pole beans. At the end of the season, each is left to produce seeds that are planted the next spring.

The big question each year involves the varieties of peppers, tomatoes, and greens. Which have withstood the heat, the wet, the drought, and the insects? A neverending combination of stressors makes my judgment inexact. How much did they bear? Was the flavor worth overlooking other faults? None are perfect; many have received second chances; and each year I'm surprised by their resilience. The purpose of those plants is to reproduce. To live.

My notes from the midsummer harvest indicated low yields of okra, peppers, and beans. The early rain hurt the larger, Big Beef tomatoes, rotting them before they could ripen. Estiva tomatoes performed poorly with good quality but scant fruit. The Ashe County sweet peppers bore more than typical for pimentos—I made a note to plant those again.

The cucumbers had been a total disaster, with few, misshapen fruits. For the upcoming planting season, I would have to use my seed saved from the 2016 crop or would need to order new cucumber seed. The tomato yields overall were down a bit, and I planned to compensate with a few more plants in 2018. Finally, I added more okra, peppers, and bean plants to the garden plan to compensate for an anticipated lack of pollinators.

Come October, the new seed catalogs would start piling up. I looked forward to selecting and trying new tomato and pepper varieties.

––––––––

The late September afternoon sun bathed the hill to the east in ruddy light. Against the dark green curtain of forest, black gum trees announced the next season with scattered leaves as red as Christmas lights. Smaller sassafras trees echoed with a few spots of bright-penny orange against velvet green. The horses were quiet and still in their dry lot at the top of the hill. The light that illuminated them was returned to me as the unusual sight of pink horses at rest.

A persimmon tree shades the path back from the barn. As I passed, I saw a glimpse of bright orange in the grass. I stooped to pick up a fruit, fallen clean from its calyx still attached to a twig far above my head. My hand closed around the perfectly ripe persimmon, its fine texture soft as babies' skin. I inhaled the faint, spicy scent that always reminds me of distant brown sugar.

By ruffling the grass aside, I found more. Skins were intact on four of five tomato-sized fruits. So far, they were untouched by the hungry. Persimmon season is always a race to gather ripe fruit before wildlife take them. So far, I was winning, but I knew that my advantage wouldn't last.

I placed three delicate fruits in a line along my forearm, propped against my ribcage, the last held loosely in my left hand. Carefully cradling them, I walked to the house to give Bill a call.

I set the fruit on the counter and picked up the telephone. "The persimmons are coming in, Bill! Do you want some?" I took a breath. "They're the big-fruited northern kind. Some have seeds you can plant if you want."

"Well, I think we could use some, thanks. How are you-all doing?"

"I'm feeling better, thanks. I'm looking forward to next year. I hope that insect specialist will be wrong about the animals not coming back. . . . How are things with Robert? Have y'all settled on plans for the bottom fields?"

"Yeah, I think that Robert has settled on planting corn down there again."

I sat down to steady myself. "Coated corn seed?"

"I guess so, he didn't say."

I knew that uncoated seed could be hard to find. I knew that a floodplain is a risky place to plant corn without fungicide protection.

My deep breaths weren't working. My voice came out tight and high, "Bill, if toxic coated corn seed is planted again in those fields, it will add more neonics to the soil and to water in our wetland. That stuff is serious poison. It'll eliminate any chance of us getting the insects back. I may as well give up on gardening here—I have no pollinators anymore."

"Well, that's what he told me he wants to plant," Bill said. "And, after all, he's leasing those fields to grow crops."

I don't remember much else. The prospect of more death at the farm erased the end of that call. I must have mumbled something in closure.

How could I have been so mistaken about how the Halting Creek fields would be used? Did I make up the nodding and acquiescence? Did I confuse politeness with agreement? Maybe. It's an easy thing to do here. When there's disagreement among people who are not family, silence is used to avoid confrontation.

I'd obviously misunderstood. I came away from the meeting with the understanding that the fields wouldn't be planted again with seeds coated with poison.

Later that week, I called Mike.

"Hey, how are you-all doing?" he started.

"Not so good. I was talking to Bill earlier. He said that Robert's planning to plant corn again in the bottom fields. I'm calling to talk to you about it."

"Now, I haven't talked to Robert, but if Bill has, then—"

I cut him off mid-sentence, my cheeks hot. "Mike, I feel like y'all are pushing us into a corner here. How are we able to enjoy our home when we can't do the things we love to do? Y'all are taking that away from us. All of it."

I paced back and forth, dining room to kitchen, gripping the phone as if to squeeze it dry. "This past summer's been hell, but I was finally able to get some answers about the cause of all the animals dying. I shared all of that with y'all. Now I hear that it doesn't matter, any of it? That it's OK to just go ahead and keep poisoning the water, killing the animals? I'd thought it was all an accident—that no one knew that the seed could cause so much harm," I said. "But now you know and still want to plant it?"

Mike was silent in response to my anger. He'd certainly never seen it before. Women here rarely show anger outside of family. And in our neighborhood of mixed cultures and world views, we're all generally on best behavior with those outside our intimate social circles.

Finally, he spoke. "I'll talk to Bill and let you know if anything changes."

9

BAD BLOOD

I HUNG UP THE PHONE, but I radiated anger. "Did they not believe me? Did they think I made it all up?" I could barely control my voice.

I turned to face Howard as he walked into the kitchen. His face formed a question. He'd heard me from the next room. I sank into a dining room chair, deflated.

"This isn't working. I don't know what to do," I said.

Howard didn't respond. His eyes searched my face.

Maybe it was because I'm a woman, about Bill's age, probably older than Mike. And I'm not part of their world—a neighbor of many years but still an outsider. We don't share a house of worship, a lifetime of proximity, or family, a combination of which often means you never lose outsider status in this small community.

Maybe I talked too much during the meeting at the garden gate. Maybe if I'd been more relaxed, I would have been comfortable letting silence rise among us. Maybe if I'd left more space for neighbors to voice their thoughts, they'd share my concerns.

Whatever the reasons, it was clear that I'd underestimated what it would take to change minds. I was up against a lot: conventional wisdom, a tradition of community self-sufficiency, and maybe most of all, the male-dominated domain of crop farming. What did I have to stand upon, to offer them in exchange for their giving up an existing source of income? My college-educated manner, my story, and a piece of paper listing incomprehensible chemical names from an out-of-state laboratory.

"I don't know, honey. I can try talking to them if you think it would help," Howard said.

"Yes, please. Whatever I've been doing has obviously had no effect." I laid my head on the table and closed my eyes. I realized that I had to step back if I wanted to achieve my goal of protecting the animals and our way of life. I thought Howard might indeed be successful where I had failed.

I'm a Southerner. The little joke is: born, not bred. My parents stole me away soon after my birth and eventually we landed in a cold, dark place full of busy, busy people—in southern New England.

The joke continues like this: I returned to my home as soon as I was old enough to escape. Because something about the South crept into my dreams and pulled at me. Maybe it was the red earth that had smeared my baby lips before my mother could snatch me away—it settled deep into my bones. Maybe it was the humidity that made my downy baby hair a halo of glory. Humidity felt like a warm embrace. Maybe it was a deep resonance with some kind of cultural memory of deprivation, of hard work and austerity, that drew me back. Southerners are strong. We know how to survive.

When I returned to the South in my early twenties, I had to relearn the culture. "Nice" is a way of life and is sometimes just skin deep. I learned everyday courtesy coupled with skepticism of outsiders. People pay attention to deeds and actions here because most everyone can talk a darn good game. I've done my best to keep that in mind; I try to conduct my life to *show* what kind of person I am.

I learned what to plant by looking at the older homes here. Everyone with a yard to their name in the early to mid-twentieth century planted sand pears, apples, and a few pecan trees. Black walnuts if there was space. Most everyone here knows how fickle factory jobs, food prices, and tax bills can be. Trees are dependable sources of food. Trees are long-lived. Trees are true.

Soon after we arrived on the farm, we met a local farmer, Harold. We hired him to build wire fences for our horses. He set heavy corner posts and pulled string to guide his lines of truncated black locust. He planted deep in the red clay, and as the fence row grew, it undulated over the rolling terrain. He worked the fence line. With electric drill in hand, he screwed insulators into the dense wood of each post. He unrolled heavy aluminum wire to create three rows of sturdy containment; he twisted metal with stout pliers to suspend corner insulators and stowed sharp ends for safety. He showed me how.

As he worked, Harold told me stories of his life growing up in our community. His family lived on a big farm nearby.

"Of course our place was in the middle of nowhere then," he said. "Town came to us."

Today, Harold's farm is an island within a sea of site-built homes on large lots. But years ago, his family ran a dairy, and the rhythm of life was defined by undulating lines of compliant cows waiting their turn to be milked each morning and evening. A huge kitchen garden fed Harold's family each year. They always planted more than they needed and gave vegetables to their neighbors. I'm sure some of their milk enjoyed the same fate.

Harold showed me where the community cannery used to be. In the days before air conditioning and cheap store-bought canned food, people used the facility to preserve an avalanche of mid-summer produce. Most of the jars were earmarked for kitchen pantries. The cannery's gone now, but when I pass the site, I imagine a cinderblock building, painted crisp white inside and out, set under trees for cool shade in summertime.

In early August, I see doors propped wide open. Industrial fans set high in doorways roar and strain to evacuate some of the oppressive heat. Indoors, it's semi-lit and the air is filled with vapor from the boiling water baths. A low murmur of companionable voices is punctuated by brisk commands delivered to girls in training. Through the mist, groups of flushed women appear; they cluster, then disperse as they move from sinks to cutting boards to water baths. As they fill jars with tomatoes, green beans, and pickled okra, all are crowned by halos of glory.

Living here has shown me how country people pull together. Like a team hitched four across. Because we are. I am convinced now that it's because of the deep memory our soil keeps in its red heart.

Ancient forests gave Southern people most of what they needed: chestnuts, elk, pigeons, and berries. Move forward thousands of years to European colonists settling a wilderness and treating the land the only way they knew how. Vast forests were cleared to make ship masts, fine houses, and farms. Once forests were converted to cropland, the soil burst with fertility and a promise of plenty for generations to come.

That promise was broken in so many ways.

The Piedmont soil was old when Europeans arrived from across the water. But they didn't know. When they cleared the ancient forests, at first the land was fertile. They thought it would always be so. Their European farming experience did not serve them well in this new place.

They didn't know that the forests had *created* that fertility and that the hot southern sun burned up the organic matter in the soil much faster than the weak northern sun they'd left behind. Years after clearing the forest, colonist farmers continued to flog the land to produce as it had when the stumps were still sound.

Their ignorance allowed bare hillsides to flow into the creeks, turning them from sparkling fish nurseries into turbid streams barely getting by. In Central Virginia and the Carolinas, within forty years of our independence from England, farmers had largely used up the soil.

When the crops failed, there was always new land to take, to break open, until those farms also failed. By the dawn of the nineteenth century, abandoned farms dotted the Piedmont landscape. People moved—over the hill, to the next county—until there wasn't an unbroken place to go. The remaining people had to do for themselves and for each other. To survive.

When the West opened up, many did move on. People packed up and traveled over the mountains and started farming the prairies. Although their farming methods didn't change, the depth of that virgin topsoil gave them more time to take without giving back.

The dust bowl of the 1930s was an emphatic rebuke to that hubris. Hugh Hammond Bennett, the soil scientist who is widely credited with saving our agricultural land during those dark days, famously said, "Take care of the land, and the land will take care of you." I'm afraid that many of us have forgotten that lesson. Because today, in addition to eroding our soil to death, we also poison the life out of it.

But it's our life too. Farming was one of our first home industries. Farming is a way to feed a family without an outside income. And farming can create wealth: farming is productive. Learning to farm develops marketable skills.

A hundred years ago, farmers could grow food without going deep into debt to buy seeds, fertilizer, and pesticides—the inputs that today's farmers struggle to afford. Back then, seed from the last crop could be saved for the next. Fertilizer was created from the animal manures and plant waste that were plentiful on a farm that included livestock, as did most farms back then. Good farmers knew their soil and how to keep it. They knew that fertile soil is a gift received from ancestors and passed on to children.

Maria Helena Semedo of the international Food and Agriculture Organization of the United Nations made headlines on World Soil Day in 2014. She proclaimed that we have only sixty more years left of farming (as we currently practice it) if we continue to consume topsoil at current rates. Sixty years if we do not change the way we grow food.

Each year, around the world, productive, fertile topsoil is becoming scarcer—more precious. Even in Midwestern farm country, the formerly rich prairie soils of the United States are disappearing. Recently, Evan Thaler studied soil condition in the corn belt; he estimates that about one-third of the area's topsoil has been completely lost. He reports that about one-third of total acres cultivated in the corn belt today are planted in nutrient- and organic-matter-poor subsoil—not in topsoil.

Yet soil quality is directly tied to how much food the land can produce. In Thayer's study, he estimated that every year, almost $3 billion of value has been lost through eroded soils in the corn belt alone. Indeed, a country's topsoil quality and agricultural productivity are a basic measure of national wealth. And a country's ability to produce food for its people is still a cornerstone of national economic security.

Mike told me his grandfather carefully maintained terraces he built on the gentle slopes. Crop rows cut across the hills rather than down to prevent erosion; the soil was managed with the goal of improving it each year.

A good farmer like Mike's grandfather managed the land as if his family's life depended upon it, because it did. It still does, but we've lost our intimate awareness of that fact.

———————

Months after I'd hung up the phone in disbelief, Bill and Mike accepted Howard's invitation to come to the farm to talk. Despite the chill of an early December evening, they didn't come to the house. They stopped to talk in the tractor shed, a space filled with familiar trappings of farm life. Scrap wood, rolls of wire, and fence insulators. White grease in tubes. Shovels, a post-hole digger, and heavy, gray suede work gloves. It smells like work in there. The men talked for almost an hour while I was up at the house making dinner.

Howard told me later that he too had met set jaws, arms tightly crossed over chests, but that they were able to find common ground over a simple shared opinion: how special our community is and how we all love living here.

"I told them that we valued the place. We have freedom outdoors, freedom to keep animals, to grow food," Howard told me. "I told them that we recognize how special it is to still have plentiful wildlife and a clean environment."

Howard told me that he ended the conversation with a simple question, "How would you feel if this situation was turned around—if it was drainage from our land that was harming yours?"

———————

Our family looked forward to a quiet Christmas together. Melissa visited from her home near the sea, accompanied by her sweet dog. She bore gifts for all.

Holidays are my favorite times to cook. We made our favorite Christmas foods: turkey roasted in a full bacon wrap; bread stuffing with sage, pecans, mushrooms, onions, and celery; greens; cranberry sauce; and green beans stored from the summer's garden. A spicy-sweet butternut squash pie is mandatory at our house after Christmas dinner, but I followed it within days with a traditional persimmon pudding using the fruit I'd frozen back in September.

We listened to Nat King Cole and other vintage carols and watched classic movies together. But while the rest of the family was intensely engaged with Trivial Pursuit, I sat alone with the laptop and searched real estate listings. I looked for houses where we could comfortably live, with enough space for a large garden. A place to go where we would live among birds and insects again. A place where I could grow fruit.

Howard stepped away from the game to fill his water glass in the kitchen, and I called him over. "Howie, look at this place I found. It's on over an acre. It has enough open area for a decent orchard and garden and is up high on a rise, so there'll be no runoff flowing onto the place."

Howard walked up behind me but didn't look at the screen. He put his hand on my shoulder. "Betsy, this thing isn't over. Let's see it through. It's too soon to make a move you might regret." Then he added, "An acre's a bit tight for the horses, isn't it? Where would they live?"

"Horses can be boarded," I said. "Please keep an open mind, that's all I'm asking."

My finger circled the black rectangular lot line on the screen. "I know this place is smaller than we're used to, but we're not going to find a replacement for the farm—we'd have to move farther out away from everybody." I looked at Howard. "I don't want to do that; we need our community."

But when I attended my monthly bee club meeting in January, I realized that it wasn't that simple. The meeting started with club business, then the president introduced the guest speaker, an apprentice who had completed her first mentored year of beekeeping. Kat spoke about her challenges as a novice: from unexpectedly having to replace a queen bee killed by workers to successfully luring bees back to water at her place to keep them out of a nearby swimming pool. It was the main event of the night.

Afterward, members milled about the meeting room talking and snacking from the refreshment table. As a bee vet, I was particularly interested to hear people discuss their bee problems. Some explained that they finally had to stop keeping bees at their homes. People cited multiple reasons: allergic or complaining neighbors, repeated colony losses. It seemed common for people to keep hives far away from where they lived. Some maintained distant bee yards to support school clubs, some to access better forage, some to add to their hives at home, and some to escape contamination.

Dan, an experienced beekeeper, mentioned that he'd struggled with repeated problems with pesticide die-offs at his place. I asked Dan where he lived.

"Over near the school. After years of fighting it, I've finally given up on keeping hives at home. My neighbor sprays for mosquitoes, and within days, my colonies are decimated. It's taken a toll on me, financially *and* emotionally." His gaze fell to the scuffed floor. My shoulders sagged with his. "I can't keep doing this," he said.

"Oh, Dan, I'm so sorry. You've been keeping bees for a long time," I said. "I can somewhat relate. I lost my blue orchard bees from insecticides too. But my situation's not on the same level of time and money invested. I hate that they market those sprays as if they were the solution to mosquito problems."

Dan lived in a wooded, large-lot subdivision, established decades ago in an area with mature trees and flowing water; yet his situation was not uncommon. Many beekeepers I've spoken to who've lost bees to pesticides described living in grassy subdivisions or wooded neighborhoods, seemingly far from agricultural fields.

I realized that moving to another neighborhood would not necessarily be the answer to ensuring bees and other insects would be there, ready to pollinate a new garden. But if there was a way to stay on the farm and make a safe place to keep animals and grow food, I wanted to do so. I wasn't convinced agriculture itself was the problem for us.

The problem was the potent pesticides—like the neonics that dissolved in water and traveled so far from the fields where they were used.

———————————

I hadn't talked to Robert since soon after I'd sent him the packet of information about what I'd discovered in the wetland. I thought back to autumn 2017. Early that fall, I'd reached out to Robert to discuss what I hoped would be a way forward for both of us. I'd asked for a time to meet so that we could talk about hay.

One sunny afternoon, I met Robert and his father at their farm. When I arrived, they were visiting with another man, and I waited by my car until they'd finished. As the visitor rolled away down the drive, we gathered.

After greetings, I laid out my story. I told them that I paid a hefty premium at the local feed store for the unsprayed hay I needed for my horses. "Because it's not sprayed, it has weeds in it like horse nettle. But it's worth it to me because I learned from the state extension service that it makes it safe for me to use the animals' composted manure in the vegetable garden."

Both men looked down at me with crossed arms.

"I'm not the only one," I began again. "There's a demand for unsprayed hay. But the feed store gets their hay from Virginia. They told me the supply's spotty. That I should stock up when I could." I continued, "A local supply of unsprayed hay sure would be nice for me and people like me. A supply to count on through the year."

Finally, Robert spoke up. "I thought you were coming over here to buy hay. We have some to sell, but it's managed to keep weeds out. We spray the fields."

"Would you consider growing unsprayed hay?" I asked.

"No."

Robert's attention moved away until his dad spoke up. "We're having a hard time finding land nearby to farm these days. There's so much development. Landowners are less willing to let us lease their land too."

I was sorry to hear that. My discovery of the contaminated wetland was not helpful to them. But they appeared committed to continuing their kind of farming wherever they *could* lease the land. And without changes to crop production, I could only hope their next lease would not be upstream from our wetland.

I'd seen how their kind of farming had changed our farm. I could not ignore the damage, and I could not repair their losses with more of my own.

_____

After the New Year passed, tightly scheduled farm and office work routines resumed. Work chafed after the relaxation of a long holiday vacation, and I craved more sleep. Evenings came too early. I missed the sunlit freedom of outdoor activities we enjoyed during the holidays. My evening drives home were defined by darkness and tight lines of glaring headlights.

The first week in January 2018 brought unusual cold and a dusting of snow. Each evening I hurried home from work to cover tender plants. Rosemary, sweet bay, and Red Russian kale all needed protection against the deep, deep freezes in the small hours of the morning. When I returned into the house each evening after chores, I pulled my foggy glasses off my face and waved them in the warm air to clear the lenses as I inquired about any calls that I may have received. I was eager to learn of plans for the Halting Creek fields and my prospects for the 2018 growing season.

I'd tried to reach out to our neighbors multiple times that week by telephone. I left messages like:

"Hey, Mike, just checking in. Can you give me a call and an update?"

"Hi, Bill, I hope y'all are well. I'm calling to learn of your plans for the upcoming year. Please give me a call."

But my calls and messages were not returned.

Sunday evening, I left the barn with protective plant covers piled high in my arms. The sun had set and the light that remained was fading fast. I shifted my load to better see the ground before my feet, but it was the sky that drew my gaze. To the west, undulating deposits of gray-green cumulus clouds lay heavily upon the yellow-tinged horizon. That evening, the western sky bore the colors of an old bruise.

Our lives had been disrupted. Well, mostly my life. Howard was able to maintain some distance, to keep his balance during the event. So why was I unmoored? More specifically, why do I feel the loss of life so deeply?

Maybe it was because my experience with death has been difficult. I've never borne it well. My parents are both gone, but I had little control over their final days. I was a bystander and helplessly suffered their loss. But sometimes I *have* more control, such as when my animals near the end of their lives. Then, my inclination and training encourage me to end their suffering.

When we've been in the sad position of tallying the happy and sad remains of a dying dog's life, I seek to protect the animal from the burden of unmanageable pain—to prevent misery. On the other hand, Howard looks for a faint tail wag, a move toward a tidbit of food. He seeks any evidence to delay the final gift of euthanasia.

"After all," he says, "life is really all they have."

He's right of course. Life is all any of us have.

Although I've spent much time immersed in nature, I think it was my years caring for people that opened my eyes and my heart to the wonder of life. As a young woman, I spent well over a decade working as a registered nurse in large medical centers. During my nursing practice, I learned that humans are somewhat fragile creatures. People thrive upon good food and secure shelter. Upon consistency, community, and connection. Upon love. From what I've observed, I know that by ourselves, we're not very strong. It doesn't take much to break us.

Maybe it was my time sitting with elders as they lay, enduring their last hours. I witnessed their bodies slowly shedding function, losing vitality. I witnessed their last breaths. Our bodies are complex and, to our limited understanding, miraculous. But it takes only a small change to shift from making-do to disaster: a weak spot spreads along the wall of an artery; stem cells go rogue in bone marrow; blood vessels relax and open wide; an electrical signal within heart muscle terminates before its time; or exposure to a toxic chemical starts the damage that changes everything.

An enduring impression was seared upon my young mind: vitality is fleeting; life is fragile.

My privilege for many years was to attend laboring mothers and to assist with births. My face was the first those newborns saw. I watched their eyes open wide in astonishment and then painfully narrow when blinded by room light. Watching a child separate from her mother for the first time elicited wonder in me but was a shock to the baby. One way to calm a newborn enduring the trauma of separation is to swaddle him snugly in a soft, heated blanket. It's an approximation of a warm, tight hug: "I'm here, you're not alone."

Sometimes I attended women and girls who labored alone. This is an existential situation. A laboring body is a body with an agenda. I remember one day, a teenager was dropped off at the hospital by *someone*. The bell to the labor and delivery suite sounded. I grabbed a prepped clipboard and walked from the nurses' station, followed the path of fluorescent glare on the linoleum-floored hall to the entrance door to greet the new arrival. An orderly pushed a squirming young woman in a wheelchair into the suite. She handed me the intake sheet, and I slipped it behind the crisp blank page for notes on my clipboard. I led them into the exam room.

The orderly said, "This is Angela. Her water broke about an hour ago. Contractions every three minutes."

Angela looked about fourteen. She wore a man's black T-shirt—the name of a local pizza parlor captioned her chest. Loose sleeves reached her elbows, but fabric stretched tight over her abdomen. Her light-blue maternity jeans had barely kept pace with the bulge of her belly, and she sat in a pool of straw-colored liquid. Her bare feet were jammed into dingy-white plastic athletic shoes—her heels had crushed the counters down to the soles.

I walked closer. "Hi, Angela, I'm Betsy. I'll be your nurse today. Is this your first baby?"

Her hand darted out and caught mine. "Mmm-hmm. It hurts really bad." She squirmed in the chair. My hand was crushed in her grip. Shallow crescent moons from her fingernails remained, lingering pale against my pink skin long after I'd reclaimed my hand. I reached out and lightly held her wrist to count her heartbeats. I'd barely secured a blood pressure cuff around her upper arm when she leaned forward in the chair, reached back with her other hand, and pushed down on her lower spine.

"My back. It *keeps* hurting." Another groan. "So much pressure." She waved at the general area toward her seat. "Where's the bathroom? I have to dookie." She straightened and craned her neck around, looking for a side door. Or an escape.

"OK, let's get you onto this table first. We need to check. Sometimes the baby can feel like that." I unfastened the cuff from the wall cord and assisted her out of the chair, over to the stepstool, and up onto the exam table. I covered her lap with a flannel blanket, slipped off her shoes, and helped her out of her dripping pants.

I leaned out the door and grabbed the sleeve of a first-year resident walking by the room. "I need a cervical check." I walked back into the room with the resident and proceeded to update her with the little I knew as she washed her hands.

The doctor pulled a stool up to the table, and we helped Angela get into position for an exam. I then took my place by Angela's shoulder and reached out for her hand. The girl clung to me. She looked up, eyes wide, mouth drawn in a tight grimace. As we worked and explained, we discovered that Angela was unfamiliar with her uterus, her vagina, or the birth process.

Angela was young and healthy. She progressed quickly during labor and became the mother of a beautiful, vigorous boy. But during my nursing practice, I was frequently astounded by the brief time I had to orient unprepared women to their situation. Active labor can induce panic among those who feel they've lost control. Swaddling's not an option. But a hand held firmly, a touch on the shoulder, a quiet, steady presence, and encouraging words can ease a woman's feeling of exquisite vulnerability. For a woman laboring alone, sometimes my support as a steadfast ally was critical to achieving calm, to building resilience, and to increasing the odds for a successful outcome. Because during childbirth, a happy ending, although probable, is not assured.

When a woman gives birth, it's like walking on a knife edge of life and death. During labor and delivery, women's and babies' bodies are in massive transition—altered blood pressures and shifting oxygen supplies. Much depends upon the relative positions of mother and baby—the mechanics of flesh and blood. Together, hearts beat out pivotal time and harmonize into the manifestation of new life. The transition must unfold perfectly, or nearly so. And in the great majority of times, everything goes well. But sometimes it does not.

The loss of a young life is uncommon but heartbreaking for all. Because life is precious. And life is all we have.

Now I've gained a broader perspective. I've learned that it is not only the support of other people that we require. As inhabitants of a shared planet, our history and destinies are entwined with other life forms: the molecules of our bodies share elements, we share DNA, and we share the ways in which our cells work to keep us healthy and alive.

We now have tools that allow us to analyze DNA and identify microbes. These tools have shown us where our closest allies live. They live within us. The members of the multitude that colonize our bodies— the microbiome of our skin, our guts, and our dark, moist places—are our closest, most intimate partners. And we live *among* microbial helpers too. We wouldn't last long without the support of the multitude intimate with plants and the living soil—they nourish us all. They balance the earth (and our lives) on the bedrock of their complex communities.

So who are we to be careless with the lives of others? We're not strong enough, not sufficient enough, to survive on our own. I know now, with certainty, that we must collaborate with and nurture the multitude, or we will perish.

———————

One evening in early January, we were busy in the kitchen getting ready for dinner. "Howie, I haven't heard from our neighbors. Have you?"

"Nope, but I haven't reached out either. I figure that they're going to do whatever they are going to do."

"Yeah, I know it's not our business—until they pollute *our* property," I said. "You know, those lower pastures aren't even safe to graze animals anymore. Not with runoff in the swale."

Looking back, I realized that three inches of rain fell during the middle of April 2014, the second season that crops were planted in the Halting Creek fields. Water flowed off the fields upstream and filled the swale in the horse pasture. Although they always had troughs of clean water, the swale was the horses' favorite source of drinking water. At the time, I hadn't seen it coming. I hadn't thought about how agricultural chemicals were used to prepare the fields in early April for spring planting.

When the horses became ill, I couldn't have imagined that it was water that may have sickened them. In my ignorance, I failed to protect my horses from toxic chemicals that may have damaged the microbial community in their guts, the community they depended upon for digestion—for their health. But in 2014, information about how Roundup kills microbes, about how Roundup dissolves in water, was not easy to find. It was the kind of thing that you already had to know about. It's still not common knowledge.

And even today, as I search, there's scant information about how Roundup alters the microbial communities in the guts of living animals—and people. A report here and there, yet no comprehensive understanding of Roundup's effects on our health, but "research points to the herbicide's potential to disrupt healthy microbiomes, including the human microbiome." While we may be sickened after damage to our gut microbes, horses depend upon a healthy population of gut microbes to digest fiber; they depend upon that intimate community for their lives.

If only I'd known, I might have saved the horses from months of pain and disability. I might have saved them from a life of confinement and separation from one of their greatest pleasures: green grass.

I'll never know for sure if the horses were sickened by Roundup, but given the timing, the nature of their illnesses, and recent information about the effects of Roundup on gut microbes, I will always wonder.

One evening in late January 2018, I pulled my head out of the refrigerator, where I'd been digging for a bag of lettuce, stood up, and looked at

Howard. "I know that you don't want to leave. But I'm struggling to keep my balance here. What can we do? How can we move forward?"

I set the bag down on the counter across the room and turned again to face him.

"Well, what are our options?" he asked. He reached for salad plates above my head. "If they're polluting our farm, it seems like that should be a crime. Maybe we should talk to a lawyer."

"Yeah . . . I don't know if it's that simple," I said. "When I spoke to that state pesticide expert back in May, he asked me to describe what happened. I didn't know what to tell him. He told me that they don't investigate unless there's intentional misuse of a pesticide. It's obvious that the tractor caught in the flood was an accident. Not intentional. Not a crime. I'm not sure if now that everyone knows about the pollution and the harm, if it would be a crime to continue. I guess we need to figure that out."

———————

Have you ever tried to find a lawyer to provide legal assistance for a pesticide contamination problem? In my experience, it's not easy.

We were at a disadvantage as the farm was not a business; we had no way to prove financial losses. I'd not kept records of the *amount* of food we produced, so we couldn't claim a value on the loss of our crops. Our livestock didn't die. I had no reason to suspect that our health had been permanently damaged.

But I knew that if toxic coated seed was planted again in creek-side fields, the contamination in the wetland would get worse. It does not take a tractor accident for the seed-coating pesticides to escape from a cornfield. Mike's dead creek showed me that.

I was sobered by the responsibility to prevent *more* contamination of the wetland. My neighbors' actions seemed out of my control. Yet it was my duty to protect the animals on our land. And so far, I wasn't doing a very good job. But whenever I felt defeated, I revisited the vivid memory of the swale water the previous spring—still, golden brown, and dead.

I contacted friends and neighbors to learn if anyone could recommend a lawyer who specialized in environmental issues. The handful of names that were offered back to me didn't lead to any attorneys who could help. So I kept looking.

Evenings were spent online searching for environmental lawyers practicing in our area. I narrowed the list to those within a sixty-mile radius and made another spreadsheet for keeping track of their names.

Each morning, I placed calls. "Hello, I'm looking for an attorney who can help us with pesticide contamination of our land. Contaminated water is flowing into our property and killing wildlife, including the pollinators I need for my garden."

Sometimes I just left a message, but most legal offices had assistants who would dutifully take my information—event, location, timing, and my name and number. Sometimes I didn't receive a return call. Among the attorneys with whom I did speak, most were discouraging. I recall many conversations that included variations on why it wasn't possible to stop a flow of water contaminated with pesticides.

One evening that busy week, I shared what I'd learned so far with Howard. The conversation started as we sat down on the couch to eat and were preparing to stream an episode of, most likely, *Deep Space Nine*.

I captured the television's remote control before Howard could grab it. "Honey, before we start, can we talk for a minute? I want to let you know what I've been learning from the lawyers." I set the remote down between us. "First of all, I'm not hearing much interest in working with us. We didn't suffer a big loss that we can hold up as proof of harm. I guess the way it works is if we wanted to sue someone, they get a percentage."

"That figures," he snorted. "I guess we're on our own then."

"The other thing I learned that does *not* help us is that the Clean Water Act has an exemption for storm-water runoff from agricultural fields. So other lawyers tell me that we're out of luck at seeking relief altogether. It seems that in 1977 they added an exemption to the Clean Water Act—it seems they didn't want to restrict a farmer's activities by making them control their own water pollution.

"But I don't know how much of an issue it was back in the day when the law was written," I said. "Maybe they were thinking of pollution like silt from erosion or nitrogen from fertilizer. Back then, most insecticides were not so water soluble. Maybe there was less pesticide runoff then? I don't know. But I *do* know that now these water-soluble neonics are used in every conventional cornfield. *And* there's more runoff and damage because of these crazy flooding rains we're getting now. Everything about growing crops has changed, but the law has not."

Later that evening, as I was thinking about the Clean Water Act exemption for field runoff, my early experiences finally made sense. Johnson couldn't collect water samples and analyze them using state resources. He wasn't interested in the wetland because he knew that it probably suffered from pesticide contamination.

When I spoke with state and local agricultural and environmental officials, I was always missing the point that the cornfield probably *was* the problem. But nobody came out and said it. Except for Stephen. Stephen wasn't even surprised when I told him about the missing frogs. He'd told me right away the cornfield was to blame.

But government officials understood that even if farm chemicals *were* the cause, there was no reason for them to spend precious time and scarce financial resources to confirm it: there was nothing they could do about it.

Back in May, *that* was the unspoken truth I'd been missing.

I better understood another experience from earlier days at the farm. I'd tried to get the pasture meadows around the swale sprayed for toxic weeds that could harm the horses, but when I told the agricultural cooperative staffer who was scheduling the application that I wanted a chemical that wouldn't hurt the frogs, he cut the conversation short. He said that he'd have to check and get back to me about a date for the work. Springtime is the right time to spray, as the weeds are young. They have to be removed before they set seed. Springtime is also the season when the swales are full of tadpoles. When I didn't hear back from him, I tried calling again. The phone went to voice mail. The co-op stopped taking calls from our number.

They knew at the time, although I did not, that there *was* no product they could use near the swale that was safe for the frogs.

I guess that I hadn't been paying attention. I'd assumed that because pesticides are each evaluated before they're approved for use, that there was minimal harm to life other than the insects they were meant to kill. The Federal Insecticide, Fungicide, and Rodenticide Act stipulates that approved pesticides "will not generally cause unreasonable adverse effects on the environment." Of course now in retrospect, now that I've learned so much more about pesticides, pollinators, and aquatic wildlife, I realize that my understanding was painfully naive.

But I wasn't ready to give up. I intended to fight for our farm—for the wildlife I loved. For the pollinators I needed. I kept making calls to find a lawyer who could help us protect our farm.

Luckily, we found Jack.

10

WEIGHT OF EVIDENCE

"YOUR SITUATION'S SOMEWHAT UNUSUAL. PEOPLE don't typically come to me for water pollution issues." Environmental lawyer Jack Tilson leaned back in his chair and faced us across his long, burnished conference table.

I thought about how the search for tadpoles led me to the dead water. Would I have just walked by if I didn't have a reason to look in the water? If so, maybe I wouldn't be here in Jack's cavernous, cold meeting room with a sack full of documents and a pit in my stomach.

"I typically represent people who've had their land contaminated by pesticides traveling through air," he said. "Pesticides blow off fields, get sprayed where they shouldn't, or evaporate off fields in hot weather. They destroy neighbors' crops or their bees. That's much more common. It's called chemical trespass."

I understood. "Yes, I've spent the last year and a half or so learning about honeybees to prepare for my new veterinary practice. I learned that beekeepers have been filing lawsuits to stop the use of coated seeds because of the effects on their bees. There are programs in place to try to protect honeybees," I said. "At my local beekeepers' club, I heard about a program called FieldWatch where beekeepers can put their hive locations on a map so that people who spray pesticides know where the bees are so they can avoid them. When I talk to beekeepers though, some report that their bees die when neighbors spray for mosquitoes—there's no program to prevent that.

"But I cultivate native bees, not honeybees," I continued. "My place was not eligible to participate in FieldWatch. And the effects of coated seed are not covered either. Nobody sprayed our land; our bees died because of the poisoned water."

Howard and I sat across from Jack and held hands beneath the massive wooden table. We shifted and squirmed in our seats. We couldn't have imagined this day at any time throughout our years at the farm. We'd resisted consulting an attorney, because our community is precious to us. We recoiled at the thought of creating bad blood, feuds, and divisions with people among whom we live. But we felt that we were out of options. The future of our farm hung in the balance. If the wetland contamination continued, our time was up to keep livestock in the lower pastures and to grow our own food.

"So, what do you have for me?" Jack asked.

I pulled printed copies of the lab reports, the emails from the wetland group, and the aerial photographs of the land from my bag. I pushed the map of the neighborhood across the table.

"Here's the floodplain. The cornfield is uphill along Halting Creek, here." I pointed out the piles of wheat straw that covered our fences. "This wheat straw is still releasing glyphosate in the upper part of the swale, where the wetland starts." I handed him the water analysis report. "That result is in the lower box marked 'wheat straw.'"

I pointed to the bottom of the page on my copy. "But if you look at the results above," I said, "the water itself was contaminated by the seed-coating pesticides that washed out of Robert's seed hopper during the flood."

"So why are you concerned with this happening again?" Jack asked. "It seems like a one-time accident."

"Yeah, that's the thing. Now I understand that the cornfield is toxic for our land even without an accident," I said. "The pesticides in the seed coating come off the seed as dust during planting. The poisonous dust in the air can kill an insect flying through it—reports from Germany documented that happening as far back as 2008. Girolami and colleagues from the University of Padua showed that bees can 'become lethally contaminated' just by flying. That poisonous dust also settles out of the air onto plants and kills even more insects. If the wind is right, the dust might even travel to our place. Once the seed is planted, if rain or a flood saturate the soil and water runs off their fields into the swale, the water-soluble pesticides travel with it. So even during normal planting, normal rain, the wetland will get more pesticide runoff. Here, I made a chart."

I dug in my bag. "The neonic on the corn seed Robert used is clothianidin. It has a long half-life, very persistent in soil and water." I pulled out another sheet. "An EPA factsheet said, 'Clothianidin has the potential for toxic chronic exposure to honey bees, as well as other nontarget pollinators.'"

I leaned back in the big leather chair. "I don't have it with me, I'll send it to you. Jesse Radolinski at Virginia Tech just published a report about their work that showed how soil and water become contaminated from planting coated corn seed. In their experiments, concentrations of a neonic in water and soil were high enough to be lethal to insects. That's just the first year!" I leaned across the table and pointed to my graph. "You can see with each year the seed is planted, the pesticide concentration in the water increases. That's why we're here. Not just because of an accident at our place. This is happening all over."

Although our experience was unusual in that it involved a tractor accident, the result—lethal contamination of water by neonic-coated seed—was not unusual at all.

"So would our situation be a trespass too, as we have evidence of toxic chemicals in our water?" I asked. I thought about the Clean Water Act exemption for field runoff and how many lawyers had dismissed our problem. "I was out in the orchard in early April a few weeks before the flood," I said. "I have photographs, evidence of all the insects and pollinators we had just before the water was poisoned. I have pictures of the bare flowers in May and June afterward."

Jack sat reading. He examined my narrative records, my timeline of events. Finally, he looked up. "Have you tried to discuss this with the Felds and the Wilsons to come to a mutually agreeable solution?" he asked.

How sensible. I felt my clenched shoulders drop half an inch. Jack's opening move involved common sense and consideration for the parties involved. I was thankful. After all, our goal was to protect our land, not to hurt our neighbors.

"The Halting Creek fields are higher than the wetland, so we get water that flows off that land," I said. "We walked the fields back in the summer to see if drainage ditches could be dug to empty runoff straight into the creek, but the slope is formidable."

I looked at Howard. "We agreed that it would take major work to form an effective barrier," he said. "And who knows how long it would last with all the floods we get these days."

"But the landowner is not on board, either," I said. "Mike told me that redirecting runoff from the crop field into Halting Creek would harm the creek. We'd discussed alternative farming methods too," I said. "Mike told me that he'd asked Robert if he could use uncoated seed or if organic methods were an option for the Halting Creek fields." Apparently, Robert didn't have the ability (or desire) to plant uncoated seed.

Indeed, uncoated crop seed, although less expensive than patented coated seed, is not always easy to find. Over 95 percent of corn seed and 50 percent of soybean seed planted in the United States today is coated with neonics. Uncoated corn seeds are typically a special order item here, and not every farm store will buy them.

Field preparation was another complication. Robert told me that he clears the fields with Roundup before planting. "If I plow the fields instead, there'll be more soil erosion," he'd told me. It was true. Floods could strip Mike's fields of loose topsoil pretty quickly. Then the creek and our downstream swale would fill with topsoil, and Mike's fields would be badly damaged—or ruined.

But continued Roundup use was a problem for the swale water. The amphibians couldn't use the wetland anymore; it's deadly to them. I couldn't let livestock near the water as they'll drink it. The horses hadn't recovered their ability to eat grass after their suspected Roundup exposure in 2014, so I knew that effects on animals' health could be serious and long-lasting. A hay crop would keep the soil in place and protect the wetland, but Robert wasn't interested and Mike had ruled it out—he didn't own the right equipment.

"We're at an impasse," I said. "That's why we came to you."

"I understand that you don't want to hurt your neighbors," Jack said. He looked up from the pile of pages on the desk in front of him. "One way forward—I'll prepare a letter to document the harm you've experienced so far and to serve as a cease-and-desist notice for the Wilsons and Felds to stop polluting your land."

Howard and I looked at each other. "That sounds about right," said Howard.

"Yes, I agree," I said. "But I'd like to look at the final draft before you send it out." The last thing we needed was to use the wrong tone and make things even worse with our neighbors.

After some drafting and editing back and forth, Jack notified us the following week that he'd sent out the approved final versions. I waited for whatever may come.

I didn't have to wait long. Late in the week, the phone rang after dinner. I recognized Mike's number, so I answered. "Hey, Mike, how's it going?"

"Well, I wanted to let you know that I received a letter from your lawyer. I need to ask you a single question," he said. "What are you going to do if we plant that field in corn again this spring?"

I took a deep breath. "If you go ahead and plant that toxic coated seed, during the next big rain I'll be standing on our property collecting the water flowing into the wetland."

"OK, I just needed to hear that." He hung up.

I thought back to the cornfield next to Halting Creek before the flood. Robert told me that in 2017, starting on April 17, he drill-planted corn seed into the prepared fields. Each seed was placed carefully at the proper depth and distance. The goal of such precision is to make sure that each corn plant will have all the sunlight and nutrition it needs to reach its full potential, to produce as much grain as possible, the highest yield.

Modern corn is a somewhat delicate plant, and the weather in spring 2017 was not favorable for a healthy crop. The extreme rainfall that produced a flood in late April continued sporadically. Water puddled in parts of the cornfield. Corn roots suffer in wet soil: less oxygen, more harmful kinds of fungus. So those areas of standing water were bad news for Robert. Corn seeds drowned beneath puddles of water, and no plants emerged. Among the plants that survived, some were small—their growth stunted.

Robert did not report using pesticides other than Roundup in his cornfield. Maybe he didn't know that neonic pesticides coated the corn seed itself. Yet they were the most potent, most toxic pesticides he used.

I saw firsthand how using neonics every time a crop is planted, every year, has consequences. We experienced those consequences every day during the summer of 2017. At the farm, we lost almost all of our flying insects. But swarms of mosquitoes thrived. Why? Were mosquitoes

Wet cornfield, May 25, 2017.

somehow resistant to the toxic effects of neonics? Maybe. Or maybe they were tolerant: able to survive higher concentrations of insecticide than expected.

Muhammad Riaz and colleagues from the Alpine Ecology Laboratory in Grenoble, France, published a report in 2013 describing their experiments with neonics and mosquitoes. In their laboratory, mosquito larvae became tolerant to five times the lethal neonic dose within eight generations of exposure. In the Piedmont of North Carolina, where we live, eight generations of mosquitoes can breed within three to four summers.

And for five growing seasons, during 2013 to 2017, our wetland and the mosquitoes that lived in it received neonic runoff from crops planted upstream next to Halting Creek. So in the floodplain, the "good" bugs declined and the mosquitoes appear to have adapted. Our local ecosystem had been completely upended.

––––––––––––

During spring 2018, we received no calls from Bill or the Wilsons. We didn't call them. Everything felt too raw and uncertain. But I missed talking with them. I missed the opportunity to chat about our farms—the land and the wild creatures we all cared about.

I work mostly among townspeople during the day. The fact that we have a farm is a curiosity and is outside of their experience. No one was interested in hearing about how a northern mockingbird defended our mulberry tree from other birds, and the result was more fruit for us; how I'd identified a new type of invasive weed; or my need for more pollinators.

We live on a hill. Sounds echo down the valley. We can hear the tractor engines of neighbors who live a mile away. So during mornings outside, I anxiously listened for the sound of Robert's new tractor pulling the planter up and down the Halting Creek floodplain. I never heard it. But I wasn't home all day, so maybe I'd missed planting time.

On springtime walks along the wetland, I edged up to the Wilsons' fields to look for a growing crop. I saw a field dotted only with weeds.

By late May, not even grass had started to grow back among the cut corn stalks.

With cautious optimism, I planted a modified garden in 2018. I left out the fully pollinator-dependent plants—cucumbers, okra, and squash—as we still had no insects. More space was made for tomatoes, beans, and peppers. I hoped for the best but was disappointed. The fruit trees and berry bushes were barren, and the 2018 vegetable garden seemed to be overrun by voles and rabbits. I received only tomatoes, and we continued to buy most of our vegetables.

Although I'd been warned by Aimée Code that the pollinators may never return, I couldn't accept the prospect of a limited food future at the farm. A lack of insects would mean an end to my fruit growing—unless I wanted to hand-pollinate my apple and pear trees. There was no way to effectively hand-pollinate my blueberries.

For pollinators to survive at the farm, the pesticides in the wetland had to degrade. But I understood that it could take years to fade away. My fervent hope was that it *would* improve over time. That a robust community of different kinds of insects could return—a healthy insect community that would support breeding birds and would provide pollinators for my garden and orchard.

I knew that I had no control over our neighbor's land, how they used it, or what they did. I didn't have control over how fast the poison would fade from the swale. But I did have control over the plants on our property.

So in spring 2018, I proceeded with my life as if the insects were only taking a short vacation. I decided to redecorate the place in preparation for their return.

My evenings of research became a pleasure that I anticipated. Instead of searching for pesticide information and reading about death and destruction, I looked for flowers, for blooming plants and shrubs to add to my pollinator plant beds. There are times of the year when nectar and pollen are scarce. That dearth of food can mean hungry times for pollinating insects. The white clover in our lawn helped a bit during the early summer dearth, but I wanted a variety of plants—native plants that would provide food for animals all season long. Plants that supported all stages of insect life, like caterpillars to fill the mouths of baby birds.

I dug new garden beds. Sheets of plastic were spread over the back floorboards of my car so that I could purchase plants as I found them. On evenings and weekends, I unloaded dripping pots of neonic-free perennials to plant. I carried home packets of organic (uncoated) annual flower seeds. I conserved blooming plants already on the farm.

Swaths of weedy henbit occupied the early spring garden beds through May. I let creasy greens bolt into tall plumes of bright yellow flowers. In late spring, lyre-leaf sage pushed inviting floral lavender tubes from tall spikes along unmown paths. I encouraged milkweeds and planted aster and goldenrod for nectar and pollen later in the year. In summer, I let forgotten corners of the yard fill up with delicate pink-daisy blooms of fleabane.

I thought back to the last weekend in April 2017 just before the flood. I'd visited the local community college to attend a Beekeepers' Association Field Day. I'd spent some of that sunny, warm Saturday among a dozen white-suited, mesh-hooded beekeepers. We learned how to get an estimate of tiny mite parasites on honeybees, an essential skill for any beekeeper who seeks to manage healthy honeybee colonies. A detour on the way home brought me to the Chatham Mills complex north of Pittsboro.

Chatham Mills' parking lot was crowded, but I found a spot far from the building and eased my car in between painted lines on pavement. I walked toward the stores and saw how slim sections of earth separated long rows of parked cars; a wider earthen bed lay between the sidewalk and the building. Everywhere I looked, plants crowded each tiny slice of soil. And those flowering plants were in bloom. On the sidewalk, I stopped and listened. A low buzzing was clearly audible, and I followed the sound. It was the drone of bumblebees, urgently visiting each of the pale yellow and purple blossoms on spikes of wild indigo. How was that possible? So many flowers in shallow, poor soil—in so little space.

That remarkable garden is Debbie Roos's creation. Debbie is a Chatham County agricultural agent, an extension specialist in sustainable

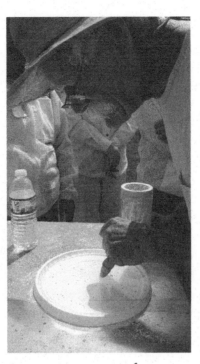

Counting Varroa mites from a
honeybee colony using the sugar
shake technique.

vegetable and fruit production for diversified small farms. Debbie understands the value of wild pollinators for a farmer's bottom line.

But nothing in nature works for free. Wild pollinators need habitat: space to nest and food to eat. Some lucky farmers do receive free
benefits from bees that live nearby. Other farmers directly support wild
pollinators with nectar plants and habitat. For most farmers without wild
pollinators, hand pollination of crops is not an option. Some invest in
honeybee colonies and manage them in wooden boxes. Some farmers
pay for colonies to visit their farms at bloom time.

People generally like butterflies, and some like bees. But many say
that they don't have enough space to support pollinators. Maybe in
response, to show how flowering plants can fit into tiny areas, Debbie started the Pollinator Paradise demonstration garden in a parking lot. She's crafted a multiseasonal display of blooms with mostly

native plants. Debbie's garden proves that it's possible for anyone with a yard or a cluster of pots to provide flowering plants to support pollinators.

Pollinators appear to be thriving at Chatham Mills. But they aren't only in the demonstration garden. The flowers in the garden add to insect habitat in the pine forest to the north and the deciduous forests to the south and east. All of those places contribute food and nesting areas to support wild pollinators. This concept—a functional landscape at a spatial scale relevant to insect needs, is emphasized by Douglas Tallamy, professor of entomology at the University of Delaware, in his book *Bringing Nature Home*.

Doug points out that it's not only the one oak tree in your small yard that insects rely upon—it's the sum total of native trees and flowering plants throughout a neighborhood. It's your oak tree plus your neighbor's willow next to a bed of bee balm. Two doors down, add the crabapple tree that rises out of a pile of leaves left over the winter as a butterfly nursery. All of these plants combine with other yards and gardens, and in total, they create a home for native insects. Anyone planting a native tree or a pot of flowers free of insecticide contamination contributes a square to the living quilt of pollinator habitat.

More of us need to plant or preserve resources for wildlife, because the integrity of the natural world is fraying. It's being picked apart field by field, river by river, forest by forest. Animals and plants fade away—gone from our world at increasing speed. Our time of living during the sixth great extinction is defined by taking more of the planet's bounty for ourselves and leaving less for the creatures who live with us and around us.

What we don't understand, what we don't *feel* deep in our bones, is that their well-being is essential to our own. Nature supports our lives in fundamental ways. Natural processes clean our air and our water, and provide us food through healthy soil and insect pollinators.

I feel it now. I've seen it. I know how it is to live in a hollowed-out world where nothing really *works* anymore. Where the water and sky are empty and quiet.

As we've developed our modern society in the name of profit and effi-
ciency, we've lost sight of the rhythms and requirements of nature. But
even if we want to support the natural world, it's not easy to make the right
choices when we don't know the full story of what's harmful and what isn't.
We're at a disadvantage when important information is hidden from us.

During my investigation and my search to learn more about pesticides, I learned of the work of Carey Gillam, an investigative journalist
who's worked for years reporting on agriculture. Gillam has a broad
perspective: she's covered the topic from the viewpoint of farmers *and*
multinational agrochemical/seed executives. A line in her 2017 book
Whitewash resonated: "For the average individual, reading through scientific research can be daunting, not to mention confusing."

Daunting for the average individual. *And* for me. And I'm an environmental scientist. I'm accustomed to reading scientific reports about
exposures to hazards in the environment, including pesticides. But during 2017, I was baffled by seemingly conflicting reports about pesticides
and health. Some of the most confusing information surrounded the
pesticide Roundup.

It was only later that I finally understood why I'd been so confused.
During late summer 2018, the first trial about cancer and Roundup
was decided in favor of Dwayne Johnson, a groundskeeper who had
developed non-Hodgkin's lymphoma after years of Roundup exposure.
Johnson's legal firm, Baum Hedlund Law, publicized internal Monsanto
emails that they'd gathered during preparation for the trial. The law
firm opened up the company's internal discussions, their schemes and
strategies, to public view.

During 2019 and 2020, as I dug deeper into Gillam's reporting and
the Monsanto emails, I learned that much of what I'd thought were honest scientific reports were actually written by the company's executives
or by academics hired by the company to write material that *appeared*
to be independent science. I'd been reading scientific reports published
in reputable journals. But I wasn't only reading honest science—I was
also reading corporate propaganda.

It was only when I learned to investigate the author names included
in the Monsanto emails that I saw the truth. Many of those contracted or

ghostwritten pieces directly countered the findings of independent scientists who reported that Roundup was associated with harm to animals or people. And I learned that independent science and scientists whose work did not support corporate messaging were apparently perceived as a potential threat.

In April 2001, William Heydens, Monsanto's toxicology and human risk assessment lead, wrote in an email to colleagues who were discussing if they should supply herbicide samples to a scientist: "Please don't do anything until we discuss this. Data generated by academics has always been a major concern for us in the defense of our products."

In one effort to counter inconvenient scientific reports, a nonprofit called Academics Review was started as an online platform that could be used to cast doubt upon independent science. Apparently, corporate-funded professors, representing themselves as independent, led the effort. Gillam reported on the phenomenon in her June 2019 article in the *Guardian*, "How Monsanto Manipulates Journalists and Academics." Monsanto executive Eric Sachs wrote in an email to one of the "independent professors" who founded the site: "The key will be keeping Monsanto in the background so as not to harm the credibility of the information."

While all the final details of how Roundup can damage human, animal, and microbial health still need to be fully investigated, we would have had much more information today if scientists had been free to study the product—if funding agencies had supported investigation into our most commonly used pesticide. Roundup was introduced to the US market in the 1970s, but until recently, scant research was published on toxicity and potential impacts on health.

Indeed, in a 2015 consensus statement, fourteen leading environmental and health scientists wrote: "Most GBH [glyphosate-based herbicide] use has occurred in the last 10 years. . . . Since the late 1980s, only a few studies relevant to identifying and quantifying human health risks have been submitted to the U.S. EPA and incorporated in the agency's GBH human-health risk assessment."

The floodgates for scientific inquiry were opened in 2015, when the World Health Organization's International Agency for Research on Cancer declared that glyphosate was a probable carcinogen. And only during the first decade of the twenty-first century were health scientists, independent of agrochemical/seed corporations, more easily finding funding and more freely publishing their work.

Over many years, widespread promotion of agricultural products and the suppression of honest science succeeded in hiding information from consumers, but also from farmers. Potential risks to farmers are not confined to their health. Risks also include soil degradation, pollinator loss, and unsustainable debt loads.

In 2017, I knew that Robert worked very hard to support both his family and his farm. Robert's dad was aging, and every year more of the farm work fell upon Robert. I can only imagine the challenges during those years: severe weather, prescriptive seed contracts, and low crop prices. Years ago, Robert took a day job to secure a steady income. During the time we've lived on our farm, Robert worked full time for a salary and farmed in his "spare" time. At first, I thought it unusual to have a farming business *and* an outside job. Now I understand this is the norm for America's family farms—in 2017, less than 30 percent made most of their income from farming.

Small farms may struggle to survive in today's global marketplace. The "median household income from farming was $210 in 2021." To increase farm income, farmers may feel pushed to buy the latest equipment, to purchase expensive, highly engineered seed designed to be planted with a selection of specific inputs like chemicals and additives with the goal of reaching higher yields per acre. It's called the "agricultural treadmill."

People can cut corners when they're stressed. In 2013, with oil prices just shy of $100 a barrel, nitrogen fertilizer may have seemed out of reach if there was to be any profit from Robert's first year of farming in the Halting Creek fields. Nitrogen fertilizer vies with seed as the most expensive of inputs needed to plant a cornfield. So to Robert, an offer of free, liquid manure from a big animal operation up the road must have seemed like a good deal. An offer too good to pass up.

Unfortunately, a farmer's financial risk does not disappear with a successful harvest. Maybe Robert and his dad were able to sell their crop at a profit. Or maybe they weren't. They had to compete against every other corn farmer in our area to sell their grain. The higher the supply, the more corn prices are pushed down. So with no control over rising input costs and with crop prices low, Robert may have been caught in the price squeeze of high expenses and low returns.

Although most of America's corn farmers don't make much of a profit from growing corn each year, others involved in corn commerce do. The United States is the largest producer of corn in the world—we produce over 30 percent of the global supply. In 2017, the total value of the US corn crop for grain was approximately $50 billion. Commodity crops are big business.

So farmers are busy people. Stretched people. Most family farmers depend upon seed distributors, farming organizations, and agricultural advisers to steer them toward the highest yields—toward profitability. Most farms in America are family enterprises. Farming can be a way of life, not just a business, and families may live *on* their farm. They want a farming income, but they also need healthy children and animals, bountiful kitchen gardens, fruit trees. Families want clean water to drink. Farm owners may prefer to build soil or at least preserve their land for their children—not to mine it.

I know that corporate efforts to control markets and to control the perception of agricultural products may seem meaningless to most of us as we focus on our day-to-day concerns. While the general public may care about farmers, their challenges may not seem like our own. But farmers grow food. Our food. Farmers steward the land, the future of our food supply. Because we're all busy, none of us have time to perform our own risk assessments of everything that we may need to buy. Many of us trust that if a chemical or product is on the market, it's safe to use.

I learned in my own backyard that I need to be more skeptical.

———————————

After my frustrating experience trying to find consistent, honest information, I fear that the glyphosate story of protecting profits regardless of the means used, of hidden information and deliberate obfuscation, may be repeated with systemic insecticides such as neonics. Because the largest use of neonics is in the coating of corn and other crop seeds, crop seed coating is an international phenomenon and is a growing source of profit for agrochemical/seed corporations.

Yet this routine use of neonics is largely invisible to us.

Today, neonics are uncommonly studied and poorly tracked—because once applied to seeds, they're exempt from regulation in the United States. As Adam Allington reported in Bloomberg Law in 2020, "When Is a Pesticide Not a Pesticide? When It Coats a Seed"; neonics that coat seed are not *recognized* as pesticides, not counted as a pesticide use. Yet this toxic coating is used in almost every cornfield planted here.

The largest use of one of our most potent insecticides is unregulated. Even though neonics commonly contaminate soil. Even though "lab studies have reported a slew of evidence that exposure to neonics is harmful to vertebrate animals" such as birds and amphibians; mammals such as rats and deer can suffer reproductive abnormalities and shortened lifespans after exposure to neonics. Even though neonic residues have been found in our drinking water, our food—the fruits and vegetables we feed our children. And even though systemic insecticides like neonics can't be washed off—they permeate every part of a plant.

But surely, the benefits to farmers, the larger crop yield, must justify the use of neonics on every corn crop, every time?

It appears not. The claims of benefits to farmers, to their bottom line, do not hold up when independent researchers investigate. As Dr. Michelle Hladik of the US Geological Survey and her colleagues state in their 2018 report: "Evidence of clear and consistent yield benefits from the use of neonicotinoids remains elusive for most crops."

Based upon reports of studies of multiple types of crops, it appears that discontinuing routine use of neonic-coated crop seed to protect wildlife, water, and soil will not cut crop yields. And farmers who use uncoated seed will pay less for that seed and reap higher profits per acre.

The sooner we transition, the better. The insects that eat crop pests and keep them under control are killed by neonics too. Those "good" insect populations, the pest predators, are a part of a healthy, diverse cropping system. And as I've seen, once animals are gone, it takes time for them to return. *If* they return.

I pray that financial, political, and regulatory obstacles that inhibit honest, transparent science are easing. In 2020, the National Toxicology Program released a review of published studies from all over the world that had been conducted to investigate potential adverse health effects associated with neonics. The report included work that studied the effects of neonicotinoids among exposed cells, among people and animals.

But they conclude that because of differences among the neonicotinoids and individual responses to exposure, there is more work to do, still much to learn. And as more scientists can study these widely used chemicals, more independent information will become available. Because only by knowing the truth of what we face can we decide if the costs are worth bearing.

In March 2019, an early flood filled the Eden River valley. After waters receded, I hiked down with mobile phone, shovel, stakes, and a mallet to see how my new elderberries and black willows were faring after their first winter in the floodplain. No bud split yet, but the twigs were supple; they survived the winter. I straightened tree tubes and firmed wooden stakes.

Work finished, I dropped tools by the trail home and walked along the wetland with my phone. In February, before the flood, I'd photographed corn cobs and stalks in massive drifts against trees and islands of dusty brown wheat straw. They looked like refuse dumps in the water. But by March, the location of the deposits of debris had changed. Water-force had pushed dead plant remnants farther downstream. The swale was fed by a diminishing supply of crop remains from the Halting Creek fields. I found no evidence of frogs or tadpoles in the wetland despite hearing tree frog song in the forest nearby.

I wasn't upset anymore, just numb.

The flood had left its mark. At the swale, branch tips were bound together above my head, encircled by Celtic knots of dead grass and twigs. The meadows bore a new burden of river debris: tree limbs and plastic trash. Near the swale, I found an unusual artifact of potential interest to Mike. I texted him and asked him to let me know the next time he'd be out in the fields—I wanted to show him.

A few hours later, Mike replied that he could meet me in the floodplain. I was glad, because we hadn't spoken in over a year. I stepped outside the house and heard his tractor. The tractor engine roared as he drove down the hill to the creek-side fields. I tracked his progress by the sound and calculated his destination—the edge of my property. I strode across the upland meadows then picked my way downhill through the dense forest undergrowth; I avoided shearing new, tender yellow-green leaves that had erupted from terminal buds. As I emerged out of the trees into the floodplain, the ground leveled and my pace quickened. When Mike shut down his machine, I was there to join him.

"Hey, Mike, how have y'all been?" I asked as he looked down at me from the tractor. A beat too quickly, I said, "If you walk over here with me, I have something to show you. The flood gave us a gift."

Mike deliberately climbed down from his seat and stopped. He looked intently at the soft ground beneath his feet.

Then, he raised his gaze, looked me in the eye, and said, "You know, you did us a favor."

11

OUR CHOICE

A thing is right when it tends to preserve the integrity, stability, and beauty of the biotic community. It is wrong when it tends otherwise.

—Aldo Leopold, 1949

MIKE SWEPT HIS HAND IN an arc over the Halting Creek fields. He ended the gesture with forefinger outstretched, pointing at the swale on his property.

"All that mess on the land. Look at that water. It still looks like a sewer down here," he said. He turned to face me. "You talked about your lost bees and how *your* garden failed, but our garden did poorly while the crops were planted around our place too."

He spat. "That stuff was sprayed all around our house, our pond. Near our well. Now we see on the TV all the lawsuits from people with cancer who used Roundup. We were living in it."

He gestured toward a massive hackberry tree edging his field. A drift of wheat straw lay a few feet up against the trunk pushed there by flood-waters. "Look at all this stuff here. I would like to know why it's still here after so many years on the ground. What is it—four years now?"

"Yes, those chemicals really changed things down here," I said. I paused and looked down. "My understanding is that the pesticides keep microbes and insects from breaking down the straw. It's not decaying the way it would on healthy land."

I walked downstream to the water at the edge of our wetland and pointed at a pile of crop residue sitting in the water. "Look here in the swale. There's straw and corn cobs, corn stalks. That's not breaking down, either. It's all sitting here. I can't get it out, and I still don't have any tadpoles or frogs coming back here." I welcomed him farther onto our land with a wave. "But, come on over here, I wanted you to see this. This is why I asked you to meet me."

I led Mike another thirty feet downstream. "It's a wood duck nesting box carried here by the last flood," I said. "We'd talked about putting some boxes up over the creek. Can we use this?"

Mike turned the large wooden box over with his boot and examined the sides. "No, squirrels have opened up the entrance. . . . It's not cypress wood. It's better to start from scratch if you want a duck box."

Later that evening, I thought about how Mike's awareness of the contamination of our soil and water had evolved. We were both aware of the land. And now, it appeared, both aware of the importance of the multitude it supported.

———————

As the summer of 2019 dawned, I eagerly awaited the return of insect life. I hoped for some recovery—2019 was the second growing season without toxic coated seed planted in the Halting Creek fields. But the orchard remained barren. Springtime looked promising, with blooms covering the trees. But the flowers were not pollinated. The blooms faded, dried, and fell, leaving no bulge of developing fruit.

There were no bees on flowers, no moths or gnats in the air. We could leave our porch light on all night long and draw no visitors. I began to suspect that Aimée, the insect specialist who told me that the bees may never return, may have been correct.

Nesting birds and bats had not returned either. For the first time in over twenty years, I didn't have the heart to plant a vegetable garden.

But late summer brought some hope. New perennial beds of mountain mint attracted an astonishing variety of wasps. They covered the flowers while drinking nectar. I spent happy hours taking photographs of their diversity, their beauty, and their work among the blooms.

My reading and studying took me down intertwined paths of discovery. One book led to another. In summer 2019, I found Jon Stika's *A Soil Owner's Manual: How to Restore and Maintain Soil Health*. He wrote: "restoring soil health requires . . . thinking of the soil as a living biologic system." Jon advocates feeding soil life through four key principles: less soil disturbance, more plant diversity, maintaining living roots in the soil, and keeping the soil covered at all times. Jon explained basic principles of soil health in a way that was easy for me to put into practice on my land.

Encouraged by Mike's awareness of his land, I bought a second copy of *A Soil Owner's Manual* and brought it to his house. No one was home, so I left the package in a plastic shopping bag hooked over the door knob. Inside the book's cover, I wrote, "Fertile land is a gift,

Double-banded scoliid wasps visited our mountain mint in August 2019.

cared for by our ancestors and now passed into our hands. I hope this book helps you as much as it has helped me."

Months later, I saw Mike. "Thank you for that book," he said. "You know my youngest son, Jason? We've been studying it together. He's interested in the farm and wants to help me improve the soil. Robert cultivated rows straight downhill and damaged our terraces. We're working to rebuild those terraces—to prevent erosion." He didn't say it, but I understood that Mike was looking forward to leaving the family land in better condition than when he had received it. For his children and for others who would follow.

Robert's oldest son, Tyler, followed Robert into farming. He's old enough now to be a full-time helper. Back in early 2016, when the Felds visited our meadows to view the wheat straw that had buried our pasture fences, Tyler had finished some years of study at the agricultural college. I asked him then how the market was for wheat in our area.

"It's real good," he had said as we walked down the meadow. "We keep it in our rotation." Indeed, during the time the Felds had grown crops uphill of our floodplain meadow, I'd seen soybean, corn, *and* wheat filling the fields along Halting Creek.

"I've seen local wheat used in bread here. Is that the main use?" I asked.

"Actually, it's more common as hog feed," he said.

"Hogs? I always think of corn when I think of hog feed," I said.

"Depending on the time of year and feed prices, wheat is a great hog feed," he said. "It supplies phosphorus and an amino acid that's low in corn."

That day, Tyler shared his knowledge with pride, and today his contributions to the family business allow more acres to be planted—more to be harvested.

In 2021, I see new fields sown with corn in my neighborhood. As farmers age out or die, their former cattle and crop fields can become a burden to the family rather than a source of income. The loss of our greatest generation provides a temporary opportunity for the Felds to lease more land to farm. But their time may be limited: in the rush for flat, buildable land, local farms are also chopped into tiny lots for new houses.

Homes for the stream of newcomers from cities across the nation who want to start a new life in North Carolina, a new life out in the country.

Our community watches with concern.

We live far from grocery stores. The pandemic made food shortages and supply interruptions common. But in 2020 we pulled together. Local farmers who'd sold their meat, milk, and vegetables to nearby restaurants and schools lost those markets during pandemic lockdowns.

Many in the community stepped up. We bought shares in farms in return for a box of meat or vegetables once a week, farmers' choice. Local dairies opened their doors a few times a week for customers to pick up fresh bottled milk. Produce, eggs, meat, flour, and dairy products became dependable and accessible—and we all knew where our food was grown. It was grown by our neighbors.

So we watch with worry as one year later, during 2021, crop farms fall one by one as fields turn into subdivisions. We watch as our precious agricultural soil is transformed into sprawling suburban development.

A southern magnolia tree stands like a sentinel on the farm. Dark-green glossy leaf-tops shine in afternoon sun; underneath each one, glimpses of mocha-brown fuzz tease. One midsummer day, the tree displayed a single large white flower. Within two days, I saw that same bloom shriveled and brown.

When a magnolia flower opens, I revel in its bright citrus perfume. I admire fleshy petals glistening like new snowfall in the sun. But I can't expect that beauty to last.

Is that what I should expect with the pollinators? Were the years of being able to feed ourselves with the garden and orchard a temporary condition? Are we moving out of the era where insects will be there for us and for the farmers around us?

Will our natural support system continue to be there to help us produce food?

The pear orchards in Sichuan province have moved out of that era. People do the insects' work. California's almond orchards are on the

Southern magnolia flower cupping shed stamens.

same path. Almond farms have largely lost wild bees, and now honey-bees struggle against contamination to do the work. Is this our inevitable future? For people or machines to do the work of insect pollinators?

I turned my back to the brown flower, walked across the yard in a dark funk, and stomped up the back stairs to the house.

I opened the door to find Howard sitting on a sturdy wooden bench in the utility room reading a letter. Taz was semi-collapsed between his legs; she sat upon one hip and rested her head against his knee. With one hand Howard absentmindedly rubbed her ear.

"Howie, I can't do it. I can't accept this as our fate."

"Accept what?" he looked up, hand stilled. The dog gently licked Howard's hand—she didn't look up. She didn't want him to stop.

"The poisoning of our land, of our children. The loss of pollinators, the loss of insects." I turned away and threw my arm out toward the garden. "The collapse of our planetary support system."

Howard set the letter down, both hands stilled. I'd broken the mood. Taz gave me a side glance as she slipped out of the room, head hung low.

Howard looked me in the eye. He seemed mildly irritated. "Betsy," he said, "you're not the only one who cares about this stuff."

Now I think that he meant that many people care and are working toward a secure food future. Because I'm learning how many of us there are.

Jonathan Lundgren is a leading voice for promoting bountiful food, healthy land, and prosperous farmers. Jonathan is an entomologist, an insect specialist. He's lived most of his life on the Northern Great Plains, surrounded by rich farmland built by primordial prairie. He studies animals, and over the last twenty years he's learned how animals, including insects, help us grow food.

"What led me down this road [was] that there was a group of farmers that I'd met that were growing conventional crops and were doing so in the absence of any pest management," he said. "It flew in the face of everything that I understood. What they taught me was that in fact pests are not inevitable. That you can design a system where pests are not a problem to begin with. What it requires is thinking about food production completely differently than we have in the past."

Jonathan runs Blue Dasher Farm as a working demonstration farm, a hub for research and education. He uses the farm to show that producing food and conserving agricultural land are not mutually exclusive. Blue Dasher Farm is not just an abstract ideal. It's a working farm. Upon the farm, Jonathan supports his family and his employees by growing crops, raising livestock, and keeping honeybees.

Jonathan cares about animals and the land—and also about farmers. Today's farmers are under great stress to make a profit and to provide for their families. But Jonathan told me that farmers have options. He demonstrates that there are other ways to farm: ways to escape the cycle of debt and soil destruction, ways to preserve water quality and to strengthen farming communities. Jonathan practices regenerative agriculture. Farmers taught him.

Now, Jonathan teaches others. He shows that by supporting healthy soil, farmers make a profit by growing healthy crops—plants more resistant to drought, pests, and disease. Crops that support *our* health. And awareness is growing; even formerly skeptical farmers such as Adam Chappell have discovered that they can escape the costly treadmill of buying new, proprietary seed and more pesticides each year. Adam farms thousands of acres in Arkansas; he grows cotton, corn, soybeans, and other crops. As he told the *Farm Journal* in 2020, his transition to a focus on soil health during annual crop production has had significant benefits for his bottom line.

"Regenerative agriculture is the future of food production," Jonathan said. "Farmers win, conservationists win, consumers win, and rural communities win." He went on to explain: Farmers win with more profit and healthier soil. Conservationists win because regenerative agriculture sustains plant, animal, and microbial biodiversity. Consumers win because the food contains fewer pesticide residues. *And* the food is more nutritious.

Regeneratively grown food is nutrient rich because "nutrient density is an essential component of regenerative agriculture," he said. And rural residents win. Local food production contributes to local jobs, local prosperity. Family farms become productive enterprises that are more economically resilient, and money circulates locally. "All of that feeds into the life of rural communities that [have] been declining for generations," he said.

"It's easy to focus on problems," he said. "But there's a lot of hope right now. And prior to understanding regenerative agriculture, I didn't have a whole lot of hope. That's a really important message that people need to take home. There is something we can do. If we invest in this, we are going to come out just fine."

––––––––––

When Melissa was a baby, I remember the overwhelming feeling of gratitude that I carried with me. She was a healthy baby—and strong. Although we had little money, we had enough to buy her a variety of good, clean food. I fed her spoonful after spoonful until the moment when she refused to take another bite. As young parents, the ability to nourish our child and watch her grow was a source of great comfort.

Healthy food for a growing child is a precious thing, a great privilege. But given Maria Helena Semedo's warning about the impending loss of our fertile soils, I fear for the future of today's babies. What about good, nourishing food for our grandchildren and the children who come later?

Today, as Maria says, much of our farmland is being abused and exploited. Farmers are working so close to the bone that they feel financial pressure to farm as many acres as possible, to cut windbreaks and to farm marginal lands such as floodplains. I fear that farmers are being exploited too.

That's why the growing global recognition of the benefits of alternative crop production such as organic farming, agroecology, and regenerative agriculture is so important—methods like these work *with* the natural world, not against it. The difference is the focus on soil health, on farming practices that actively build fertile soil and produce food with less chemical contamination. Living soil not only provides us nutritious, clean food. Healthy soil also holds carbon out of the air. Regenerative crop production is an essential part of addressing climate change. Healthy soil is a planetary life preserver.

Successful farmers are pragmatists: if one wishes to make a living as a farmer, one must secure a profit. Farmers are increasingly seeing the benefit for their bottom line and reaching for the opportunities afforded by alternative markets, by non-GMO and organic certification, with both hands.

Regenerative farmers learn to notice small changes on their land. This power of observation, watching the fields and responding to weather and other sporadic events, requires mental flexibility and curiosity. Happily for everyone who eats, the challenges and rewards of growing food aligned with nature's rhythms afford an opportunity to earn a sustaining income on less acreage. This appears to be attractive to young farmers.

We need young farmers; the average age of farmers in the United States is about fifty-seven years. Many farmers are aging out of the business. But according to the US Department of Agriculture's 2019 Organic Survey, a higher percentage of organic farmers are young farmers (less than thirty-five years old), and a higher percentage of new farmers report farming organically. *And* a larger percentage of organic farmers report farming as their primary occupation. This is good news indeed for our future food security: A future where small farms can sustain themselves financially while preserving resources needed to farm. A future where farming is a viable career choice for many and where farms are healthy places to raise children.

Late September 2020 brought an extended period of warm, dry weather. Outside the barn door, a flower bed exploded with color in afternoon sun. Towering above all, yellow blooms of swamp sunflower held court, visited by pollinators of many kinds: precious bumblebees, slim honeybees, and darting hoverflies. Many buzzing, all moving. The air was disrupted by pollinators arriving, leaving, inspecting the flowers from millimeters away—hovering. Some looked, some smelled, some tested each flower's scent, each electrical charge, to know if it was time to land, advantageous to gather.

I reluctantly left the animals and their buzzing industry and walked into the barn to finish chores. But afterward, as the sun was descending in the west, I leaned on the broom and turned to face the light. The seven-foot-tall sunflowers with their four-inch discs of yellow leaned precariously westward as if pulled toward the last rays of the day. In the still, warm air, I heard only contented horses chewing. A shaft of late-day sun splintered off by the door, fell upon the aisle floor. Bees, flies, and gnats fluttered, glided, and crossed within the golden spotlight. Those featured pollinators reminded me of the abundance we enjoyed before the cornfield contaminated our farm.

The growing season of 2020 was a turning point. We received fruits that require pollination for the first time since 2017. Apples, pears, even cucumber plants were fertilized by insects, mostly eastern carpenter bees. In 2021, bumblebees and some ground-nesting bees returned. In 2022, we received a good blueberry crop. A few songbirds returned to the farm. It's not the way it was. But it may never be. For me, it's a recent improvement. And I rejoice.

On a cool October morning, I lift a water bucket in the horses' paddock and turn to movement fifty feet to the north. A buff-brown deer, a doe, steps carefully. Her shape is difficult to distinguish from the backdrop of forest. The doe slowly forges her way across the road cut between forest and meadow edge. She moves soundlessly; her large, stout body reveals her age and experience. Stilled, I focus carefully within the tangled brown, tan, and green at her tail and look for followers. Another doe appears. She is slim, smaller. Maybe her second year here? The trailing fawn has lost her spots but is still a baby. She closes the gap to her elders in wild caprioles, then dawdles. She explores each plant she encounters with eyes, nose, and mouth. Her young mother waits patiently inside the safety of wood edge. The fawn leaps to join her, and together, they melt from view.

I know the Eastern phoebe who calls insistently from the tulip tree above. The phoebe's a local resident. She established one of two active nests at the farm this year. Her raspy voice reassures me as I work: "I'm here. You're not alone."

At twilight, on the way home after chores, I see movement above. A little brown bat hunts in the still air twenty feet above me. A questing bat means flying insects. I throw my arms wide, lean back, and shoot vibrant blue waves of gratitude toward the bat, the sky, the universe. The bat circles above me and disappears over the tree line. Leaving me, feet firmly planted on earth.

I am one of many. A small part of the multitude that is humanity, an unstoppable force shaping the planet. Together, we form a wave of change that washes over the land. Change is the constant. But how will we direct it? Will we continue excessive consumption that pushes planetary decline? Or will we work together to manifest a healing tide of constructive action?

I've seen our careless yet exquisite power over life and death. I witnessed about forty pounds of corn seed changing a myriad of lives for years, maybe forever. The experience was a burden, a trauma, but ultimately a gift. Now I can't ignore the reality of our power. My power. My power's a small force that, when added to others pushing and pulling together, will decide our fate and the fate of our children.

We all live on the knife edge. As we move through our lives, by our every choice, our every action, we create our future. We're at the tipping point. It could go either way. Many of us *feel* the edge now as we become aware of changing climate, changing societies, changing economies, and the rapid loss of life on our planet. Together, we'll determine where we go.

Do we choose the side with a bright, healthy future for our children? A future of prosperity and civil society in harmony with the rhythm and realities of the planet. Or will we choose to continue frantic extraction, taking as much as we can each day? Extraction that will lead to a future of poverty and hardship? A future of punitive limits for many and tenuous enclaves for the few?

Today, I align my actions with my hard-won knowledge. I strive to use my money and my time wisely. I seek to fashion my words and make choices in agreement with my new understanding. In some ways, this is the most power I have.

Early morning in autumn, I push open the door of the house and emerge into a cool atmosphere and a barely perceptible fog. The water clings lightly to my skin until my heat, my internal fire, pushes it off as vapor. Vapor coalesces as it cools and rejoins other water droplets in the air.

The gray form of the barn looms ahead. It remains in dawn shadow. But the sun rises behind the pine trees to the east. Golden shafts of light escape through the boughs and illuminate the ground in scattered patches. I walk directly into a beam, stop, and close my eyes; I turn my face to our star. The need to conserve life, the hope for a planet in balance draws me onward—*that's* my focus, my guiding light.

I stay long enough to feel my face warm. And then, with purpose, I step forward.

EPILOGUE

As I wrote this book, problems associated with the widespread use of neonicotinoid-coated seed came into sharper focus. Consider: in the United States, once a liquid pesticide mixture is poured onto crop seed and dried, it ceases to *be* a pesticide in the eyes of the law. One of the biggest obstacles to protecting people and animals from poisoning by systemic pesticides like neonics is that for regulatory purposes, pesticide-coated seeds are "treated articles," exempted from regulation under the Federal Insecticide, Fungicide, and Rodenticide Act. This lack of regulation creates uncertainty among local and state governments as to how they should address toxic coated seed accidents and seed disposal.

The result is that even today, seeds coated with potent neurotoxic pesticides can be spilled, can be planted every year in the same land, can be spread widely over the landscape without recognition or acknowledgment of their toxicity. The result is a steadily growing risk of poisoning—for soil and water, for wildlife, for pets, and for people.

In April 2018, as I drove down a local road, I struggled to understand what I was seeing. Up ahead, half a lane was bright red and the color covered about twenty feet of asphalt. I stopped, got out of my car, and bent down over the strange red substance. It was toxic coated sorghum seed. Apparently, when a tractor traveled between fields, the seed hopper opened and the seed dropped onto the road. The spill was next to a home and near a pond—*uphill* from a pond.

I went to the door of the home and was able to rouse the occupant. Together we took turns pushing a broom and loading seed tipped from a dust pan into black plastic garbage bags; we swept about thirty pounds of seed from the road. As we worked, a county deputy drove by and laughed at us for working so hard in the sun. But by 2018, I knew that if we'd left the bright red seed on the road, it would harm local animals and potentially kill life in the pond below. But also I worried that children who play on the quiet, residential street may have been attracted to gather and play with the colorful pea-sized balls.

We worked diligently to clear the area, but some of the seeds were lodged in asphalt crevices and in the grass beside the road. For some days afterward, when I drove by, I saw birds pecking along the pale red roadside for the last "edible" morsels of seed.

We swept toxic coated sorghum seed from the road.

I learned later from department of transportation officials that they would not deploy a costly vacuum truck to remove a coated seed spill; they would send a sweeper truck to clear the travel lanes. So if we *had* sought help that day, all thirty pounds of toxic seed would have been pushed onto the grass beside the road.

In 2021 I learned of a small Nebraska town dealing with unimaginable levels of seed-coating pesticide contamination. And it had been for years. Starting in 2015, the AltEn ethanol plant in Mead was no longer an average ethanol plant turning corn kernels into fuel additives. The Mead plant was trying something different: instead of buying corn from local farmers, they received unsold toxic coated seed from agrochemical companies.

AltEn used the coated corn seed to make ethanol, an accepted use of the seed, but the distilling process left behind large piles of depleted seed—also known as wet distillers grains or "wet cake." Processed wet cake from ordinary corn is valuable as an animal feed. But processed wet cake from the pesticide-coated seed could not be fed to animals. It was too toxic. So it sat in piles on the ground around the plant. For years.

The stench from the rotting piles of wet cake was hard to ignore. And it was not just the smell. Residents complained of health problems among family members and animals—for years. Reporters took notice.

The situation at AltEn made international news when Carey Gillam reported in early 2021 that all was not well in Mead, Nebraska: "People reported eye and throat irritation and nosebleeds. Then colonies of bees started dying, birds and butterflies appeared disoriented and pet dogs grew ill, staggering about with dilated pupils."

Christina Stella of Nebraska Public Media picked up the story later in the year and made a documentary about the impacts of the AltEn contamination on the community of Mead. She reported that the piles of wet cake grew from thirty-six thousand tons by the end of 2017 to an estimated eighty-four thousand tons that covered sixteen acres by the time the plant ceased operations in spring 2021. In addition to the piles of rotting wet cake, large, open lagoons of contaminated wastewater were stored on site. She wrote that the contaminated water "could have filled more than 260 Olympic-sized swimming pools."

Prior to 2019, as the volume of waste grew around the plant, the state approved a disposal method: land application of lagoon water and wet cake onto local farm fields. The land application spread seed-coating pesticides over larger areas of the community. This exposed more residents to toxic chemicals. In 2019, Nebraska officals detected about ten different pesticides in samples from fields where the wet cake had been spread. Stella goes on to report, "One chemical—clothianidin—was being applied to land at 85 times the EPA limit and showed up in the liquid waste at nearly 300 times the safety limit for drinking water."

But large volumes of pesticide-contaminated water remained at the plant site. During heavy rains, toxic water flowed off AltEn property into local waterways. The Keiser family owns property about six miles downstream from AltEn. The family treasured their large pond, which was stocked with bass and rich with wildlife. But in 2016, they were shocked to find a large fish kill. After that, their pond continued to deteriorate. As Chris Dunker reported for the *Lincoln Journal Star*, Mr. Keiser described their pond's water in 2021: "It's about as sterile as you can get."

Toxic coated seed spills are common, as are seeds that are left at the soil surface during planting. In 2016 and 2017, Charlotte Roy at Minnesota's Department of Natural Resources and her colleagues studied Minnesota crop fields for the presence of exposed coated seed and seed spills. They reported: "Seeds are abundant and widely available on the soil surface for wildlife consumption during the spring planting season."

And today we know more about how birds are harmed or killed by neonics. As Gabriele Giuseppe Distefano summarized in a 2022 report about neonicotinoids in sea birds, "Exposure to sublethal concentrations of neonicotinoids, even after a single dose, has been shown to affect birds' physiology significantly." Birds are harmed directly by eating toxic coated seeds, or indirectly by eating poisoned insects, crustaceans, or fish; by drinking contaminated water; or from malnutrition due to a loss of prey.

So the AltEn disaster in Mead, Nebraska, may be an unusual situation. But it's also a cautionary tale.

Consider the inherent contradiction within each toxic coated seed: pesticides are chemical tools designed and used to kill some forms of life; seeds are our ancient partners—many can be used as food by themselves, and all contain the opportunity for new plant life. When opposites are combined into one, there's the risk of confusion or cognitive dissonance.

So what are these candy-colored nuggets? Are they potent pesticides? Or are they precious seeds? They're both.

In my own experience, when I spoke to seed salesmen, to farmers, and to state and local officials, I witnessed a common lack of understanding about potential health risks and environmental damage posed by exposure to toxic coated seed. I encountered confusion among many as to whether they should be treated as ordinary seeds, as toxic waste, or as something else. And if they were something else, what to do with them?

Until we eliminate this confusion about what exactly is the nature of toxic coated seed, until we clarify the identity of these products and how to safely manage them, there will be more reports of contaminated land, dead wildlife, and disrupted lives; we will continue to casually destroy our fellow inhabitants of the natural world, our partners who make life on earth possible for all of us.

ACKNOWLEDGMENTS

My deepest appreciation to my patient and supportive husband, Howard, who sat alone on the couch too many evenings to count. Loving thanks to Flor, who encouraged me to speak my truth. Deep gratitude is extended to the animals and plants, the land and water, the multitude that support us here. Many thanks for the authoritative scientific work of Christy Morrissey, Dave Goulson, Michelle Hladik, Francisco Sánchez-Bayo, Christian Krupke, Rick Relyea, Margaret Douglas, John Tooker, Robin Mesnage, staff members of the Xerces Society, and many, many others. Without the courageous investigative work of scientists, I would never have known what had killed the animals. I would like to thank the neighbors, colleagues, community members, and North Carolina officials who provided information and helped move my investigation forward. Much appreciation for the support, assistance, and encouragement I received from Jay Levine, Dave Goulson, Sylvia, Erin Zimmerman, and Elizabeth Sams. I'm grateful for my readers: William Butcher, Michelle Aronson, and especially Mari Trosclair, whose loving support throughout served to provide a platform from which I could reach higher. Many thanks to members of the North Carolina Writers Network who showed me the way and to members of my Creative Nonfiction course, whose comments improved multiple scenes within this work. Much appreciation and thanks to my hardworking and talented agent, Leslie Meredith; to the team at Chicago Review press, including my acquiring editor Jerry Pohlen, copyeditor Michelle Williams, managing editor Devon Freeny, and publicist Bianca Maldonado. And thanks to my first editor, Jill Rothenberg, who tirelessly reminded me: "Dialogue, dialogue!"

Additional supporting notes, photographs, and videos from this story are available at my website: www.elizabethhilborn.com.

NOTES

1. The Mystery

"biodegradable and won't build up": Attorney General of the State of New York, Consumer Frauds and Protection Bureau, Environmental Protection Bureau, In the Matter of Monsanto Company, Respondent, Assurance of Discontinuance Pursuant to Executive Law § 63(15). New York, NY, Nov. 1996. False Advertising by Monsanto Regarding the Safety of Roundup Herbicide (Glyphosate), 3–4, http://big.assets.huffingtonpost.com/fraud.pdf.

its active ingredient targeted and interrupted an enzyme: Klaus M. Herrmann and Lisa M. Weaver, "The Shikimate Pathway," *Annual Review of Plant Physiology and Plant Molecular Biology* 50 (1999): 473–503, https://doi.org/10.1146/annurev.arplant.50.1.473.

4. Empty Nest

he exposed frogs and toads to Roundup: Rick A. Relyea, "The Lethal Impact of Roundup on Aquatic and Terrestrial Amphibians," *Ecological Applications* 15, no. 4 (2005): 1118–1124, https://doi.org/10.1890/04-1291.

Roundup loves water: W. A. Battaglin, M. T. Meyer, K. M. Kuivila, and J. E. Dietze, "Glyphosate and Its Degradation Product AMPA Occur Frequently and Widely in U.S. Soils, Surface Water, Groundwater, and Precipitation," *Journal of the American Water Resources Association* 50, no. 2 (2014): 275–290, https://doi.org/10.1111/jawr.12159.

"The markets for seeds": Josh Sosland, "Biden Initiative Targets US Ag Sector," *World Grain*, July 12, 2021, https://www.world-grain.com/articles/15537-biden-initiative-targets-us-ag-sector.

"As the structure of the marketplace has changed": Mary K. Hendrickson and Harvey S. James Jr., "The Ethics of Constrained Choice: How the Industrialization of Agriculture Impacts Farming and Farmer Behavior," *Journal of Agricultural and Environmental Ethics* 18 (2005): 278, https://doi.org/10.1007/s10806-005-0631-5.

5. Red Zone

"We grieve only for what we know": Aldo Leopold, *A Sand County Almanac with Essays on Conservation from Round River* (New York: Oxford University Press, 1966; Seventh Printing, 1974), 52.

Raymundo described crying into her dive mask: Chelsea Harvey, "'I Cried . . . Right into My Mask': Scientists Say Guam's Reefs Have Bleached Four Years Straight," *Washington Post*, August 3, 2016, https://www.washingtonpost.com/news/energy-environment/wp/2016/08/03/i-cried-right-into-my-mask-these-coral-reefs-have-seen-a-devastating-four-years-of-bleaching/.

"I grieve what is happening": Margaret Renkl, "I Will Not Rest Until This Garden Grows," *New York Times*, February 26, 2021, https://www.nytimes.com/2021/02/26/opinion/winter-gardening-wildlife.html.

"Just as grief over the loss": Neville Ellis and Ashlee Cunsolo, "Hope and Mourning in the Anthropocene: Understanding Ecological Grief," *Conversation*, April 4, 2018, http://theconversation.com/hope-and-mourning-in-the-anthropocene-understanding-ecological-grief-88630.

a loss of over 80 percent of insect biomass: Caspar A. Hallmann et al., "More than 75 Percent Decline over 27 Years in Total Flying Insect Biomass in Protected Areas," *PLoS ONE* 12, no. 10 (2017): e0185809, https://doi.org/10.1371/journal.pone.0185809.

6. Moving Water

"The Same Pesticides Linked to Bee Declines": Elizabeth Royte, "The Same Pesticides Linked to Bee Declines Might Also Threaten Birds," *Audubon*, Spring 2017, https://www.audubon.org/magazine/spring-2017/the-same-pesticides-linked-bee-declines-might.

can't "be removed from fruits or vegetables": Quan Zhang et al., "Dietary Risk of Neonicotinoid Insecticides Through Fruit and Vegetable Consumption in School-Age Children," *Environment International* 126 (2019): 672–681, https://doi.org/10.1016/j.envint.2019.02.051.

"a single corn kernel with a 1,250 rate": Erin Hodgson and Christian Krupke, "Insecticidal Seed Treatments Can Harm Honey Bees," Iowa State University, Extension and Outreach, Integrated Crop Management, April 6, 2012, https://crops.extension.iastate.edu/cropnews/2012/04/insecticidal-seed-treatments-can-harm-honey-bees.

about a pound of glyphosate: Office of Chemical Safety and Pollution Prevention, "Glyphosate: Response to Comments, Usage, and Benefits" (memo), Environmental Protection Agency, April 18, 2019, https://www.epa.gov/sites/default/files/2019-04/documents/glyphosate-response-comments-usage-benefits-final.pdf, 13.

some states in the middle third of the country use three times: Pat Dempsey, "Breaking Down the Use of Glyphosate in the U.S. Midwest," Center for Investigative Reporting, May 26, 2019, https://investigatemidwest.org/2019/05/26/breaking-down-the-use-of-glyphosate-in-the-u-s/.

about five million pounds: Office of Chemical Safety, "Glyphosate" (memo), https://www.epa.gov/sites/default/files/2019-04/documents/glyphosate-response-comments-usage-benefits-final.pdf, 18.

analysis of toxicology studies prompted them to declare: International Agency for Research on Cancer, World Health Organization, *Some Organophosphate Insecticides and Herbicides*, IARC Monographs on the Evaluation of Carcinogenic Risks to Humans, vol. 112 (Lyon, France: IARC, 2015), full monograph: https://publications.iarc.fr/Book-And-Report-Series/Iarc-Monographs-On-The-Identification-Of-Carcinogenic-Hazards-To-Humans/Some-Organophosphate-Insecticides-And-Herbicides-2017, "Glyphosate," section 10: https://monographs.iarc.fr/wp-content/uploads/2018/06/mono112-10.pdf.

reported that urinary concentrations of glyphosate: Paul J. Mills et al., "Excretion of the Herbicide Glyphosate in Older Adults Between 1993 and 2016," *JAMA* 318, no. 16 (2017): 1610–1611, https://jamanetwork.com/journals/jama/fullarticle/2658306.

found neonics in hair samples: Jean-Marc Bonmatin et al., "Residues of Neonicotinoids in Soil, Water and People's Hair: A Case Study from Three Agricultural

Regions of the Philippines," *Science of the Total Environment* 757, no. 25 (2021): 143822, https://doi.org/10.1016/j.scitotenv.2020.143822.

about 50 percent of people in a nationally representative survey: Maria Ospina et al., "Exposure to Neonicotinoid Insecticides in the U.S. General Population: Data from the 2015–2016 National Health and Nutrition Examination Survey," *Environmental Research* 176 (2019): 108555, https://doi.org/10.1016/j.envres.2019.108555.

plant residues still contained glyphosate for months afterward: Laure Mamy, Enrique Barriuso, and Benoît Gabrielle, "Glyphosate Fate in Soils When Arriving in Plant Residues," *Chemosphere* 154 (2016): 425–433, https://www.science direct.com/science/article/pii/S0045653516304039?via%3Dihub.

"detections in groundwater . . . started after 500 days": US EPA, "Preliminary Pollinator Assessment to Support the Registration Review of Imidacloprid," January 4, 2016, persistence in soil: 13, mobility: 52, https://www.motherjones.com/wp-content/uploads/epa-hq-opp-2008-0844-0140.pdf.

"Even the best clinical trials": US Food and Drug Administration, "FDA-TRACK: Center for Drug Evaluation & Research—Post-Approval Safety Monitoring," https://www.fda.gov/about-fda/fda-track-agency-wide-program -performance/fda-track-center-drug-evaluation-research-post-approval-safety -monitoring.

These final mixtures can be much more toxic: Robin Mesnage and Michael N. Antoniou, "Ignoring Adjuvant Toxicity Falsifies the Safety Profile of Commercial Pesticides," *Frontiers in Public Health* 5 (2018): 361, https://doi.org/10.3389 /fpubh.2017.00361.

since 1997, developmental disabilities have steadily increased: Benjamin Zablotsky et al., "Prevalence and Trends of Developmental Disabilities Among Children in the United States: 2009–2017," *Pediatrics* 144, no. 4 (2019): e20190811, https://doi.org/10.1542/peds.2019-0811.

"We assert that the current system in the United States": American College of Obstetricians and Gynecologists et al., "Project TENDR: Targeting Environmental Neuro-Developmental Risks: The TENDR Consensus Statement," *Environmental Health Perspectives* 124, no. 7 (2016): A118–A122, https://doi .org/10.1289/EHP358.

"Unfortunately, industries are allowed to market": Bruce P. Lanphear, "The Impact of Toxins on the Developing Brain," *Annual Review of Public Health* 36

(2015): 211–230, https://www.annualreviews.org/doi/pdf/10.1146/annurev -publhealth-031912-114413.

High-quality scientific reports were published in the first decade: María Teresa Muñoz-Quezada et al., "Neurodevelopmental Effects in Children Associated with Exposure to Organophosphate Pesticides: A Systematic Review," *Neurotoxicology* 39 (2013): 158–168, https://doi.org/10.1016/j.neuro.2013 .09.003.

7. Bees Please (Queen's Dance)

"clothianidin is practically non-toxic to water fleas": Environmental Protection Agency, "Clothianidin and Thiamethoxam: Proposed Interim Registration Review Decision, Case Numbers 7620 and 7614," docket nos. EPA-HQ-OPP-2011-0865 & EPA-HQ-OPP-2011-058 (January 2020), 39, https:// www.epa.gov/sites/default/files/2020-01/documents/clothianidin_and _thiamethoxam_pid_final_1.pdf.

wild bees contribute about $3 billion worth of value each year: John E. Losey and Mace Vaughan, "The Economic Value of Ecological Services Provided by Insects," *BioScience* 56, no. 4 (2006): 311–323, https://doi.org/10.1641/0006-3568(2006) 56[311:TEVOES]2.0.CO;2.

Another report stood out from the others: Jennifer Hopwood et al., *How Neonicotinoids Can Kill Bees: The Science Behind the Role These Insecticides Play in Harming Bees*, 2nd ed. (Portland, OR: Xerces Society for Invertebrate Conservation, 2016), https://xerces.org/sites/default/files/2018-05/16-022_01_XercesSoc _How-Neonicotinoids-Can-Kill-Bees_web.pdf.

"We are mostly affected by pesticides": "Kenyan Farmers Pollinate Crops by Hand After Pesticides Kill Off Insects," *Afro News*, March 22, 2021, https://afro.news/2021/03/22/kenyan-farmers-pollinate-crops-by-hand -after-pesticides-kill-off-insects/.

"Pear trees are sprayed once each week": Tang Ya, Xie Jia-sui, and Chen Keming, "Hand Pollination of Pears and Its Implications for Biodiversity Conservation and Environmental Protection: A Case Study from Hanyuan County, Sichuan Province, China," unpublished report submitted to the International Centre for Integrated Mountain Development (ICIMOD), 2003, 13–16, https:// documents.pub/document/hand-pollination-of-pears-and-its-implications -for-pollination-natural-pollinators.html.

8. Harvest

at levels similar to the concentrations I found in our wetland: Christy A. Morrissey
    et al., "Neonicotinoid Contamination of Global Surface Waters and Associ-
    ated Risk to Aquatic Invertebrates: A Review," *Environment International* 74
    (2015), 291–303, doi: 10.1016/j.envint.2014.10.024, https://www.sciencedirect
    .com/science/article/pii/S0160412014003183?via%3Dihub.

a recent study from Purdue University scientists: Adam Alford and Christian H. Krupke,
    "Translocation of the Neonicotinoid Seed Treatment Clothianidin in Maize,"
    PLoS ONE 12, no. 3 (2017): e0173836, doi: 10.1371/journal.pone.0173836,
    https://journals.plos.org/plosone/article?id=10.1371/journal.pone.0173836.

"We have been attacked in the past": Stéphane Foucart and Stéphane Horel, "'Mon-
    santo Papers': The Pesticide Giant's War Against Science," *Le Monde*,
    June 1, 2017, https://www.lemonde.fr/planete/article/2017/06/01/monsanto
    -operation-intoxication_5136915_3244.html.

9. Bad Blood

"Take care of the land, and the land will take care of you": Ciji Taylor, "PBS
    Film Explores History of Dust Bowl and Founding of USDA Agency,"
    National Resource Conservation Service, US Department of Agriculture,
    February 21, 2017, https://www.usda.gov/media/blog/2012/11/16/pbs
    -film-explores-history-dust-bowl-and-founding-usda-agency.

we have only sixty more years left of farming: Chris Arsenault, "Only 60 Years
    of Farming Left If Soil Degradation Continues," *Scientific American*,
    December 5, 2014, https://www.scientificamerican.com/article/only
    -60-years-of-farming-left-if-soil-degradation-continues/.

about one-third of total acres cultivated in the corn belt: Evan A. Thaler, Isaac J.
    Larsen, and Qian Yu, "The Extent of Soil Loss Across the US Corn Belt," *Pro-
    ceedings of the National Academy of Sciences* 118, no. 8 (2021): e1922375118,
    https://doi.org/10.1073/pnas.1922375118.

safe for me to use the animals' composted manure: "Herbicide Carryover in Hay,
    Manure, Compost, and Grass Clippings," North Carolina State Extension Pub-
    lications, February 19, 2020, https://content.ces.ncsu.edu/herbicide-carryover.

"research points to the herbicide's potential to disrupt healthy microbiomes": Pere
    Puigbò et al., "Does Glyphosate Affect the Human Microbiota?" *Life* 12, no. 5
    (2022): 707, https://doi.org/10.3390/life12050707.

pesticides *"will not generally cause unreasonable adverse effects"*: "Summary of the Federal Insecticide, Fungicide, and Rodenticide Act," US Environmental Protection Agency, September 12, 2022, https://www.epa.gov/laws-regulations /summary-federal-insecticide-fungicide-and-rodenticide-act.

10. Weight of Evidence

bees can *"become lethally contaminated" just by flying*: V. Girolami et al., "Aerial Powdering of Bees Inside Mobile Cages and the Extent of Neonicotinoid Cloud Surrounding Corn Drillers," *Journal of Applied Entomology* 137, nos. 1–2 (2013): 35–44, https://doi.org/10.1111/j.1439-0418.2012.01718.x.

"Clothianidin has the potential for toxic chronic exposure": Office of Prevention, Pesticides and Toxic Substances, "Name of Chemical: Clothianidin; Reason for Issuance: Conditional Registration" (fact sheet), US Environmental Protection Agency, May 30, 2003, https://www3.epa.gov/pesticides/chem_search /reg_actions/registration/fs_PC-044309_30-May-03.pdf.

published a report about their work that showed how soil and water become contaminated: Jesse Radolinski et al., "Transport of a Neonicotinoid Pesticide, Thiamethoxam, from Artificial Seed Coatings," *Science of the Total Environment* 618 (2018): 561–568, https://doi.org/10.1016/j.scitotenv.2017.11.031.

Over 95 percent of corn seed: John F. Tooker, Margaret R. Douglas, and Christian H. Krupke, "Neonicotinoid Seed Treatments: Limitations and Compatibility with Integrated Pest Management," *Agricultural & Environmental Letters* 2, no. 1 (January 2017): https://acsess.onlinelibrary.wiley.com/doi/epdf /10.2134/ael2017.08.0026, 4.

mosquito larvae became tolerant to five times the lethal neonic dose: Muhammad Asam Riaz et al., "Molecular Mechanisms Associated with Increased Tolerance to the Neonicotinoid Insecticide Imidacloprid in the Dengue Vector *Aedes aegypti*," *Aquatic Toxicology* 126 (2013): 326–337, https://doi.org /10.1016/j.aquatox.2012.09.010.

a functional landscape at a spatial scale relevant to insect needs: Douglas W. Tallamy, *Bringing Nature Home: How You Can Sustain Wildlife with Native Plants* (Portland, OR: Timber Press, 2007).

"For the average individual, reading through scientific research can be daunting": Carey Gillam, *Whitewash: The Story of a Weed Killer, Cancer, and the Corruption of Science* (Washington, DC: Island Press, 2017), 91.

The law firm opened up the company's internal discussions: Baum Hedlund Aristei & Goldman, "Monsanto Papers | Secret Documents," December 2, 2019, https://www.baumhedlundlaw.com/toxic-tort-law/monsanto-roundup-lawsuit/monsanto-secret-documents/.

"Please don't do anything until we discuss this": William F. Heydens, email to Erik Jacobs et al., April 10, 2001, exhibit 8 of case 3:16-md-02741-VC, document 192-8, filed March 15, 2017, document page 138, https://usrtk.org/wp-content/uploads/2017/03/192series.pdf.

Gillam reported on the phenomenon in her June 2019 article: Carey Gillam, "How Monsanto Manipulates Journalists and Academics," *Guardian*, June 2, 2019, https://www.theguardian.com/commentisfree/2019/jun/02/monsanto-manipulates-journalists-academics.

"The key will be keeping Monsanto in the background": Eric Sachs, email to Bruce Chassy, November 30, 2010, https://www.usrtk.org/wp-content/uploads/2016/01/Sachs-AR.pdf.

"Most GBH [glyphosate-based herbicide] use has occurred in the last 10 years": John Peterson Myers et al., "Concerns over Use of Glyphosate-Based Herbicides and Risks Associated with Exposures: A Consensus Statement," *Environmental Health* 15, no. 19 (2016): 4, https://doi.org/10.1186/s12940-016-0117-0.

And only during the first decade of the twenty-first century were health scientists: S. H. Zyoud et al., "Global Research Production in Glyphosate Intoxication from 1978 to 2015: A Bibliometric Analysis," *Human and Experimental Toxicology* 36, no. 10 (2017): 997–1006, https://doi.org/10.1177/0960327116678299.

less than 30 percent: Christopher B. Burns and James M. MacDonald. *America's Diverse Family Farms*, 2018 ed., US Department of Agriculture, Economic Research Service, December 2018, https://www.ers.usda.gov/webdocs/publications/90985/eib-203.pdf, 14–17.

"median household income from farming was $210 in 2021": "Farm Household Well-Being: Farm Household Income Estimates," US Department of Agriculture, Economic Research Service, December 1, 2022, https://www.ers.usda.gov/topics/farm-economy/farm-household-well-being/farm-household-income-estimates/.

farmers may feel pushed to buy the latest equipment: J. Gordon Arbuckle and Chris Kast, "Quality of Life on the Agricultural Treadmill: Individual and Community Determinants of Farm Family Well-Being," *Journal of Rural Social*

Sciences 27, no. 1 (2012): 84–113, https://egrove.olemiss.edu/cgi/viewcontent
.cgi?article=1424&context=jrss.

30 percent of the global supply: M. Shabandeh, "Corn in the U.S.–Statistics and Facts," Statistica, November 17, 2022, https://www.statista.com/topics/986 /corn/.

approximately $50 billion: M. Shabandeh, "Production Value of Corn for Grain in the U.S. from 2000 to 2021," Statistica, May 6, 2022, https://www.statista.com /statistics/190876/production-value-of-corn-for-grain-in-the-us-since-2000/.

neonics that coat seed are not recognized as pesticides: Adam Allington, "When Is a Pesticide Not a Pesticide? When It Coats a Seed," Bloomberg Law, January 27, 2020, https://news.bloomberglaw.com/environment-and-energy /when-is-a-pesticide-not-a-pesticide-when-it-coats-a-seed.

"lab studies have reported a slew of evidence": Elizabeth Royte, "Widely Used Neonic Insecticides May Be a Threat to Mammals, Too," *Food & Environment Reporting Network/National Geographic*, February 5, 2022, https://thefern.org/2021/02 /widely-used-neonic-insecticides-may-be-a-threat-to-mammals-too/.

"Evidence of clear and consistent yield benefits": Michelle L. Hladik, Anson R. Main, and Dave Goulson, "Environmental Risks and Challenges Associated with Neonicotinoid Insecticides," *Environmental Science and Technology* 52, no. 6 (2018): 3329–3335, https://pubs.acs.org/doi/full/10.1021/acs.est.7b06388.

studied the effects of neonicotinoids among exposed cells: Windy A. Boyd et al., "NTP Research Report on the Scoping Review of Potential Human Health Effects Associated with Exposures to Neonicotinoid Pesticides," research report 15 (Internet), Research Triangle Park (NC), National Toxicology Program, September 2020, https://www.ncbi.nlm.nih.gov/books/NBK563583/.

11. Our Choice

"A thing is right when it tends to preserve the integrity": Aldo Leopold, *A Sand County Almanac* (New York: Oxford University Press, 1949; reprint ed., New York: Robert Finch, 1987), xxvi.

"restoring soil health requires . . . thinking of the soil": Jon Stika, *A Soil Owner's Manual: How to Restore and Maintain Soil Health* (CreateSpace, 2016), 42.

"What led me down this road": Author interview with Jonathan Lundgren, April 16, 2020.

even formerly skeptical farmers such as Adam Chappell: Chris Bennett, "A Skeptical Farmer's Monster Message on Profitability," *Farm Journal*, July 7, 2020, https://www.agweb.com/news/crops/crop-production/skeptical-farmers-monster-message-profitability.

higher percentage of organic farmers: National Agricultural Statistics Service, *2019 Organic Survey Data Release*, US Department of Agriculture, October 22, 2020, https://www.nass.usda.gov/Surveys/Guide_to_NASS_Surveys/Organic_Production/pdf/2019_Organic_Executive_Briefing.pdf, 38–39.

Epilogue

"People reported eye and throat irritation and nosebleeds": Carey Gillam, "'There's a Red Flag Here': How an Ethanol Plant Is Dangerously Polluting a US Village," *Guardian*, January 10, 2021, https://www.theguardian.com/us-news/2021/jan/10/mead-nebraska-ethanol-plant-pollution-danger.

Christina Stella of Nebraska Public Media picked up the story: Christina Stella, "The Smell of Money: Mead, Nebraska's Fight for Its Future," Nebraska Public Media, August 4, 2021, https://nebraskapublicmedia.org/en/news/news-articles/the-smell-of-money-mead-nebraskas-fight-for-its-future/.

The Keiser family owns property: Chris Dunker, "'It's About as Sterile as You Can Get'—Storm, Wastewater Runoff from AltEn Traveled Miles Downstream for Years," *Lincoln Journal Star*, July 4, 2021, https://journalstar.com/news/state-and-regional/nebraska/it-s-about-as-sterile-as-you-can-get-storm-wastewater-runoff-from-alten-traveled/article_a3b264a0-36bf-5d6c-9dfc-4ab10851e875.html.

"Seeds are abundant and widely available": Charlotte L. Roy et al., "Multi-Scale Availability of Neonicotinoid-Treated Seed for Wildlife in an Agricultural Landscape During Spring Planting," *Science of the Total Environment* 682 (2019): 271–281, https://doi.org/10.1016/j.scitotenv.2019.05.010.

"Exposure to sublethal concentrations": Gabriele Giuseppe Distefano et al., "The Ubiquity of Neonicotinoid Contamination: Residues in Seabirds with Different Trophic Habits," *Environmental Research* 206 (2022): 112637, https://doi.org/10.1016/j.envres.2021.112637.

ABOUT THE AUTHOR

Elizabeth Hilborn, DVM, is a veterinary specialist in honeybee medicine at Bee Well Mobile Veterinary Services. An avid gardener and fruit grower, she's fed family and friends with fresh produce from her family's farm in North Carolina for decades. She has served for over twenty-five years as an environmental epidemiologist with the US Environmental Protection Agency, where she writes about her studies of the health effects of emerging infectious diseases, extreme weather, and water pollution.

Courtesy of House